A Brief Introduction
to US Politics

A Brief Introduction to US Politics

Robert McKeever and
Philip Davies

PEARSON
Longman

Harlow, England • London • New York • Boston • San Francisco • Toronto • Sydney • Singapore • Hong Kong
Tokyo • Seoul • Taipei • New Delhi • Cape Town • Madrid • Mexico City • Amsterdam • Munich • Paris • Milan

Pearson Education Limited
Edinburgh Gate
Harlow
Essex CM20 2JE
England

and Associated Companies throughout the world

Visit us on the World Wide Web at:
www.pearsoned.co.uk

First published 2006

ISBN-10: 0-582-47341-1
ISBN-13: 978-0-582-47341-6

British Library Cataloguing-in-Publication Data
A catalogue record for this book is available from the British Library

Library of Congress Cataloging-in-Publication Data
A catalogue record for this book is available from the Library of Congress

10 9 8 7 6 5 4 3 2 1
11 10 09 08 07 06

Typeset in 10/12.5pt ITC Century by 35
Printed and bound in Great Britain by Ashford Colour Press Ltd, Hampshire

The publisher's policy is to use paper manufactured from sustainable forests.

Contents

Preface

This short version of *Politics USA* is intended for the student or teacher who needs an introduction to the essential features of the American political system. The United States is a complex democracy. Its structural roots date from the eighteenth century, as do its founding concepts of popular sovereignty and republicanism. Yet in the two centuries and more since the Constitution of 1787 was created, the United States has undergone dramatic change. A political system designed for thirteen states aligned along the Atlantic coast must now serve the needs of a diverse, continental nation that possesses economic and military prowess beyond the imagination of the Founding Fathers.

This book aims to provide its readers with a coherent and succinct account of how contemporary American politics blends enduring principles with the realities and demands of the present day. Our goal is to build an understanding of American politics in a logical series of steps. We begin with a brief overview of American society today that sets the scene of the analysis to come. The first two chapters then introduce you to the constitutional framework of American politics and the fluid concept and practice of federalism. While these subjects may be considered 'dry', they are essential to a sound understanding of politics in the United States. As with the book as a whole, we aim to provide an intelligent but accessible analysis to constitutionalism and federalism. Key terms and concepts are explained in a way that enables the reader to employ them with confidence.

We move next to the major features of the representative process: elections, of course, but also the main players in electoral politics, such as parties, interest groups and the media. We also analyse the challenges to democracy presented by an electoral system highly dependent upon television and awash with interest-group money.

The following three chapters examine the major institutions of the federal government – the presidency, the Congress and the Supreme Court. These embody the constitutional principle of the separation of powers, but we explain how these three institutions are simultaneously independent yet constrained by each other. We pay particular attention to the evolution of these institutions since

1787, since none plays its role quite as envisaged by the framers. Above all, we provide a clear analysis of the powers and limitations of these central elements of national government.

One of the inevitable features of a short introductory text is a relative paucity of examples and case studies. In order to counter this, we conclude the book with two chapters that show the way that government and politics work in connection with the system's main outputs: domestic and foreign policies. Readers are thus able to gain knowledge of the main policy issues that constitute the American political agenda today, but are also able to evaluate the way in which the system as a whole works.

Finally, we hope that by providing an accurate, up-to-date and accessible introduction to American politics, we also stimulate a desire to learn more about this unique and powerful country that we, the authors, continue to find fascinating.

The authors are particularly indebted to Morten Fuglevand, who conceived the project in the first place and who brought it to fruition with his customary patience and good humour.

Bob McKeever
Phil Davies

Acknowledgements

We are grateful to the following for permission to reproduce copyright material:

Figure 2.1 © Empics; Figure 2.2 © Ann Johansson/ Corbis; Figure 3.2 from the U.S. Senate Collection, Center for Legislative Archives; Data in Box 3.3 is from http://elections.gmu.edu (McDonald, M.P., 2001); Figure 3.3 © Empics; Figure 3.4 © Empics; Table 3.6 from www.cnn.com/elections/2004; Figure 4.1 © Kirk Anderson; Figure 5.1 © Ron Sachs/ Corbis; Figure 5.2 © Bettmann/Corbis; Table 5.2 from *Mass Media and American Politics*, Pew Research Centeer (Graber, D., 2002); Figure 6.1 © Jim Young/Reuters/Corbis; Figure 6.2 © Brooks Kraft/Corbis; Figure 6.3 © Steve Sack; Figure 6.4 © Steve Sack; Figure 6.5 © Empics; Figure 7.1 from *Parties, Politics, and Public Policy in America*, 9th Edition, CQ Press (Keefe, W.J. and Hethereington, M.J., 2003); Figure 8.2 © Bob Gorrell; Figure 10.1 © Miroslav Zajic/Corbis; Figure 10.2 © Getty; Tables 10.1 and 10.2 from Statistical Abstract of the United States, 2004–2005, US Census Bureau; Figure 10.3 © Mark Fiore.

In some instances we have been unable to trace the owners of copyright material, and we would appreciate any information that would enable us to do so.

This book is dedicated with love to Heather McKeever and to Rosamund Davies

Introduction: American government and politics

Understanding the political system of any country depends in part upon understanding its culture. By culture we mean the values, traditions and aspirations of a nation. These in turn are in part dependent upon the social make-up of the country, its economic system and the way it interacts with the rest of the world. Viewed through the prism of culture, the American political system in the early twenty-first century presents a fascinating but complex picture.

For anyone coming new to American politics, the first thing to understand is that the United States is a very diverse country. There are 50 States with many geographical, political and cultural differences between them. The politics and culture of Texas, for example, are very different from those of New York, California or Vermont. There is also a tremendous diversity of ethnic and racial groups, so that it is no longer a simple matter to describe a 'typical American', even though non-Americans are still tempted to use stereotypes. Most striking of all, perhaps, are the different lifestyles to be found in the United States. The country that led the world in such matters as feminism, gay rights and youth culture is also a country where many are

deeply religious and adopt a traditional standpoint in their opposition to these developments.

America, of course, has been marked by diversity from the start. Immigrants from a variety of European countries encountered Native American tribes and then forcibly introduced African slaves into the country. Huge swathes of what is now American territory, including California and Texas, were populated by Hispanics. Some of the immigrants were fleeing religious persecution, and so different Christian sects flourished in the American colonies. Later waves of immigrants brought even more religious diversity, as Jews and Orientals, for example, found a home in America. On the economic front, there were early differences between the mercantile economy of New England and the plantation economy of the South.

Diversity, then, is nothing new. As a result, one of the principal challenges for the American political system has always been to accommodate diversity while providing for effective government at the national level. In the second half of the twentieth century, a new dimension was added by the emergence of the United States as a superpower. Now the obligations of the United States did not stop at its own shores or the boundaries of the New World. Rather they stretched around the globe and led to wars in places such as Korea and Vietnam.

The end of the Cold War brought only a temporary respite from global responsibilities and engagement. The Iraqi invasion of Kuwait in 1990 and the outbreak of vicious wars in the former state of Yugoslavia demonstrated that only the United States could create and police a peaceful global order. Moreover, by the end of the twentieth century, the process of globalisation meant that the United States had a considerable stake in maintaining order in the world. The increasing interconnectedness of national economies and the international dimensions of problems such as global warming, AIDS, terrorism and poverty left the United States with little option but to remain closely engaged with the rest of the world. The terrorist attacks of September 11th, 2001, deeply reinforced that imperative to engage the power and influence of the United States on a global scale.

To say that the United States is the only country that has the capacity to provide leadership to the world does not mean that it can easily achieve its foreign policy goals. There are limits to America's military capacity and there are constraints imposed by domestic factors, including public opinion and the claims on the public purse of domestic programmes such as Social Security and Medicare. Indeed, most Americans are usually far more concerned with domestic priorities than with foreign policy goals. The political system of the United States must enable the government to be strong and effective in promoting defence, national security and protecting America's interests abroad, while simultaneously fulfilling the domestic ambitions of its people.

In the first decade of the twenty-first century, however, the American people are divided over what those domestic ambitions should be. Of course, all Americans want a prosperous economy, well-paid jobs and low rates of crime. There is a sharp divide on the other hand about socio-moral or 'lifestyle issues'. The 'hot button' issues here are abortion and gay rights. Behind these, however, are more fundamental differences over the role of religion in private and public life and the authority of traditional ways of thinking and acting.

These issues lie at the root of the so-called Red–Blue divide in the contemporary United States. Blue Americans, those with essentially liberal cultural values, live mainly in the urban and suburban areas which form the great cities of the Northeast, the industrial Midwest and the West Coast. Most vote Democrat. Red Americans, more socially conservative and religious, live in the predominantly rural areas of the South, the Great Plains and the Mountain States. And they vote Republican. Typical Blue areas are New York, Los Angeles and Boston; typical Red areas are Texas, Wyoming and Mississippi.

Of course, the Red and Blue divide is something of a simplification and it has been frequently argued that many areas and whole states should really be considered 'Purple'. For example, states such as Florida and Pennsylvania are evenly balanced between liberals and conservatives, Democrats and Republicans. Furthermore, individual Americans may be Blue on some issues but Red on others. Nevertheless, the Red–Blue divide does capture a basic truth about contemporary American politics, namely that ideological and partisan divisions are strong, and growing stronger, making political leadership and consensus more difficult to deliver.

Moreover, because Americans are quite evenly divided along Red–Blue lines, elections are close and hard fought. In 2000, for example, the successful candidate, the Republican George W. Bush, actually won fewer popular votes than his Democrat rival, Vice-President Al Gore. In the United States, however, presidential elections are determined not by the national popular vote but by the number of electoral college votes that each state is allocated. In 2000, the election came down to which candidate had won the state of Florida, but this was not easy to determine. Bush appeared to have won by a narrow margin, but the Gore campaign challenged the fact that some votes had not been counted because the voting machine had not punched clean through the ballot papers. A lengthy judicial wrangle followed, and in the end the United States Supreme Court stepped in and in effect awarded the state – and the presidency – to Bush.

The 2000 election only added to the bitterness of the divisions in America. Many Democrats believed that Bush had stolen the election and deplored the fact it was the most conservative justices on the Supreme Court who had ruled in his favour. President Bush won again in 2004. Although no one challenged the legitimacy of that election, the margin of victory was narrow. It demonstrated once again that the country was sharply and evenly divided.

The American political system is under considerable pressure in the first decade of the twenty-first century. Its foreign policies require unity and strong leadership, while on the domestic front the people are divided and half of them reluctant to be led by President George W. Bush. The foreign policy agenda is fraught with difficulty, as are some of the main domestic policy issues. The obvious question that arises is: is the American system of government and politics well-equipped to deal with these difficult challenges? What are its strengths and what are its weaknesses? Does it really serve the interests of the country that President Abraham Lincoln described as 'the last best hope of mankind'?

Chapter 1

The Constitution and constitutionalism

This chapter examines the origins, development and impact of the single most important document in American politics – the Constitution of the United States. The Constitution provides not only a framework for government in America, but also a way of thinking about government. For inseparable from the Constitution is the idea of constitutionalism – the belief that all things governmental and political must comply with the principles set out in that document. The US Constitution was drafted in 1787 and came into force in 1789. Yet it is no mere historical relic. Because it has been regarded as a 'living document', subject to new interpretations as well as formal amendment, it has developed in line with the socio-economic and political transformation of America from a rural, eastern seaboard nation to a post-industrial, continental power that dominates the world in so many respects. As you might expect, just as America has not achieved this transformation without struggle and contention, so too the Constitution has been fought over and its development has been far from smooth. Nevertheless, it remains the keystone of American government and any understanding of American politics must begin with an appreciation of the Constitution and constitutionalism.

The origins of the Constitution of 1787

The Constitution of 1787 has philosophical roots in the progressive European thought of the eighteenth century, but its driving force was a distinctly practical consideration: how to replace British colonial rule with a government that was effective but not repressive. The United States had been wrestling with this problem since the Declaration of Independence in 1776, but even after the successful conclusion of the War of Independence in 1783, it still had not found a solution. Part of the difficulty lay in the fact that achieving independence and implementing self-government were distinctly different projects, and Americans took some time to make the transition from the one to the other. It was also the case that the people who provided the momentum for independence were not the same as those who seized the initiative to write a new constitution in 1787: not only did they have different goals, but, to some extent, different interests and ideologies too. The outcome was that the more radical thought behind the Declaration of Independence was, in part, replaced by the more pragmatic conservatism of the Founding Fathers. As a consequence, the Constitution emerged as an innovative document that combined radicalism, conservatism and sheer pragmatism. That combination is still evident today and each element needs to be understood by any student of contemporary American politics and government.

The Declaration of Independence and the American Revolution

Historians disagree over the causes of the American Revolution. Some argue that economic rivalry between American and British merchants fanned the flames of revolution, while others point to American resentment of new taxes being imposed on them without consultation. A third view is that Americans were simply developing a national self-consciousness that led naturally to the desire to rule themselves. All of these probably played their part. Certainly the period from the end of the Seven Years War between Britain and France (1756–63) until the Declaration of Independence in 1776 saw rising tensions over clashes of economic interests. The British tried to tax Americans more heavily and to control trade more strictly in the interests of British merchants, both with the aim of recuperating some of the expenses of the war with France. It is also logical that such clashes would increase awareness that British and American interests were not identical and that greater self-rule was desirable in order to nurture America's distinctive needs.

Where there is broad agreement among historians is that most Americans were reluctant revolutionaries. Indeed, many of those who felt obliged to back the movement for independence saw themselves as fighting to restore the rights of Englishmen, rather than to abandon the political traditions of the Mother Country. In effect, the independence activists were immersed in a political debate between Whigs and Tories in Britain that dated back to the English Civil War. The Whigs took their cue from the writings of the English philosopher, John Locke. Accordingly, they opposed the notion of the divine right of kings to rule as they see fit and believed that each man has natural rights, granted to him by God, that no king or parliament could take away. They also accepted Locke's belief that governments depend ultimately on the consent of the people: if a government violates the social contract between the ruler and the ruled, then the people have the right to change their government.

Only when they finally realised that they could never persuade George III to accept their Whig agenda, did the Americans turn to independence. As Michael Heale put it, 'The only course left was rebellion, a rebellion which was begun . . . not so much against the British constitution as on behalf of it' (Heale, 1977, p. 34). In this sense, it can be misleading to think of the independence movement as *revolutionary*. Certainly there was no intention to overthrow the economic or social order that prevailed in the colonies. On the other hand, the mere act of overthrowing an established monarchy through a popular uprising was a radical step. Indeed, the main purpose of the Declaration of Independence was less to announce independence than to justify it. Moreover, the act of fighting for independence did bring forth more radical thinking.

One manifestation of this was the contrast between the new state constitutions that followed in the wake of the Declaration of Independence and the colonial systems of government that preceded them. While the War of Independence was emphatically not fought to create a democracy in America, it did inspire a strengthening of democratic elements in the new constitutions. For example, while no state formally abolished property qualifications for the franchise, states such as New

Box 1.1

The Declaration of Independence (1776) and equality

Jefferson's Declaration consists for the most part of a long list of somewhat contentious accusations levelled at King George III. However, it is best remembered and celebrated for its ringing proclamation of the equality of all men, their possession of unalienable rights, and popular consent and sovereignty as the legitimate basis of government:

'We hold these truths to be self-evident, that all men are created equal, that they are endowed by their Creator with certain unalienable rights, that among these are Life, Liberty and the pursuit of Happiness.

That to secure these rights, Governments are instituted among Men, deriving their just powers from the consent of the governed, That whenever any Form of Government becomes destructive of these ends, it is the Right of the People to alter or abolish it, and to institute a new Government . . .'

Much debate surrounds Jefferson's claim that 'all men are created equal', given the existence of slavery in the American colonies. Indeed, Jefferson himself was a slave-owner. How can this contradiction be explained, if not by sheer hypocrisy or unconscious racism? In terms of political theory, Jefferson was simply restating John Locke's premise that, in the state of nature prior to the formation of society, all men are created equal by God. At the same time, Jefferson and some others were clearly aware that slavery was wrong and could do untold harm to America at some point in the future. Of course, they were proved right as a bitter conflict soon developed over the abolition of slavery which culminated in the Civil War (1861–65). The Declaration's statement of equality was at odds with slavery and, for that reason, it became a rallying cry for abolitionists. Other groups, most obviously women, have also invoked the Declaration of Independence in their struggles for liberty and equality. It has thus proved an invaluable tool for those determined to make American practice match the promise of the American Revolution.

Thomas Jefferson.

Hampshire, Pennsylvania and Georgia eased them to the point where there was near-universal white male suffrage. Another democratic spurt came in the form of frequent elections to state legislatures, something which increased popular control of political elites.

At the national level, however, the most obvious radical development was the decision to replace a monarchy with a republic. Whig theory allowed for both monarchical and republican systems of government, but even in the years immediately prior to independence, most Americans thought of republicanism in pejorative terms. It was a close relative of the even more alarming concept of democracy, which was equated with 'mob rule'. Yet practical considerations pushed Americans into republicanism, including the impossibility of finding an American royal family to replace the British one. Embracing a republic, however, required a deliberate and careful attempt to distinguish it from democracy. As a result, American constitutionalism after independence was based on incorporating democratic elements of government, while ensuring that they were contained by elitist counterbalances.

While most of those who led the independence movement retained aristocratic or even monarchist leanings, there were more radical voices, such as that of Thomas Paine, the English pamphleteer, and Sam Adams, the Massachusetts politician. These radicals pushed hard in the direction of popular control of government. Between 1776 and 1789 they were engaged in something of a political struggle with the conservatives to control America's political destiny. The historian Donald Lutz argues that

---

Box 1.2

Thomas Paine's *Common Sense*
The Rule of Law Should Replace the Rule of Kings

In his famous work *Common Sense*, published on the eve of the War of Independence in 1776, Paine sought to reassure those who feared the vacuum that would be left by the overthrow of the monarchy. The rule of the king, he said, would be replaced by the rule of law.

Thomas Paine.

'But where says some is the King of America? I'll tell you Friend, he reigns above, and doth not make havoc of mankind like the Royal of Britain. Yet that we may not appear to be defective even in earthly honors, let a day be solemnly set apart for proclaiming the charter; let it be brought forth placed on the divine law, the word of God; let a crown be placed thereon, by which the world may know, that so far as we approve of monarchy, that in America THE LAW IS KING. For as in absolute governments the King is law, so in free countries the law ought to be King; and there ought to be no other.'

Paine was considered a dangerous radical by the British and, indeed, by many Americans. With hindsight, however, Paine was simply in the vanguard of the movement for American democracy and his ideas came to be embraced by most Americans.

the radicals had the upper hand at first, but had lost their grip by 1787. As a result, 'the political theory underlying the Declaration of Independence of 1776 is not the same as that underlying the Constitution of 1787. The theory of consent implicit in the Declaration not only does not naturally evolve into the Constitution but in some important respects is contradictory to it' (Lutz, in Graham and Graham, 1977, p. 61).

Whatever the nuances of political theory and the clash of interests and factions, there remains a common core to American politics in the period 1776–87. The most important was a commitment to republicanism and a government based on popular consent. This embraced political ideas and rhetoric that facilitated, over time, the emergence of a modern democracy. In short, while the War of Independence was not fought to create a democracy and while the Constitution did not produce one, both contained seeds of democracy that were to germinate and flourish in time.

The Articles of Confederation 1781–1789

The Articles were America's first constitution and they embodied the spirit of 1776. The Americans had fought to overthrow a distant, centralised government. It was logical, then, to replace it with government close to the people and that meant government at the state level. As a result, the Articles provided only for the very weakest of national governments. There was no national executive or judiciary at all. And the national legislature – the Congress – was so constituted that it was, as Merrill Jensen put it, 'the creature of the state governments and thus, ultimately, of the electorate of the states' (in Latham, 1956, p. 16). Each state, regardless of size, had one vote in the Congress. And, without any effective means of ensuring compliance with such decisions as were agreed, states could simply renege on their commitments. The Congress had no independent power to raise revenue and, as the end of the war came into view, the states were even less inclined than before to attend to national issues.

There were those in the country who believed that a stronger national government was both necessary and desirable. Becoming known as the Federalists, they were alarmed by certain developments in the post-independence years. For example, the Congress was showing few signs of being willing to honour the national debt that had grown up to pay for the war. If the United States failed to repay this, it was unlikely that bankers would be willing to invest further in America. This would undermine economic development and prosperity. Another problem was the growing tendency of states to behave as economic rivals, imposing trade barriers on each other's goods. Yet another major problem was defence and social order. Federalists feared that a weak United States might yet fall prey to the colonial designs of European powers still present on the continent. Moreover, there was alarm at internal unrest, such as the so-called Shay's Rebellion in Massachusetts in 1786–87.

These issues prompted the Federalists to call for the amendment of the Articles of Confederation. Delegates from the states were asked to gather in Philadelphia in 1787 to discuss proposed changes. However, once the Constitutional Convention was in place, it staged a political coup. Rather than working on amendments to the Articles, it called instead for a new constitution to be drafted along Federalist lines. Supporters of the Articles of Confederation, the Anti-Federalists, had shown themselves fatally complacent by not attending in sufficient numbers at Philadelphia. When a new constitution was duly produced, the Anti-Federalists were already on the back foot and never recovered. The Constitution of 1787 was ratified by the required nine states and came into operation in 1789.

The philosophy and design of the Constitution

The differences between the philosophy of the Declaration of Independence and that of the Constitution of 1787 can, to a significant degree, be explained by differences in purpose. The Declaration was a justification for an anti-colonial war.

The Constitution was intended to produce a government that would consolidate independence and take the country forward. The Founding Fathers therefore took the core philosophy of the Declaration but applied it to the practical task of gaining agreement on a new and more effective national government system. Political principle was combined with pragmatism to produce a unique document. At the heart of the new Constitution lay a number of key features that embodied both pragmatism and principle.

Federalism

It was noted above that under the Articles of Confederation the national government was 'the creature of the states'. One major problem for the Philadelphia Convention, therefore, was how to transfer enough power from the states to the national government to make it effective, without transferring so much that the states would never allow it. This was solved by compromises in two key respects. First, the powers of the national or *federal* government would be specified or *enumerated*. The logic was that any power not specifically granted to the federal government remained in the possession of the state governments. This logic was later reinforced by the Tenth Amendment to the Constitution (see Bill of Rights below). Secondly, the states were given control of the upper chamber of the Congress, the United States Senate. This was achieved in two ways. First, the states were given equal representation in the Senate: two senators per state, regardless of population. Secondly, the state legislatures were given control over the selection of their senators. Since no national legislation could be approved without the consent of the Senate, the states could use their power base there to block any unwanted expansion by the federal government.

Popular consent and representation

While all the Founding Fathers agreed that the legitimacy of government depended ultimately upon popular consent, they did not agree on how much direct involvement the people should have in government. Some, like James Madison, were convinced that the lower chamber of the Congress, the House of Representatives, must be directly elected by the citizenry. He believed that the stability of the government would depend considerably on whether the people had faith in its ability to reflect their moods and demands. Others, like Elbridge Gerry, thought this unwise. His experience in his home state of Massachusetts had convinced him that the people were often misinformed and too easily misled by 'designing men'. However, with the people shut out of the selection of the president, the senators and the justices of the Supreme Court, the more democratically-minded delegates carried the day on the House of Representatives. This was to be the major democratic element in the new Constitution.

The separation of powers

The principle of the separation of powers was a familiar one by 1787. As expounded by the French political thinker, Baron de Montesquieu, in his book *On the Spirit of Laws* (1748), the separation of powers in government would help to prevent despotism. And while Montesquieu thought the British government was based on such a separation, Americans believed that they had been in danger of tyranny because of George III's attempt to subvert it. For the Founding Fathers, then, the separation of powers into legislative, executive and judicial branches of government came quite naturally.

The problem at Philadelphia was how to turn the separation of powers into functioning government institutions. And while it was important to ensure that none of these institutions would become too powerful, it was also important that all three of them should be able to function effectively together. The Convention devoted considerable time to the construction of the three institutions and all three required compromise between the delegates. One of the thorniest issues was the process of selecting the various office-holders. If, as was at first suggested, the president (executive) was to be chosen by the Congress (legislative), would this not undermine the separation of powers by allowing the control of one office by another?

Box 1.3

The separation of powers and the selection process

Executive Branch   **The President**
Chosen by the electoral college, composed of state delegations whose members are selected in a manner determined by each state legislature

Legislative Branch   **The Congress:**
The House of Representatives
Members chosen directly by the voters in each state district

The Senate
Members chosen by state legislatures in any manner they wish

Judicial Branch   **The Supreme Court**
Justices chosen jointly by the president and the Senate. The president nominates Supreme Court justices and the Senate confirms or rejects them.

In the end, the Convention came up with selection systems that differed for each institution and that avoided placing selection in the hands of another institution acting alone.

Checks and balances

The separation of powers was complicated, however, by the further imposition of checks and balances on each institution. The president was given a veto over any bill passed by Congress, although this could be overridden by a two-thirds majority of both the House and the Senate. The Congress, for its part, could restrain the activities of the president through its control of finances, *the power of the purse*. Each chamber of Congress checked the other, because all bills have to be passed in identical form by both the Senate and the House before they become law. This ability to intervene in the powers exercised by other branches of government had both negative and positive aspects to the exercise of federal power. As already noted, it made it difficult for any branch to become dominant to the point of tyranny. Moreover, because representatives of many different interests and viewpoints could influence national policy-making, the system was highly consensual.

However, the other side of that coin was that the system would prove difficult to coordinate and allowed entrenched minorities to block action that might benefit the majority. This tension between majority and minority power is a major feature of American government to this day.

Ratification of the Constitution

The Convention decided that each state should be given the opportunity to debate and approve the new Constitution. It would come into force once nine of the thirteen states had ratified it. As a result, there was a national debate over the new Constitution, featuring the Federalists, who supported it, and the Anti-Federalists who opposed it. Both sides produced some thoughtful and persuasive pamphlets. Most famously, for the Federalists, James Madison, Alexander Hamilton and John Jay authored the *Federalist Papers*. Intended principally to persuade the voters of New York State to ratify the Constitution, they have come to be regarded as an authoritative explication of the constitutional design. However, for all the insight they yield into the minds of the framers, it should not be forgotten that they are as much propaganda as an objective

Box 1.4

The Federalists v. the Anti-Federalists, i

The Federalist Papers   No. 10

In the 10th *Federalist*, James Madison famously argued that a large republic, as opposed to either a small republic or a democracy, would prevent any faction from seizing control of the government and using its power to abuse the rights of citizens. The dangerous faction could be a majority or a minority of the people.

'AMONG the numerous advantages promised by a well-constructed Union, none deserves to be more accurately developed than its tendency to break and control the violence of faction. The friend of popular governments never finds himself so much alarmed for their character and fate, as when he contemplates their propensity to this dangerous vice. He will not fail, therefore, to set a due value on any plan which, without violating the principles to which he is attached, provides a proper cure for it. . . .

By a faction, I understand a number of citizens, whether amounting to a majority or a minority of the whole, who are united and actuated by some common impulse of passion, or of interest, adversed to the rights of other citizens, or to the permanent and aggregate interests of the community. . . . A republic, by which I mean a government in which the scheme of representation takes place, . . . promises the cure for which we are seeking. Let us examine the points in which it varies from pure democracy, and we shall comprehend both the nature of the cure and the efficacy which it must derive from the Union.

The two great points of difference between a democracy and a republic are: first, the delegation of the government, in the latter, to a small number of citizens elected by the rest; secondly, the greater number of citizens, and greater sphere of country, over which the latter may be extended.

The effect of the first difference is, on the one hand, to refine and enlarge the public views, by passing them through the medium of a chosen body of citizens, whose wisdom may best discern the true interest of their country, and whose patriotism and love of justice will be least likely to sacrifice it to temporary or partial considerations.'

However, Madison conceded, this might not be enough to prevent scheming men from acquiring the power of government and using it for malevolent purposes. The critical safeguard, he argues, is to have a large republic in which the multiplicity of interests, groups and individuals makes it difficult for a majority to form; and even if it does, it makes it more difficult for that majority to act.

'The smaller the society, the fewer probably will be the distinct parties and interests composing it; the fewer the distinct parties and interests, the more frequently will a majority be found of the same party; and the smaller the number of individuals composing a majority, and the smaller the compass within which they are placed, the more easily will they concert and execute their plans of oppression. Extend the sphere, and you take in a greater variety of parties and interests; you make it less probable that a majority of the whole will have a common motive to invade the rights of other citizens; or if such a common motive exists, it will be more difficult for all who feel it to discover their own strength, and to act in unison with each other. Besides other impediments, it may be remarked that, where there is a consciousness of unjust or dishonorable purposes, communication is always checked by distrust in proportion to the number whose concurrence is necessary.'

What Madison was in effect arguing for was a pluralist republic. That theme of pluralism has run throughout American political history ever since.

analysis of the Constitution. Nevertheless, certain of the *Federalist Papers* are rightly viewed as authoritative statements of the philosophy and hopes of the Founding Fathers, as they set about persuading their fellow citizens of the merits of the new Constitution.

The Anti-Federalists also put their case to the people of the several states through pamphlets and newspapers. One such Anti-Federalist critique of the new Constitution was published as *Letters from the Federal Farmer*, written by either Richard Henry Lee of Virginia or Melancton Smith of New York, or possibly by both. Another anonymous Anti-Federalist was 'Brutus', thought to be Judge Robert Yates of New York. Brutus did not simply disagree with the Federalists over such issues as the merits of a large republic, he was quite prophetic in seeing how the federal government would acquire increasing powers at the expense of the states.

The Anti-Federalists feared a centralised and distant government. They cherished the independent powers of the states and believed that the new Constitution would erode the autonomy of the states. They also feared that there were those who harboured aristocratic or even monarchist sentiments and who would try to use the powers of the federal government for the benefit of the social and economic elite. Unsurprisingly, such fears were widespread and the Federalists only narrowly won the ratification campaign. Even then they had to promise to enact a Bill of Rights that, in the main, emphasised the limits of the new federal government. Moreover, the Anti-Federalist current remained powerful in the new political system, and does so even to this day. Not for nothing do contemporary candidates for national office campaign 'against Washington' and promise to make the federal government hear the voice of the 'ordinary folks' back home.

Box 1.5 The Federalists v. The Anti-Federalists, ii: The Anti-Federalists

'Brutus', Letter in the *New York Journal*, 18 October 1787

Article I, Section 8 of the proposed Constitution was at first glance an unobjectionable statement allowing Congress to use its specified powers through 'all necessary and proper' laws. Brutus, however, correctly foresaw that Article I, Section 8, could be later interpreted to allow Congress a wide array of powers going well beyond those enumerated in the Constitution. Sure enough, in the case of *McCulloch* v. *Maryland* (1819), the US Supreme Court did precisely that and thereby endowed the Congress with an indeterminate number of 'implied powers'. The outcome today is that there is hardly any subject on which Congress may not legislate if it wishes to.

'How far the clause in the 8th section of the 1st article may operate to do away all idea of confederated states, and to effect an entire consolidation of the whole into one general government, it is impossible to say. The powers given by this article are very general and comprehensive, and it may receive a construction to justify the passing of almost any law. A power to make all laws, which shall be *necessary and proper*, for carrying into execution, all powers vested by the constitution in the government of the United States, or any department or officer thereof, is a power very comprehensive and definite [indefinite?], and may, for ought I know, be exercised in a such manner as entirely to abolish the state legislatures. . . .

It is not meant, by stating this case, to insinuate that the constitution would warrant a law of this kind; or unnecessarily to alarm the fears of the people, by suggesting, that the federal legislature would be more likely to pass the limits assigned them by the constitution, than that of an individual state, further than they are less responsible to the people. But what is meant is, that the legislature of the

Box 1.5   continued

United States are vested with the great and uncontroulable powers, of laying and collecting taxes, duties, imposts, and excises; of regulating trade, raising and supporting armies, organizing, arming, and disciplining the militia, instituting courts, and other general powers. And are by this clause invested with the power of making all laws, *proper and necessary*, for carrying all these into execution; and they may so exercise this power as entirely to annihilate all the state governments, and reduce this country to one single government. And if they may do it, it is pretty certain they will; for it will be found that the power retained by individual states, small as it is, will be a clog upon the wheels of the government of the United States; the latter therefore will be naturally inclined to remove it out of the way. Besides, it is a truth confirmed by the unerring experience of ages, that every man, and every body of men, invested with power, are ever disposed to increase it, and to acquire a superiority over every thing that stands in their way. This disposition, which is implanted in human nature, will operate in the federal legislature to lessen and ultimately to subvert the state authority, and having such advantages, will most certainly succeed, if the federal government succeeds at all. It must be very evident then, that what this constitution wants of being a complete consolidation of the several parts of the union into one complete government, possessed of perfect legislative, judicial, and executive powers, to all intents and purposes, it will necessarily acquire in its exercise and operation.'

Box 1.6

The Bill of Rights

The idea of a Bill of Rights had been raised at the Philadelphia Convention but had been rejected. Many believed that the structure of government, characterised by separation of powers, federalism and checks and balances, provided sufficient protection for basic rights. However, during the ratification campaigns, Federalists were forced to concede on this point and promised to begin enactment of the Bill of Rights as soon as Congress met. They were duly enacted and ratified in 1791. Many of the rights protected in the first ten amendments now apply to the states as well as to the federal government. However, it should be emphasised that as originally conceived, they were designed to limit the power of the federal government and preserve state power and citizens' rights. This is most evident in the wording of the First and Tenth Amendments.

The First Amendment

'Congress shall make no law respecting an establishment of religion, or prohibiting the free exercise thereof; or abridging the freedom of speech, or of the press; or the right of the people to assemble, and to petition the government for a redress of grievances.'

The Tenth Amendment

'The powers not delegated to the United States by the Constitution, nor prohibited to it by the states, are reserved to the states respectively, or to the people.'

The development of the Constitution

The fact of agreeing a new Constitution did not mean that the system would necessarily work. Indeed, the sheer novelty of the framers' design was enough to cast doubt on its viability. However, the first generation of national office-holders included many such as Presidents George Washington, Thomas Jefferson and James Madison who honoured the terms of the Constitution while implementing it with flexibility and intelligence. Some clauses of the Constitution were quietly dropped. Thus President Washington at first applied literally the requirement that treaties be ratified with the 'advice and consent' of the Senate. When he asked for advice on a treaty, the Senate took so long to study it that Washington lost patience. Thereafter, he and other presidents simply sent agreed treaties to the Senate for approval: consent was still required, but not necessarily advice.

Two developments that were to prove of enormous importance were the advent of political parties and a power of judicial review vested in the Supreme Court.

Political parties

Madison and many other framers disapproved of parties. They were factions within the meaning of *The Federalist* no. 10 and thus likely to be selfish and harmful to the general welfare. The Constitution was designed to inhibit their emergence, yet they became a feature of national government during the very first presidential administration, that of George Washington (1789–97). Based on the Federalist/Anti-Federalist debate, President Washington found it preferable to surround himself with those who shared his Federalist philosophy. President Thomas Jefferson (1801–9), who garnered the support of the Anti-Federalist current in forming the Democratic-Republican party, took things further by his strategic collaboration with fellow party members in Congress. Although parties briefly disappeared during the so-called 'Era of Good Feelings' (1812–24), they soon re-emerged and remain to this day. Parties are virtually unavoidable in a system with free elections. It is testimony to the Constitution of 1787 that, although it was not designed to cater for them, it has easily been able to encompass their activities. Moreover, if the Constitution did not prevent the rise of parties, as Madison had wished, it did help to ensure that American parties would be weaker than in comparable political systems.

Judicial review of the Constitution

The most important development in the history of the Constitution was the emergence of the United States Supreme Court as its sole, ultimate interpreter. This occurred in the landmark case of *Marbury* v. *Madison* (1803). The Constitution had failed to make clear which institution or group of institutions should have authority to interpret the Constitution. Federalists strongly believed that the Supreme Court should have this power, but Jeffersonians believed that each of the three branches of government had the right to interpret the Constitution. However, for reasons explained in Chapter 8, the Supreme Court successfully claimed a monopoly of the right to declare state and federal laws unconstitutional in 1803. Thereafter, the Court usually took a flexible approach to constitutional questions and, in particular, often showed a shrewd awareness of when statesmanship should trump strict principle in the interpretation of the words of the Constitution. Chief Justice Marshall gave voice to the need for flexibility in his famous dictum in *McCulloch* v. *Maryland* (1819). He said that the Constitution was intended to endure through the ages 'and consequently, to be adapted to the various crises of human affairs'. The notion of flexibility in the Constitution is crucial to the success of the United States. Its society, economy and international role have undergone several transformations since 1789, and only a constitution adaptable to such change could survive.

One of the most important developments in constitutional interpretation involves the First Amendment to the Constitution. Originally viewed as a restriction only on the federal government, the Supreme Court in the twentieth century gradually

Box 1.7

Substantive due process: the magic of constitutional interpretation

The Fifth Amendment to the Constitution reads in part:

'[no person shall] be deprived of life, liberty, or property, without due process of law'

The Fourteenth Amendment has a similar clause, restricting the state governments from doing the same. The wording implies that a certain legal *process* has to be observed by government before citizens can have basic rights taken away. Starting in the nineteenth century and then gathering pace in the twentieth century, the Supreme Court began to interpret the clause as meaning that there were some rights that were so fundamental to a citizen's liberty, that governments could not take them away even if they observed the proper procedures. This new judicial doctrine was called 'substantive due process'. In the contemporary era it has become a subject of sharp debate between the justices of the Supreme Court and has caused considerable controversy outside the Court. This is because 'liberty' has no fixed meaning except that which the justices choose to give it. And in recent decades, a majority of justices have held that it includes a woman's freedom to choose an abortion or a homosexual's freedom to engage in sexual acts with others of the same sex. Substantive due process thus provides a striking example of how judicial interpretation of the Constitution can change to fit the emergence of new societal values and conceptions of liberty.

interpreted its clauses to restrict state governments as well. As a result, states as well as the federal government may not abridge freedom of speech and the press and, in the modern era, this means, for example, that there are few government limits on political or artistic expression. The Supreme Court gradually applied other restrictions on the federal government to the state governments, giving rise to the concept of the 'nationalisation of the Bill of Rights'.

Even more controversially, the 'due process' clauses of the Fifth and Fourteenth Amendments have been expanded to cover more than the procedural rights they originally guaranteed, and are now held to protect rights that were far from the minds of the Founding Fathers.

Sometimes, however, the Court has not proved adaptable enough in its application of the Constitution, with disastrous consequences. Most important, in the case of *Dred Scott* v. *Sandford* (1857) the Court refused to allow Congress a last chance at finding a compromise on slavery. Instead, the Court came down wholly on the side of slave-owners' property rights and thereby helped to cause the Civil War (1861–65). Again, in the first third of the twentieth century the Court upheld a notion of property rights that was probably similar to that held by the framers themselves. When the Great Depression (1929–39) arrived, however, the government needed new powers to deal with the emergency, and some of those new powers infringed that traditional understanding of property rights. As a result the Court clashed with President Roosevelt's New Deal and only saved its independence when it finally recognised the need to adapt to a new concept of government power to regulate property rights.

Constitutional amendment

As well as flexibility of interpretation and adaptation by the Supreme Court, the Constitution has also endured thanks to formal amendment. There have been relatively few amendments – twenty-seven, including the ten that make up the Bill of Rights. Some have been of relatively minor importance, such as the most recent regulating the salaries of members of Congress. Many, however, have been of monumental importance, such as the so-called Civil War amendments (Thirteenth, Fourteenth and Fifteenth) that abolished slavery and advanced equality for black Americans. Others have fundamentally altered the country's political institutions by changing the way the Senate is elected (Seventeenth) and limiting the terms of office of the President (Twenty-second). Still others have extended the right to vote to women (Nineteenth) and 18-year-olds (Twenty-sixth).

The process of constitutional amendment is, however, very cumbersome. Proposed amendments have to be approved by either a two-thirds majority of both houses of Congress or two-thirds of the state legislatures. That is, in itself, difficult to achieve. However, the proposed amendments must then be ratified by three-quarters of the state legislatures. These 'super-majoritarian' requirements empower minorities to defeat even popular proposed amendments. As a result, the difficulty of amending the Constitution serves the legitimate purpose of ensuring that the founding principles of American government cannot easily be altered. Only measures acceptable to the great majority of citizens and states will pass muster.

On the other hand, the formal amendment process is often too rigid a method of responding to those crises and fundamental changes that all nations may endure over the centuries. The Supreme Court, through flexible interpretation of the Constitution, has thus become an informal constitutional convention. While there is not a hint in the Constitution that the Court was intended to play such a role, the fact that it has emerged to do so is testimony to the pragmatism of American constitutionalism. And it is precisely that pragmatism which has permitted the Constitution not only to survive the transformation of the United States since 1787, but to become the most revered document in American politics.

Chapter summary

The Constitution of 1787 was inspired by the desire 'to form a more perfect union'. The chief goal of the framers was to strengthen the national government so that the United States could become safe and prosperous. At the same time, it sought to preserve the philosophical principles of the War of Independence, especially the notion that all government was dependent upon the consent of the governed. This synthesis was achieved by introducing a national legislature, executive and judiciary, while controlling their behaviour through the separation of powers and a system of checks and balances. Although it created a republic rather than a democracy, there were sufficient democratic elements to secure the consent of the governed and for a democracy to emerge with the passage of time. One of the main reasons that the Constitution endures until this day is that it has been applied flexibly, in order to incorporate the new demands that arise from changing times and circumstances.

Discussion points

1. Was the War of Independence a revolutionary movement?

2. Did the framers get the balance right between preventing tyranny and constructing an effective national government?

3. What were the main purposes behind the demand for a Bill of Rights?

4. What are the major sources of flexibility in the Constitution?

5. Were the framers right to make the amendment of the Constitution so difficult?

Further reading

On the ideas and events behind the movement for independence and the Constitution of 1787, see, for example, Michael Heale's *The Making of American Politics, 1750–1850* (London: Longman, 1977) and Jack P. Greene's *Understanding the American Revolution: Issues and Actors* (Charlottesville: University of Virginia Press, 1995). On the Constitution, see R. Maidment and J. Zvesper's *Reflections on the Constitution* (Manchester: Manchester University Press, 1989) and Jack Rakove's *Original Meanings: Politics and Ideas in the Making of the Constitution* (New York: Vintage Books, 1997).

References

Heale, M. (1977) *The Making of American Politics, 1750–1850* (London: Longman).

Jensen, M. (1956) 'The Articles of Confederation', in Latham, E. (ed.) *The Declaration of Independence and the Constitution* (Boston, Mass.: D.C. Heath).

Lutz, D. (1977) 'Popular consent and popular control, 1776–1789', in Graham, G.J. and Graham, S.G. *Founding Principles of American Government* (Bloomington: Indiana University Press), p. 61.

Chapter 2

Federalism

The politically minded citizens of the United States felt competing pressures in the late eighteenth century. They were the proud defenders of a new nation, established in a spectacular stand against the imperial might of Great Britain, but were still vulnerable to predation by strong European powers. The requirement to establish a government system with strength enough to build and maintain the nation's presence on a difficult international scene suggested that a strongly centralised authority was needed. America's population had also developed significantly differing political cultures within the boundaries of distinct colonies and this varied heritage militated against governmental centralisation.

American federalism attempts to answer these competing demands of the system. The structure has proven so resilient that the original states and those added since have retained their individuality in many ways into the third century of America's history as an independent nation. Functions are performed separately and in combination by states, and by the nation, in a way that adds complexity to the American polity, but that provides a flexibility that continues to lie at the core of policy-making and implementation in the United States.

The states were there from the start

The United States has always been a nation of variety. Even the thirteen states that made up the nation in the late eighteenth century already contained populations that were different in their origins and ancestry, in their religious beliefs, in their business interests and their commercial motivations. To some degree the original states had originated, grown and developed around these differences, and competition and separation between states was clearly evident in the early days of American independence, in tension with the generally accepted wish to cooperate within a national structure.

The Articles of Confederation recognised the force of state feeling, speaking of a 'Perpetual Union', but pointing out that 'each state retains its sovereignty, freedom and independence.' This union was clearly made up of states that were in some way seen as equal entities, regardless of size. In the Continental Congress the states had delegations of different sizes, but when decisions were called for they were made on the basis of one vote per state. When the Continental Congress was not sitting authority was passed to a Committee of the States, on which each state had one delegate.

While this initial form of central government for the United States of America had an impressive list of powers delegated to it by the states, it remained a relatively weak authority in what was, even in its original form, a fairly large nation for its time. Conscious of their different origins, and different traditions, the states were not eager to surrender power to the centre, and at times their actions did not meet even the limited obligations that they agreed in support of the central administration. The Continental Congress found national authority difficult to progress in these circumstances.

While some defended the loose confederation as a vibrant environment in which the states could develop their individual responses to their populations' individual needs, other opinions were voiced, concerned that the balance of authority was too much dispersed from the centre. Some political opinion at state level was resistant to moves towards the Philadelphia Convention of 1787, but opinion within some states was becoming sympathetic to the need for greater cooperation at the centre to be somehow sanctioned within the United States.

Box 2.1

The position of the states in 'The Articles of Confederation and Perpetual Union'

This original instrument of American government was constructed to be very conscious of state power. While this probably helped speed the evolution of the United States of America it also limited the strength of its national authority. Federalism scholar Joseph Zimmerman (1992) argues that under the Articles of Confederation the Continental Congress had five major defects:

1. States failed to honour their obligation to fund the national treasury. Congress could not levy taxes. States were expected to contribute, but many of them failed to do so, leaving the national government finances in a critical state.

2. States did not feel obliged to honour nationally initiated legislation or agreements, and Congress had no authority to enforce laws and treaties, or any sanction against those individual states who ignored them.

3. States moved quickly to establish trade tariffs. Business across state boundaries was hampered by barriers of taxes and fees, and Congress had no authority over commerce between states.

4. States could not rely on the support of national armed forces for common defence. In spite of a continuing threat from European forces in North America, and from disharmony within the states, the weak national treasury did not provide the resource for reliable military response.

5. States could dissolve the Union.

The states in the Constitution

Given the significance of the individual states in the early history of the nation it is not surprising that the tension between the states and central authority should surface in several ways, and feature in some of the major compromises that were negotiated on the way to a ratified US Constitution.

Led by James Madison, the delegates to the Philadelphia Convention from Virginia proposed that states be represented in the new national government according to their population. This did not find favour with the smaller states, who felt that

---

Box 2.2

National Powers and State Powers in US Federalism

The US Constitution delegates many powers expressly to the US federal government, particularly in Article I, Section 8, where the powers of Congress are enumerated. The constitution also allows the federal government 'to make all laws which are necessary and proper . . . in the Government of the United States', an 'elastic clause' that broadens central government authority. At the same time the Constitution reserves to the states those powers not specifically given to the federal government, or denied to the states. The boundaries between state and federal authority remains negotiable, and through US history many decisions in the federal courts have contributed to the shifting definition of federalism.

The powers of the US federal government include those:

- to lay and collect national taxes, duties, imposts and excises;
- to provide for the common defence and general welfare of the United States;
- to conduct foreign affairs through diplomacy, and to maintain the armed forces;
- to regulate commerce with foreign nations and between the states;
- to borrow, print and coin money;
- to enforce federal laws;
- to declare and conduct war.

The powers of the state governments include those:

- to establish local governments;
- to provide important services such as education;
- to conduct elections;
- to pass laws on marriage, divorce, wills and domestic relations;
- to exercise state level police power in support of the public welfare.

Powers held concurrently by federal and state governments include those:

- to borrow money, spend money and impose taxes;
- to establish courts;
- to charter and regulate banks;
- to pass, enforce and interpret laws.

their interests would not properly be protected in a system that could be dominated by those states with large populations.

In the compromises that emerged from a summer of debate in Philadelphia state rights were embedded in a number of ways into the proposed constitution. The US Senate, one of the two chambers of the US Congress, was to be made up of two senators from each state, regardless of size, and the senators were to be appointed by the states, through their legislatures. The members of the electoral college, the vehicle for electing the president of the United States, were also to be appointed in a manner chosen by the state legislatures, and the members were only to meet in their separate state capitals. The number of electoral college members allocated to each state was made equal to the state's total numerical representation in the US House and the US Senate, building in the weighting towards small states that equal representation in Senate affords.

While representation in the House of Representatives was designed to be distributed according to the census record of population, the integrity of state borders was protected. No congressional constituency border was allowed to cross a state border, and the states retained the authority to draw the boundaries of the congressional districts within their state borders. The integrity of those state borders was also protected within the Constitution, and cannot be altered without the approval of the state.

The Tenth Amendment of the US Constitution makes it clear that powers not expressly granted to the national government, or prohibited to the states, were 'reserved to the states respectively, or to the people'. In this arcane phraseology we find the constitutional foundation stone of the federal system in the United States. Finally, all of these protections for state authority and participation are protected by a system of constitutional amendment that requires massive state input.

Dealing with differences

Federalism emerges from the US Constitution as one of the core concepts of US government and politics. In a federal system there is a central government and a layer of sub-national governments. Both elements derive their power directly from the citizens and exercise authority directly over the population that elected them.

The central national government (the federal government) consists of those separated, checked and balanced branches – the presidency, Congress, judiciary – established by the US Constitution, and now headquartered in Washington, DC. The various governments of the individual states, their position in the system also guaranteed by the US Constitution, meet in each of the capital cities of America's fifty states.

The US Constitution embeds history into any understanding of contemporary America. Constitutional provisions have been amended, and reinterpreted, but the core documentary foundation of the USA remains intact to a large extent as it was over two centuries ago. The success of governance in twenty-first century America owes a great deal to the strength and the versatility of this historic document.

Federalism institutionalises the states' and the federal governments in a relationship that has to be worked at in order to succeed. The working out of that relationship is important in the defining of an active federal system that can operate to satisfy the various needs of its citizens at national, state and local level.

Federalism also works to create spaces within which the historical variety that has contributed to the nation can still have impact. Waves of immigration from different parts of the world have introduced ethnic variety to the United States throughout its history. A feature of this immigration is that different periods were characterised by the dominance of particular ethnic, national and racial groups, whose settlement patterns have had long-term impact within the federal system.

The early immigrant communities congregated in geographically defined areas, often settling where the experience of the first migrants of that nationality signalled the existence of opportunities. Scandinavian farmers, for example, colonised mid-western agricultural states such as Minnesota and Wisconsin. German brewers also ended up in the

Figure 2.1 Flags of the individual states grace the south lawn of the Alabama Capitol in Montgomery, which flies the American and state flags over the dome (AP Photo/Dave Martin).

Source: © Empics

Midwest. Irish and Italian communities made use of opportunities in the nation's major cities, which were growing rapidly when these groups were entering the country. Other national groups who moved to the USA in large number in the late nineteenth and early twentieth centuries, such as Polish immigrants, were attracted to the then burgeoning areas of heavy industrial production. Geographical proximity can also be important, and in recent decades there have been increasing concentrations of Asian populations on the West Coast, of Latin American groups in the South and Southwest, and of Cubans in Florida.

Immigrant groups old and new often remain identified at least in part by the variety of their ethnic and religious heritage. The celebration of these differences, whether by Italian-Americans, Cuban-Americans, Irish-Americans, Vietnamese-Americans or other hyphenated-Americans, has become almost perversely a definition of a community's 'Americanness' – partly a nostalgic statement about the nations left behind, but primarily a witness to the community's place in pluralist America.

This web of historic and contemporary demography is laid over a nation where resources – natural, social, and fabricated – are not evenly distributed. For example, traditional heavy industries developed in the nineteenth and twentieth centuries around areas where raw materials could be extracted; similarly, oil extraction has prompted related business in Alaska and in the southern states; the concentration of prestigious universities, for example in Massachusetts and in California, has aided the development of modern, research-based industries in these states; agribusiness regimes of various kinds are dependent on particular predictabilities of weather, water and soil.

The characteristics of America's states and localities continue to reflect the amalgamation of interrelated ethnic, commercial, historical and geographical factors such as these. State boundaries give a political shape and context which can act to maintain these cultural and economic diversities, along with related differences in social and religious organisation, in the face of all homogenising pressures. The protective borders of the states create the environment in which state political cultures,

and local government political cultures can develop sensitive to these important differences. State and local politics reflects this rich variety, and the federal system of government affords these differences a continuing and active place.

Dual federalism

In the scholarship on federalism there are a number of concepts that compete to encapsulate the relationship between the federal and state governments. Commonly there is a distinction drawn between 'dual federalism', a model said to apply to the whole period from America's founding to the early twentieth century, and 'cooperative federalism', covering roughly the last century, and sometimes subdivided into shorter periods. Some scholars are uncomfortable with the apparent concreteness of these categories, and prefer to consider federalism as a steadily evolving system of intergovernmental relations.

The model of dual federalism posits that the national and state governments operate as equals, with authority in separate spheres that do not overlap. The theory assumes that the national government does not stray from the list of powers enumerated in the Constitution, since to do so would breach the boundary of its proper sphere of influence. More prosaically, this is sometimes called 'layer cake' federalism, envisioning the federal and state government structures as layers that might touch but remain identifiably separated and independent within their jurisdictions.

Some scholars have challenged this image, pointing out that even in the early days of federalism there were interventions by the federal government into areas that might be considered reserved to the states, for example, as the federal government intervened to support transport and communications developments that promoted the spread of settlement into the land mass of North America. Nevertheless, it is fair to say that through the nineteenth century most domestic affairs were considered to be the concern of state and local governments.

Dual federalism did not necessarily equate with weak central government. The history of the

Supreme Court has been peppered with cases that deal with a variety of content, but revolve on the relationship between states and the federal government. For example in 1819 the case of *McCulloch v. Maryland* considered the authority of the US Congress to charter a national bank. The Supreme Court's decision in support of the Congress meant much more than the establishment of a new financial institution, since it used the 'elastic', or 'necessary and proper' clause to find the 'implied powers' that gave Congress this authority, and simultaneously underlined that federal law was the supreme law of the land.

Throughout the nineteenth century different challenges came through the courts, creating a body of precedent and helping define the scope of national government power, but by 1860 a wholly different and more tangible challenge was emerging with the approach of a civil war between the states of the Union. The differences between northern and southern states had already produced major legal battles, but tensions simmered on. Southern states argued that they had the authority to nullify federal law in order to protect their way of life and its culture of slavery. With the election of Abraham Lincoln to the presidency southern states began to declare their secession from the Union. Under President Lincoln the North refused to accept that union was a mere creature of the states. The victory of the North was a practical confirmation that the states owed a duty of loyalty to the nation.

Cooperative federalism

Crises such as the US Civil War can have lasting impact on the structure of government. In the USA they have often been associated with a temporary centralising of authority, some aspects of which have not always faded away when the crisis itself has declined in significance. In the first half of the twentieth century the pace of technological, industrial and demographic changes might have been enough to provoke a sense of crisis in some. The Wall Street Crash and the subsequent Great Depression made many feel that unusual responses were needed to face these unusual times, and President Franklin D. Roosevelt responded with a

battery of programmes in the New Deal that helped shift federalism into a new form.

The economic burdens of unemployment, the collapse of business confidence, the failure of industrial investment, and the need for social welfare responses in the 1930s were beyond the experience or resource base of the states. The federal government role in domestic policy expanded dramatically as it moved in to initiate and support domestic welfare, job creation, price and production control in the commercial, financial, industrial and agricultural sectors, all in the name of solving the economic crisis that had fallen upon the United States.

One of the key features of this increased federal government involvement is the federal 'grant-in-aid'. This is a distribution of national funds to states for specific policy purposes. This form of transfer was used first in the late nineteenth century, but it was the Sixteenth Amendment to the US Constitution, passed in 1913, and authorising the federal government's right to collect income tax, that significantly altered the ability of the federal government to use this facility. The national income tax gave federal government a resource much greater than had existed before – a foundation on which a more cooperative relationship could be built between levels of government, and in which the voice of the federal government could be heard clearly stating policy objectives.

Fiscal federalism – spending (and raising) the revenue

It is clear that state and local government cannot be disregarded as small or parochial. For example, the general expenditure by the US federal government in 1999 was $1,465,796 million. Almost 19 per cent of this ($274,872 million) was spent on defence. A further $580,488 million (39.6 per cent) was reserved for nationally paid pensions and health care benefits. Of the total federal outlay, just $610,436 million was left for other spending, some of which went into domestic programmes. In the same year combined state and local spending, all on domestic programmes, amounted to $1,398,533 million – substantially more than the direct spending on domestic policy that could be made by the federal government. This is the consistent pattern of government spending in the USA.

In individual policy areas states regularly spend twice as much as the federal government on welfare. State and local governments outspend the federal government on health services and hospitals by almost five to one. On higher education, state and local governments spend ten times more than the federal government. Highways, and police, prisons and probation services are other policy areas supported primarily by state and local governments.

In some policy areas, state and local governments are especially important. For example, while the federal government spent $637 million on primary and secondary education in 1999, state governments spent $2,925 million, and local governments made an outlay of $336,946 million, well over 500 times more than the federal government. Education is the single largest item in local government budgets, amounting to 41.4 per cent in 1999.

In addition to the policy areas already discussed, with fire protection, policing, sanitation and a wide variety of other functions dealt with at this level it is clear to see that, within the federal system, state and local government is critical in the provision of public services that have a direct effect on the day-to-day lives of Americans. The state and local control of such a wide spectrum of areas provides the opportunity for different communities to design policy agendas suitable to their needs and their political culture. It also allows the possibility of different local and state governments confronting similar issues in alternative and different ways. Forums exist for state governors, state attorneys-general, city mayors and many other government officers to discuss the issues that they have in common in the search for innovative and successful policies. This is one significant way in which the states and localities continue to perform a role encapsulated in Supreme Court Justice Louis Brandeis' description of the states as America's 'laboratories of democracy'.

The federal grant-in-aid support of states and their local governments has grown over the past generation, both in terms of dollars and as a percentage of total federal outlays, but looks relatively constant when expressed as a percentage of gross domestic product, and as a proportion of expenditure from state and local sources. This provides further evidence for the growth of state and local governments as the focus of domestic policy spending, though only a proportion of that money is raised directly by state and local governments.

In 2001, the largest single element within the estimated $316,265 million total federal grants-in-aid was $141,793 million, or nearly 45 per cent of the total, for health policy expenditure, most of which was to help underwrite the states' Medicaid programme expenditure. Other large elements were $69,627 million (22 per cent) for income security programmes such as food stamps and child nutrition; $46,844 million (14.8 per cent) for education and employment services; and $35,264 million (11.2 per cent) for transportation. Smaller elements went to support policies such as natural resources, agriculture, community development, justice and veterans benefits.

The federal government gains influence through the grant-in-aid programme since, as the collector and distributor of these funds, it is in a position to demand terms and conditions for their receipt of funds. Decisions on the distribution of grants will be affected by government priorities, and funding may be designed to satisfy multiple aims. The federal government is in this happy position since it collects over 68 per cent of all the tax revenue collected by governments in the USA, almost all from income tax.

State and local governments do not have the same relatively easy access to tax revenues. State and local income taxes raise only a fraction of the national take, and are supplemented by sales taxes (most important to states), property taxes (providing almost three-quarters of local government tax revenue), and an increasingly wide range of other revenue streams.

With only one exception the states are required to balance their budgets, and while there are ways to finesse this limitation, they certainly cannot plan to run constant, and even growing, deficits, as happens regularly at the federal level. Their own-sourced revenue is therefore particularly subject to broader changes in economic conditions.

Table 2.1 Federal grants-in-aid, 1970 to 2001

	Total grant ($ million)	As percentage of state/ local govt expenditures from own sources	As percentage of all federal outlays	As percentage of GDP
1970	24,065	29.1	12.3	2.4
1975	49,791	34.8	15.0	3.2
1980	91,385	39.9	15.5	3.3
1985	105,852	29.6	11.2	2.6
1990	135,325	25.2	10.8	2.4
1995	224,991	31.5	14.8	3.1
2000	284,659	31.3	15.9	2.9
2001 (est.)	316,265	n/a	17.0	3.1

Source: Constructed from data on US Bureau of the Census website: http://www.census.gov

Table 2.2 Grants-in-aid by policy area, 2001

	Total grant ($ million)
Energy	479
Natural resources and environment	5,092
Agriculture	842
Transportation	35,264
Community and regional development	8,739
Education, employment, training, social services	46,844
Health	141,793
Income security	69,627
Veterans benefits and services	445
Administration of justice	4,465
General government and miscellaneous	2,675
Total	316,265

Source: Constructed from data on US Bureau of the Census website: http://www.census.gov

The 1990s saw a period of economic growth in the USA, and some states, such as California, did particularly well.

The sharp reversal of the stock exchange boom, accelerated by post-September 11th, 2001 economic anxieties, hit state governments particularly hard. Reported state government reserves fell by more than 75 per cent in the three years to 2003, leaving many states in considerable fiscal stress. New York raised taxes in 2003, while California cut spending, for example by halting planned road-construction. Kentucky saw a decline in child care provision, while Michigan cut its budget for environmental enforcement by one-third. Federalism does not solve such problems, but it does create a context in which the states may be able to show flexibility, individuality and innovation in their various responses.

Table 2.3 State and local government general revenue sources, 2000

	$
Property tax	249,177,604,000
Sales tax	215,112,414,000
Individual income taxes	211,660,682,000
Corporation income taxes	36,058,903,000
Other taxes	160,341,511,000
Total other charges	223,479,819,000
Other own revenue	153,541,798,000
Own-source revenue	1,249,372,731,000
Intergovernmental revenue (inc. grants-in-aid)	291,949,750,000
Total general revenue	1,541,322,481,000

Source: Constructed from data on US Bureau of the Census website: http://www.census.gov

Table 2.4 State and local government combined general
expenditures, 2000

	$
Elementary and secondary education	365,180,872,000
Public welfare	233,350,301,000
Higher education	134,351,694,000
Health and hospitals	127,341,578,000
Prisons and corrections	48,805,439,000
Police	56,798,071,000
Highways	101,335,910,000
Interest on debt	69,813,738,000
Other	365,790,018,000
Total direct expenditure	1,502,767,621,000

Source: Constructed from data on US Bureau of the Census
website: http://www.census.gov

The states and their local governments in US federalism

Fixing the parameters of the balance of power and authority between federal and state governments has occupied a good deal of political and legal energy ever since the nation was founded. Washington DC is the hub of the federal political structure, and politics at the national level often dominates political discourse. The undoubted significance of the national government should not, however, mask the considerable importance of state and local government in the United States.

For the most part, state government structures follow the national style. Forty-nine of the states have bicameral legislatures, modelled on the example of the two chambers of the US Congress, the House of Representatives and the Senate, although sometimes in the states these chambers have been given different appellations. Nebraska is the sole exception, with a single chamber (unicameral) state legislature, where all the members are state senators. Nebraska also has the distinction of being the only state where the legislature is nominally non-partisan. Unlike the situation in all the other forty-nine states, candidates for election to the state legislature in Nebraska do not stand as political party nominees. Elsewhere in the country the state

political parties are key to the elections process, and the state legislative bodies are organised along party lines after the election.

State governors and lieutenant governors fill the leading executive positions in each state, but many states elect other members of the executive branch too. Various state level ballots offer the opportunity to vote for state treasurer, attorney-general, secretary of state, and other statewide offices, and in about half the states members of the state judiciary are also subject to election.

The design of local government is very much the creature of the state. This allows for regional decision-making, and consequently there is considerable variation in sub-state government patterns across the nation. There is a tendency to reflect the federal model in the practical operation of state–local relations, although the constitutional guarantees that exist for states in the federal system are absent at the local level.

Eighty-eight thousand governments

Counties, cities and other general purpose governments are common, but among local governments the most numerous perform specified functions. There are almost 49,000 school districts and special districts set up to serve purposes such as the running of schools, and the organisation and administration of drainage and irrigation districts, power authorities and public housing authorities.

General purpose local governments make up almost 39,000 more units – counties, municipalities, towns and townships. In June 2002, the US Bureau of the Census counted 87,576 separate governments in the United States. The national government in Washington is one of these and the individual state governments constituted fifty more. The rest of these government units consisted of the immense variety of local governments throughout the nation.

With such considerable governmental diversity, accurate generalisations are inevitably rare. American federalism preserves the opportunity for local communities, within the parameters of the US Constitution and inside their own political boundaries, to take local responsibility for differentiations in local politics and policy implementation. The result is a system of domestic politics and government containing myriad variations between states, and between other governments within states.

There has been a trend over the last generation towards greater activity at state and local level, and this has continued into the twenty-first century. At local government level there has been a growth in the number of governments as well as the number of employees within local government, but these recorded very different rates of expansion. In the thirty years up to 2002 the number of local governments grew by 11.8 per cent, but the last of these decades was a period of relative stability in the number of local governments, with the number expanding at less than 1 per cent, and that rate slowing in the second half of the decade. Over the whole thirty-year period the number of general purpose local governments has remained almost static, but the number of schools districts has declined by 9.1 per cent, while the number of special districts with other functions has increased by 24.8 per cent. This expansion in the use of special districts accounts for almost all the growth in the number of local governments in the past three decades.

Employment trends in state and local government confirm the shift towards the significance of states and localities in the American federal system. While the number of federal (central) government employees fell over the whole thirty-year period to 2002, and showed a dramatic fall of 413,000 (13.3 per cent) in the final decade of that period, both state and local government employment grew steadily and considerably throughout this time.

In the thirty years between 1972 and 2002 the number of employees at state government level rose by 71.5 per cent. While the greatest growth came in the middle of this period, there was still a rise of 12.2 per cent in the number of state employees in the decade to 2002. At the local government level almost 4.7 million new jobs were created between 1972 and the end of the twentieth century, showing a 58.6 per cent growth over the whole period, and with a rate of increase still very solid at the end of this time. In the 1970s state and local governments employed almost 11 million people, less than four times the workforce of the central government. By the beginning of the twenty-first century

Table 2.5 Federal, state and local governments

	Federal	State	Local
1972			
Number of units	1	50	78,218
Employees	2,832,000	2,957,000	7,970,000
1982			
Number of units	1	50	81,780
Employees	2,862,000	3,744,000	9,235,000
1992			
Number of units	1	50	86,692
Employees	3,103,000	4,521,000	10,930,000
2002			
Number of units	1	50	87,525
Employees	2,690,000	5,072,000	12,639,000
			(1999 figure)

Source: Constructed from data on US Bureau of the Census website: http://www.census.gov

Table 2.6 US local governments come in many forms

Counties	3,034
Municipalities	19,429
Townships	16,504
Sub-total – General purpose local governments	38,967
School districts	13,506
Special districts	35,052
Sub-total – Special purpose governments	48,558
Total – Local Governments	87,525

Source: Constructed from data on US Bureau of the Census website: http://www.census.gov

state and local governments paid nearly 18 million employees, almost seven times as many employees as the central government had on its payroll.

Local government can be 'special', local democracy may be 'direct'

The structure of local government offers a particular way in which differences across the nation can be expressed within the governmental structure. County governments are almost ubiquitous in the states, excepting only Rhode Island and Connecticut, although not all county governments have exactly the same range of functions. Towns and township governments exist in a total of twenty states, concentrated in the Northeast and Midwest United States, but only some of the New England states maintain the tradition of annual town meetings, a general meeting of local citizens to take the town's major political decision, and make its major political appointments.

Across the USA there is a patchwork of thousands of local governments designed to undertake particular functions. Special districts have a certain degree of administrative and financial independence, and come in many forms. More than 90 per cent of special districts have been created to perform single functions. The biggest sub-group of special districts is devoted to delivering elementary and secondary education. While amalgamation has reduced the number of school districts considerably over the past generation there were still 13,506 in 2002.

Many other special districts are dedicated to functions such as the provision and management of drainage, flood control, irrigation, and soil and water conservation. Fire protection, housing and community development, and water and sewerage provision are also often dealt with by special district governments, and in some states they might deal with cemetery upkeep, or mosquito control. Some states put particular faith in this form of local government, and over half of the nation's special districts are accounted for by only eleven states.

Some states provide another form of citizen access to their political system, through the 'direct democracy' of initiative, referendum and recall elections. The forms of participation differ, but

Figure 2.2 Whether gay marriage should be formally recognised has been a contentious issue in recent elections at state and federal level.

Source: © Ann Johansson/Corbis

Box 2.3

The fifty states and gay marriage

The states have the responsibility for the details of marriage and divorce law. There are differences between states regarding such details as minimum ages and periods of notice, and the state of Nevada in particular has become known for the lack of bureaucracy surrounding the marriage ceremony. These differences notwithstanding, individual states recognise marriages performed in other states.

This comity has been strained in the growing debate over gay marriage. In 1996 the US Congress passed the federal Defence of Marriage Act, which prohibits federal recognition of same-sex marriages, and which allows states to refuse recognition to gay marriages performed in other states.

As well as the emotional value that a formal marriage might provide to a couple, the institution of marriage is associated with all kinds of rights and responsibilities. Taxation, inheritance and pensions may all be affected by marital status. The right to be involved when a 'next of kin' is needed to make a decision does not automatically transfer to a life partner of the same sex.

The Massachusetts Supreme Judicial Court ruled in 2003 that the state's constitution guaranteed equal rights to gay couples, and from May 2004 same-sex marriages were performed in that state. There were others around the nation who felt that their local laws were gender-neutral. Decisions made locally in San Francisco, California, and by county officials in Portland, Oregon and Multnomah County, New Mexico, also allowed the issue of marriage licences to some gay couples.

Gay marriage became a major issue in the 2004 election, when various groups of local state legislators and conservative citizen activists inserted questions on the ballot in eleven states: Arkansas, Georgia, Kentucky, Michigan, Mississippi, Montana, North Dakota, Oklahoma, Ohio, Oregon and Utah. In all of those states the vote favoured amendments to the state constitutions to define marriage as applying only to heterosexual couples.

As of early 2005, most states had laws prohibiting gay and lesbian marriages. Some states were introducing further legislation, or state constitutional amendments, to reinforce marriage as a heterosexual institution. Anti-gay marriage activists indicated that the issue would continue to be pursued in state legislatures and that initiatives would appear on more state ballots, while gay and lesbian advocate groups were taking their case to the courts in a number of states. There was some political momentum for federalising the issue by amendment to the US Constitution.

The states face a difficult situation. Most Americans oppose gay marriage, but only a minority of the public support a US constitutional amendment on the topic, and a solid majority of citizens are in favour of some legal recognition of the civil union of same-sex couples. In Vermont, for example, state law defines marriage as between man and woman, but additionally, since 2000, a state of civil union between partners in same-sex relationships has provided access for Vermont's gay couples to state-level marriage benefits. California, Hawaii and New Jersey have similar formulae for providing some rights.

In general the position of homosexuals in the USA has improved in recent decades but, as in many civil rights battles before, this is a slow and uneven process. As the states confront the gay marriage issue the pattern of responses will reflect the differing political cultures of the fifty states.

over half the states, the District of Columbia, and a number of sub-state governments give the voters an opportunity to comment directly on legislative measures through initiative propositions and/or referenda which are included on the election day ballot.

In many states these political forms have been dormant or used only occasionally since they were first introduced, early in the twentieth century, but there have been high profile examples of their use, and the popular use of initiative propositions has increased over the past generation. For example, in California, Massachusetts, Colorado, Michigan and Oregon, propositions have been used in single-issue campaigns to cap local taxation rates, legalise the medical use of marijuana, abolish bilingual education in schools, attempt to limit the size of hog farms, and to try to introduce an assisted suicide law. State-level democracy was startlingly evident on election day 2004, when voters in eleven states were presented with ballot questions on gay marriage (see Box 2.3).

In addition, in about one-third of states a public petition can force a special recall election. The single question put in a recall election is whether

Table 2.7 Special district government by function (not including school districts), 2002

	Percentage
Natural resources (drainage, flood control, irrigation, soil and water conservation)	19.9
Fire protection	16.2
Water supply	9.7
Housing and community development	9.7
Sewerage	5.7
Cemeteries	4.7
Libraries	4.4
Parks and recreation	3.7
Highways	2.2
Health	2.1
Hospitals	2.1
Education (school buildings)	1.5
Airports	1.4
Utilities (electric, gas, public transport)	1.4
Other single function districts	6.2
Multiple function districts	9.0

Source: Constructed from data on US Bureau of the Census website: http://www.census.gov

Table 2.8 States making greatest, and least, use of special districts, 2002

	Number
Illinois	3,145
California	2,830
Texas	2,245
Pennsylvania	1,885
Kansas	1,533
Missouri	1,514
Colorado	1,414
Washington	1,173
Nebraska	1,146
New York	1,135
Indiana	1,125
Louisiana	45
Hawaii	15
Alaska	14

Source: Constructed from data on US Bureau of the Census website: http://www.census.gov

the current incumbent in an office should be confirmed in that position for a full term, or be removed from the position before the term of office has ended. Governor Gray Davis of California was removed from office by a very high profile recall election in 2003, when he was replaced in office by Arnold Schwarzenegger.

Has federalism stopped being cooperative?

While federalism allows for regional adaptation and change, the continued existence into the 1960s of apparently unassailable racist regimes in some southern states threatened to bring this devolutionary system into disrepute. This served to underscore that state governments generally had at that time failed to adapt to modern political needs. Many state legislatures met only briefly, relied wholly on amateur politicians, and restricted their governors to single, short terms in office. Sometimes individual regimes were corrupt, and the local political environment often limited, rather than encouraged, change.

States found themselves under pressure from the federal government and the federal courts to confront the social and political problems of the late twentieth century. Many resisted for some time, but over time the nation's states responded appropriately.

State legislatures now meet regularly and take a creative approach to policy development. A broader tax base has provided a more solid fiscal foundation. State policy initiatives in education, environmental policy, health care and employment training have increasingly served as models for the national agenda.

Evidence of the increased respect for modernised state government can be found in the number of state governors who have been presidential candidates in recent years. Governors Carter, Reagan, Clinton and Bush have all made the transition to that national office, and other governors have challenged for it.

The period since this modernisation of state governments began has been interpreted by some as a time when states have come back into their own. President Reagan's 'New Federalism' plans sought to thrust many programmes into the hands of the states, and to increase state autonomy in the implementation of programmes funded by federal grants. While the federal funding stream declined in these years, these moves increased the states' experience in policy-making and implementation.

At the same time the Supreme Court's 1985 decision in *Garcia* v. *San Antonio Metropolitan Transit Authority* appeared to weaken the ability of state and local governments to resist federal government legislative pre-emption – in this case the imposition of the Fair Labor Standards Act on state and local governments, with its contingent costs.

In the 1990s the leaders of America's subnational governments became increasingly vocal in their dismay at the number and expense of federal legal requirements for which there was no equivalent federal funding stream. These 'unfunded mandates' give the national government effective control over part of the state and local budget, by determining part of the policy agenda, and demanding that it be underwritten from state and local budgets. After the Republican congressional election successes of 1994 the US Congress passed

the Unfunded Mandate Reform Act (1995), requiring more careful consideration of any legislation that would impose an unfunded mandate totalling more than $50 million. The legislation may have imposed extra steps but it has not outlawed the unfunded mandate, and pressing issues, such as increased security concerns, can still result in costs legislated in Washington, DC, but falling on subnational governments.

The turn of the new century has seen an apparent shift in the Supreme Court towards a more vigorous consideration of federalism. The Court's 1995 decision in *United States* v. *Lopez* declared unconstitutional the Gun-Free School Zones Act (1990). This legislation had made possession of a gun within 1,000 feet of a school into a federal crime. Advocates of states' rights believed that the Act interfered with states' law enforcement authority. Other decisions in similar vein have followed, as Pickerill and Clayton (2004) say, 'invalidating a series of federal statutes, ranging from the Violence Against Women Act to the Gun-Free School Zones Act to the Brady Bill to the Age Discrimination in Employment Act'. These authors go on to point out that while the Court seems to have 'rediscovered constitutional doctrines and limitations on federal power . . . not used since the New Deal' (p. 233), the decisions have generally been by the tightest of Supreme Court margins, five votes to four.

The debate over the nature of American federalism continues to be live and lively, affected by the contexts of local, state and national politics, the pragmatic requirements of funding in any political system, and of decisions made in every branch of the national government. Voices are regularly raised in concern that the defences for state autonomy are eroding. Certainly as technology and communications become increasingly fast there may be an increasing sense of national agendas taking precedence. On the other hand there remain considerable differences between the states. A few moments of thought would suffice to compose a simple list of economic, geographic, environmental and demographic reasons why the citizenry of, say, Alaska, Florida, New Mexico or Idaho are likely to have different policy questions high on their agendas. It is a commonplace to point out that California's gross domestic product would put it among the top nations in the world, but it is no less true that other states also have 'nation-sized' economies. All of these are run by state governments that will continue to press the value of their place in the US federal system.

the opportunity for locally dominant groups to reject cultural and political progress. It is not unusual for federal principles to be tested in the Supreme Court, and recent decisions have maintained an emphasis on the rights and individuality of the states.

Chapter summary

In the federal system of the United States of America the national government and the state governments each have a direct relationship with the electorate. If the move from the Articles of Confederation to the US Constitution shifted the balance of authority somewhat to the national government, the states have always retained considerable autonomy. The position of the states is protected constitutionally, and the continuing role of federalism is encapsulated especially in the Tenth Amendment.

The USA is a large and heterogeneous nation. The history of immigration and American national development is imprinted in the differences between states. The variety of natural resources, weather patterns and geographical features are reflected in the industries, businesses and agricultural enterprises of the different states. The states allow the development of local and regional politics in response to these differences within the nation.

The relationship of the states to the national government has changed over time, with closer intergovernmental relationships evolving in recent decades. The federal government has the most effective fund-raising source in the shape of income tax, and federal grants to state and local governments have a huge impact on domestic policies. It is still true though that most domestic policy spending is accomplished at state and local government levels.

The states devolve some authority to local governments, and altogether there are almost 88,000 government units in the USA, some of which operate within very specific policy areas. Many states also offer their citizens the opportunity to vote directly on issues through various forms of referenda that appear on the ballot.

Federalism continues to adapt. The system allows local political and economic reaction to local pressures. At best this encourages the sharing of good practice between local governments, but it can also provide

Discussion points

1. The American federal system was invented as a pragmatic way of bringing the states together as a nation in the late eighteenth century. In the twenty-first century, what are the main benefits to the nation of a system that retains such a strong role for its states?

2. The evolution of the US federal system has resulted in a national web of almost 90,000 different local 'governments'. What are the benefits and the costs of such a network?

Further reading

Joseph Zimmerman's *Contemporary American Federalism: The Growth of National Power* (Leicester: Leicester University Press, 1992) remains an authoritative introduction. David Walker's *The Rebirth of Federalism* (2nd edn, Chatham, NJ: Chatham House, 2001) provides an impressive history and analysis of American federalism. The author found useful Alan Grant's essay 'Devolution and the reshaping of American federalism', in Grant's own edited collection, *American Politics: 2000 and Beyond* (Aldershot: Ashgate, 2000).

References

Pickerill, J.M. and Clayton, C.W. (2004) 'The Rehnquist court and the political dynamics of federalism', *Perspectives on Politics*, vol. 2, no. 2 (June), pp. 233–48.

Zimmerman, J.F. (1992) *Contemporary American Federalism: The Growth of National Power* (Leicester: Leicester University Press).

Chapter 3

Elections and the electorate

This chapter begins with an examination of the complex arrangements made by the framers of the Constitution for the election of the president and members of Congress. We shall see how these arrangements have changed over time and how they translate into political practice in the modern day. We then turn to an analysis of how American voters respond to election campaigns.

The constitutional framework of elections

The Constitution of 1787 was founded upon the principle of popular sovereignty, the notion that government ultimately derives its authority from the consent of the people. This did not mean, however, that the framers were committed to democracy as we understand it today. While they favoured a *republic*, they were opposed to creating a *democracy*, which many of them equated with mob rule. The constitutional framework for elections, therefore, attempted to blend the principle of popular sovereignty with a desire to restrict the power of the people to actually govern the country.

You are already familiar with the idea that the Constitution's 'separation of powers' and 'checks and balances' were intended as anti-majoritarian devices. To reinforce these restraints on democracy yet further, the framers decided that separate institutions would be elected by separate constituencies, operating separate electoral procedures. In other words, the president, the Senate and the House of Representatives would be chosen in different ways, by different people and at different times. Rival institutions would thus check each other by representing the interests of rival constituencies.

The House of Representatives

The House was intended to be the popular, democratic institution of the federal government. Consequently, its members would be kept close to the people in the following ways:

1. By being directly elected by the voters.
2. By frequent elections – every two years.
3. By representing relatively small, local constituencies, apportioned by population.

Originally, the Constitution envisaged the House containing one representative for every 30,000 people. The subsequent growth in population, however, has made this apportionment redundant: on the basis of the 1990 census population figure of over 248 million Americans, constituencies of 30,000 would create a House with 8,270 representatives. Congress has therefore fixed the number of representatives at 435 and growth in population simply means that the size of House constituencies, or *districts*, increases accordingly. Today, a House district contains on average approximately 570,000 persons.

Apportionment by population means that some states send many more members to the House of Representatives than others. Every state is entitled to at least one representative, and this is the case with Wyoming (population 501,000) and Vermont (population 619,000), for example. The largest states fare much better: California (population 35,484,000) has 53 representatives and Illinois (population 12,654,000) has 19.

Members of the House, however, are not intended primarily to represent state interests, but rather the interests of their district – and these can vary considerably even within the same state. For example, the New York inner-city voters of Harlem have very different needs and concerns from rural constituents in upper New York state.

Members of the House, both individually and collectively, are obliged to keep in close touch with constituency opinion by the fact that they serve for only two years before facing re-election. With such a short period between elections, voters are unlikely to forgive or forget any representative who

has seriously offended public opinion on a salient issue. As a result, representatives keep in constant touch with constituency opinion by, for example, making frequent trips back home from Washington and conducting polls in their district on major issues.

Some critics argue that two-year terms make representatives virtual 'slaves' to public opinion and have advocated replacing them with four-year terms. They also argue that it means that representatives spend too much of their time on electioneering in one form or another, and too little of their time on government duties. Whatever the merits of these criticisms, however, the present system does help fulfil the framers' aim of subjecting the House of Representatives to more popular influence than any other branch of the federal government.

The Senate

The representative functions of the Senate were intended to be significantly different from those of the House. First, instead of representing the voters per se, the Senate was to represent the states. As such, every state is entitled to two senators, regardless of population. Thus, while we saw above that Wyoming has one representative and California fifty-three, both these states have two senators. This system was a concession to the least populous states, who feared being swamped in the national legislature by the largest states. In line with this representative function, senators are elected by the voters of the whole state.

The second major representative difference is that whereas the House was designed to be the popular chamber, the Senate was designed to be a more 'aristocratic' chamber which checked the popular will. In fact, as many historians have pointed out, the framers thought of the Senate's relationship to the House as somewhat similar to that between the British House of Lords and House of Commons. In line with this aristocratic bent, senators were not originally to be elected directly by the voters. Instead, the legislatures of the states would each decide for themselves how to elect or appoint US senators. This system remained in operation until replaced by the Seventeenth Amendment, ratified in 1913, which instituted the direct election of senators by the voters.

The Constitution further distances senators from popular control by giving them a six-year term of office. This enables senators to take a more long-term and independent view of issues than representatives. If a senator goes against his or her constituents' views on an issue, the chances are that by the time the next elections come around the voters' memories will have faded and their political passions cooled.

Nevertheless, the framers established yet another device that protects the Senate as a whole from the popular political pressures of the moment: *staggered elections*. While all senators serve six-year terms, they are not all elected at the same time: one-third of senators come up for re-election every two years. This means that even if a ferocious political wind should blow in any election year, fully two-thirds of the senators will be electorally unaffected by it. While the House can change direction radically as a result of one year's election results, the Senate is much more resistant to sudden change – hence, its ability to act as a brake upon the House.

The presidency

The president and the vice-president are the only politicians in the United States who are elected by a national constituency. Logically enough, then, they were intended primarily to advocate and represent the national interest, as opposed to state interests (Senate) or local interests (House of Representatives).

Just as the presidency's representative function is different from those of the Senate and House, so too are its terms of office and its mode of election. The president serves a four-year term and, since the passage of the Twenty-second Amendment in 1951, is restricted by the Constitution to a maximum of two terms of office. In fact, however, the very first president, George Washington, had established the custom of not seeking a third term and the Constitution was only amended in the wake of Franklin D. Roosevelt's break with this precedent. The fear which lies behind the two-term limit is of a president who can combine executive power with personal electoral popularity and thereby gain unhealthy control over the rest of the political system.

As a result of the different terms of office for president, Senate and House, it takes four years and three successive elections to complete a full electoral cycle for the federal government.

Box 3.1

Federal government election cycle, 2004–2008

2004   Presidency
         House – All 435 seats
         Senate – 1st one-third of seats

2006   House – All 435 seats
         Senate – 2nd one-third of seats

2008   Presidency
         House – All 435 seats
         Senate – 3rd one-third of seats

The electoral college

The method of electing the president is again different from anything else. The first thing to note is that Article II, Section 1(ii) of the Constitution established an indirect method of election, once again taking the direct choice of president out of the hands of the ordinary voters. The framers had several reasons for this. First, the least populous states feared that the most populous would always supply the president. Secondly, the framers did not believe that in such a large country the ordinary people would have sufficient knowledge of the qualities of presidential candidates. Thirdly, the framers were wary of too much popular control over the choice of president, fearing that this would encourage demagoguery. They preferred a statesman rather than a tribune as president.

The president therefore would be chosen by an electoral college, in which each state had a number

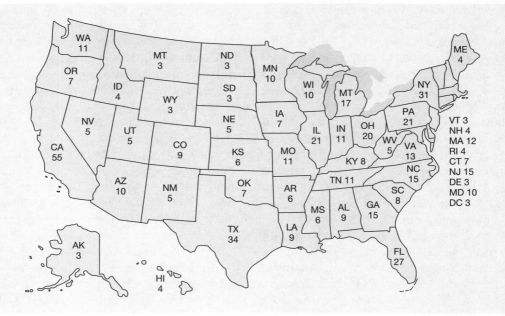

Figure 3.1 Electoral college map, 2004–2008.

Source: www.electoral-vote.com

of delegates, called electors. It was left to the states themselves to decide how they would choose their electors. Originally, most state legislatures simply appointed them, but the practice quickly developed of holding some kind of popular vote on the question. By 1832, only South Carolina did not permit a popular vote. Even so, electors were not bound to vote for any particular candidate in the electoral college; rather, they were supposed to use their wisdom and experience to select the best potential president. Today, however, with the exception of the odd maverick, electors cast their vote for the candidate who has won the popular election in their state.

Electoral college arithmetic

The number of electors for each state is fixed by adding the number of its representatives to the number of its senators. To calculate the number of electors from any state, then, is easy. For example, as we saw above, Illinois has two senators, like every other state, and nineteen members in the House. Therefore the number of delegates in the electoral college from Illinois is twenty-one. Wyoming,

one of the least populous states with just one representative, has three votes in the electoral college; and California, the most populous, has fifty-three representatives and therefore fifty-five electoral college votes.

The total number electors in the electoral college, then, is equal to the number of representatives and senators in the Congress, plus three from the federal District of Columbia: that is, 538 altogether.

Any presidential candidate must win over half the electoral college votes and therefore the minimum number required for victory is 270.

Electoral strategy

In an important sense, the American presidential election is not just one single election but rather fifty-one separate elections in the states and the District of Columbia. What determines victory is not the percentage of votes won in the national popular ballot, but the number of electoral college votes obtained by winning the elections in the states. For example, a candidate who takes California by a single vote bags all its fifty-five electoral college votes. The same candidate then loses, say, Illinois (twenty-one electoral college votes) by 1,000,001 votes. Although she is now 1 million votes down on her opponent in the national popular vote, she is nevertheless ahead 55–21 in the vote that counts, the electoral college vote.

It is thus not necessary to win 50 per cent of the *popular* vote in order to win the presidency. In 1992, Bill Clinton became the fourteenth president in America to do exactly that. Indeed, on four occasions, most recently in 2000, it has not even proved necessary to win more of the popular vote than one's chief opponent. Of the two-party vote, George W. Bush won 49.7 per cent compared with 50.3 per cent for Al Gore: yet despite winning more than half a million more votes than Bush, Gore lost the electoral college battle by four votes, 267–271.

Moreover, even where a candidate wins both the popular vote and the electoral college vote, the margin of victory in the latter is often a gross distortion of the former. Thus, a candidate who

appears to have won a landslide in the electoral college may only have won the popular vote by a relatively narrow margin. In 1992, for example, Bill Clinton took only just over two-fifths of the popular vote, but more than two-thirds of the electoral college vote. It is important to bear this in mind when considering how much of a mandate a winning presidential candidate can claim.

Presidential candidates must therefore adopt the electoral strategy of winning states, rather than the national popular vote per se – and, of course, they must seek above all to win the states with the most electoral college votes. In theory, a candidate could win the presidency by carrying just the eleven largest states, including California, New York, Illinois, Texas and Florida. In practice, such a clean sweep of the big states is achieved only in the greatest of landslides. Bill Clinton, for example, had to carry the twentieth largest state before he secured victory in 1992. In 1996, however, he needed victory in only fourteen states to garner enough votes to win re-election. In 2000, Al Gore carried only twenty states, plus the District of Columbia. However, because his victories included six of the nine largest states, he came within a whisker of winning the presidency.

Third party candidates

The electoral college, combined with the simple majority voting system in nearly all states (first past the post, winner takes all), not only exaggerates the mandate of the victorious candidate, it seriously disadvantages any third party candidate. In 1992, for example, Ross Perot took almost 19 per cent of the national popular vote, yet because he failed to come first in any state, he received no electoral college votes at all. Other third party candidates have fared little better.

The difference between Ross Perot in 1992 and George Wallace in 1968 was that, although Perot had broader appeal nationally, Wallace had a strong base in the South which enabled him actually to win some states.

Strong third party candidates, however, pose a significant potential problem under the electoral college. If the contest between the Democratic and

Table 3.1 Minority presidents

Percentage of popular vote	President	Year of election
49.72	Kennedy	1960
49.54	Polk	1844
49.52	Truman	1948
49.24	Wilson	1916
48.50	Cleveland	1884
48.27	Garfield	1880
48.14	Bush[a]	2000
47.95	Hayes[a]	1876
47.82	Harrison[a]	1888
47.28	Taylor	1848
46.05	Cleveland	1892
45.28	Buchanan	1856
43.42	Nixon	1968
43.29	Clinton	1992
41.84	Wilson	1912
39.82	Lincoln	1860
30.92	Adams[a]	1824

[a] Fewer popular votes than main opponent
Source: *National Journal*, 5 November 1992, p. A40; figures for 2000 calculated from Pomper *et al.*, 2001, pp. 133–4

Table 3.2 Third party candidates in recent elections

Candidate	Year	Party	Percentage of popular vote	Electoral college	Percentage of electoral college
Ralph Nader	2004	Independent	0.35	0	0
Ralph Nader	2000	Green Party	2.7	0	0
Ross Perot	1996	Reform	8.5	0	0
Ross Perot	1992	None	19	0	0
John Anderson	1980	National Unity	6	0	0
George Wallace	1968	American Independent	13	46	8

Source: Adapted from *National Journal*, 5 November 1992, p. A40; Pomper *et al.*, 1997, p. 178; Pomper *et al.*, 2001, p. 133

Republican candidates is close, then a third candidate with some electoral college votes could hold the balance of power. The framers of the Constitution did anticipate this and they provided that, where no candidate has a majority of electoral college votes, the election shall be decided in the House of Representatives. For this purpose only, however, each state delegation in the House, rather than each representative, is entitled to one vote. Although this mechanism has not been invoked for over a century, the mere possibility that a 'maverick' candidacy could throw the electoral process into confusion generates periodic calls for the reform of the electoral college system. Until a crisis actually materialises, however, nothing is likely to be done. Meanwhile, the United States continues with this arcane method of choosing its president.

Presidential nominations

The presidential election itself always takes place on the Tuesday after the first Monday in November, but the campaign for the presidency begins long before that. The first task of anyone seeking the presidency is to secure the nomination of one of the major political parties. Both the Democratic and Republican parties hold a *nominating convention* in the summer prior to the November election. The delegates at these conventions choose who shall be the party's nominee for the November general election. For the candidates, then, the goal is to ensure that a majority of the convention delegates are committed to support them. This is achieved by winning votes in pre-convention elections.

The primary campaign

There are two methods prevalent today for selecting convention delegates: the *primary election* and the *caucus election*. The rules governing these elections vary somewhat between states and between the Democratic and Republican parties, but the broad outlines are as follows. In the period between February and June of election year, each state holds either a primary or a caucus election for each of the parties. Since 1968, more and more states have opted to hold primaries, mainly because these elections make it easier to meet the technical rules governing issues such as the gender and racial composition of state delegations to the convention. Whereas in 1968 there were just seventeen primaries, in 2004 the Democrats held caucuses in only thirteen states.

In a primary election, participants simply enter the polling booth and cast their vote for the delegate or presidential candidate of their choice. Caucuses are more time-consuming. Voters physically gather in rooms and may spend several hours determining who they will support.

Both primaries and caucuses may be either 'closed' or 'open'. If 'closed', then only those voters officially registered as Democrats may vote in the Democratic primary or caucus, and the same for the Republicans. If the election is open, however, officially registered independents or even members of the other party may opt to vote in either the Democratic or Republican choice.

The number of convention delegates from each state is not purely a function of its population or even size of electorate. Rather it depends to a significant degree on the number of those who voted for the party in recent elections. As a result, the number of delegates from a state is different for the Democratic and Republican conventions. Nevertheless, it is still the most populous states which send the most delegates to the convention, so, as in the November election, candidates must try to win primaries and caucuses in the larger states.

Although candidates will not campaign hard in every state primary, serious contenders will try to collect a winning number of delegates to take to the convention. This means that the campaign must be planned well before the first primaries and caucuses take place. This has become even more true of recent elections, because of the tendency towards 'frontloading' the primaries and caucuses. Thus, in 2004, a nomination campaign which began with the Iowa caucus on 19 January, was effectively over by 9 March, when only four state primaries remained to be held.

Advantages and disadvantages of the primary system

Primaries were introduced in the early twentieth century as a means of democratising the selection of presidential nominees by removing the corrupt control of the process by party bosses. Today, that democratisation can be criticised both as having gone too far and as having not gone far enough.

In regard to the former, critics argue that the elimination of party boss control has gone so far that the parties have lost almost any real say in who gets their nomination. In 1968, the Democratic party establishment was able to impose the nomination of Hubert Humphrey, the incumbent vice-president, even though he had not entered a single primary. The outcry against this led to the rule changes which encouraged more primaries and required any serious candidate for the nomination to enter at least some of them.

The results of these changes were, however, unsatisfactory to many Democrats. Candidates could now appeal directly to the voters in primaries, thus bypassing the need for support from the party establishment. This led to the nomination of candidates such as George McGovern (1972) and Jimmy Carter (1976), men who were in significant ways at odds with traditional Democratic policies. McGovern lost heavily to his Republican opponent, while although Carter won the presidential election, the lack of enthusiasm he generated among other Democrats, particularly in Congress hampered his ability to govern and contributed to his defeat by Ronald Reagan in 1980.

The Democrats in particular, then, have fiddled with the rules governing primaries and nominating conventions continuously since 1968, in an attempt to produce a popular, winning nominee and a subsequently successful president. Changes introduced for the 1992 election, for example, included mandatory proportional representation and an increase in the number of convention 'super-delegates' appointed by the party establishment to 750 – about 20 per cent of all delegates (Cook, 1991). Over the years, however, the results of such changes have not been encouraging. In the ten presidential elections between 1968 and 2004, the Democrats have won only three times. In truth, the nominating system is just one factor in explaining the Republican ascendancy in this period, and probably a minor one at that.

Despite these rule changes, it can be argued that the nomination process is not very democratic in practice. Most obviously, voter turnout in both primaries and caucuses is very low. In recent elections, the average turnout in primaries has been 21 per cent, and in caucuses just 7 per cent (Wayne, 1996, p. 91). In 1988, in the key opening primary in New Hampshire, 34 per cent of the electorate voted; and in the very first test, the Iowa caucus, the turnout was just 10 per cent (Cook, 1991). In 2004 the turnout in the Maryland Democratic primary was 23.7 per cent of those registered to vote. Moreover, the relatively few people who do bother to vote tend to be the committed partisans of both parties and are not necessarily typical of the electorate at large. The risk is that the party will find itself with a relatively extreme nominee who has pleased the activists but who alienates the more typical voter at the general election in November.

Perhaps the greatest disadvantage of the primary system, however, is the danger of self-inflicted damage upon the party's eventual nominee. In a long and fiercely fought nomination campaign, candidates will seek not only to enhance their own image and prospects, but also to undermine those of their competitors. This can sometimes erupt into bitter conflict between candidates from the same party, bordering on political fratricide. Even incumbent presidents seeking renomination do not always emerge from this phase of the campaign unscathed.

Presidential election campaigns

By custom, the general election campaign begins after the Labor Day holiday in September. The two-month campaign, however, rarely determines who shall become president, since 'for the vast majority

Figure 3.2 In 1948 the polls gave Truman no chance of winning re-election, but he pulled off the greatest surprise in the history of presidential elections.

Source: From the US Senate Collection, Center for Legislative Archives

of citizens in America, campaigns do not function so much to change minds as to reinforce previous convictions' (Polsby and Wildavsky, 1995, p. 162). Thus, candidates who trail their opponent in the opinion polls on Labor Day usually do the same in the real poll on election day. The last surprise result in this respect occurred in 1948, when Harry Truman defeated Thomas Dewey against all the pundits' expectations: but that was in the days when opinion polling was much less accurate than it is today.

In more recent times, only Hubert Humphrey's late rally in 1968 threatened to reverse the September opinion polls, although many elections show something of a swing towards the governing party candidate as election day nears. Of course, in very close elections, such as in 2000 and 2004, the final weeks of the campaign may be important, since even a very small switch of voter allegiance can make a difference.

The fact is, then, that most people have already made up their minds by Labor Day. While the campaign is by no means irrelevant, it is rarely decisive. This is not surprising once we appreciate that Americans engage in what is sometimes called *retrospective voting*. This means simply that the election tends to be a referendum on the past four years. If the nation has experienced both peace and economic prosperity, the party currently in power is likely to be re-elected, especially if an incumbent president is standing again (Polsby and Wildavsky, 1995, p. 166). If, on the other hand, the country is in serious trouble at home or abroad, the rival party is likely to win.

There was considerable debate over which issues had really mattered to the voters in 2004. Partly this was to do with the way the questions were put. In exit polls, voters were asked to choose from a list of issues provided to them. A Pew Research Center survey instead left it up to voters to volunteer the issue that mattered most to them. As we can see from Tables 3.3 and 3.4, the form of the question makes a significant difference.

There is also a lack of clarity about what voters understand by such terms as 'moral values'. Nevertheless, these polls do yield an approximate indication of what motivated voters in any given

Table 3.3 Voters and issues in the 2004 election

What mattered most in your vote?

	Fixed list[a] (%)	Open end[b] (%)
Moral values (Net)	27	14
Moral values	–	9
Social issues[c]	–	3
Candidate's morals	–	2
Iraq	22	25
Economy/jobs	21	12
Terrorism	14	9
Health care	4	2
Education	4	1
Taxes	3	1
Other	4	31
Honesty/integrity	–	5
Like/dislike Bush	–	5
Like/dislike Kerry	–	3
Direction of country	–	2
Leadership	–	2
Foreign policy	–	2
Don't know	1	5
	100	100

[a] First choice among the seven items provided on the exit poll list
[b] Unprompted verbatim first response to open-ended question
[c] Abortion, gay marriage, stem cells
Source: PEW Center, 2004

election. Thus, in 2004 a large number of those who voted for President Bush were most concerned with moral issues, whereas Kerry supporters were most exercised by the issue of the war in Iraq. Also Bush voters were especially concerned with terrorism, while Kerry voters were more worried about the state of the economy. What is definitely unusual about 2004, however, is how low down the list of concerns came the economy and jobs – just 12 per cent of the voters nominated that as the issue that mattered most to them. Indeed, with Iraq and terrorism so prominent, it may be best to view 2004 as a 'wartime' election.

Usually, however, the state of the economy is the most important single factor in elections. For all his foreign policy problems in 1980, the main cause of President Carter's defeat was dissatisfaction with the economy. The importance of the economic issue was again clearly illustrated in 1992 when, despite

Table 3.4 Wide gap over the issues that matter

	Fixed list[a]		Open end[b]	
	Bush voters (%)	Kerry voters (%)	Bush voters (%)	Kerry voters (%)
Moral values (Net)	44	7	27	2
Moral values	–	–	17	1
Social issues[c]	–	–	6	1
Candidate's morals	–	–	4	[a]
Iraq	11	34	11	39
Economy/jobs	7	36	3	21
Terrorism	24	3	17	[a]
Health care	1	8	[a]	4
Education	2	6	0	1
Taxes	4	2	2	[a]
Other	5	3	34	30
Honesty/integrity	–	–	6	4
Like/dislike Bush	–	–	5	5
Like/dislike Kerry	–	–	5	2
Direction of country	–	–	2	3
Leadership	–	–	4	[a]
Foreign policy	–	–	0	4
Don't know	2	1	6	3
	100	100	100	100
Number of cases	(309)	(258)	(285)	(284)

[a] First choice among the seven items provided on the exit poll list
[b] Unprompted verbatim first response to open-ended question
[c] Abortion, gay marriage, stem cells
Source: PEW Center, 2004

a wide perception of his foreign policy record as excellent, President Bush was defeated by an equally wide perception that the economy was stagnant and unlikely to improve under his guidance. His opponent Bill Clinton had learned the lesson of past elections. In order to ensure that his campaign team never lost sight of the issue that could bring him victory, he had a sign prominently displayed at campaign headquarters which said simply, 'It's the economy, stupid!'

Nevertheless, a vibrant economy does not guarantee victory, as Vice-President Al Gore found to his cost in 2000. The 1990s had witnessed an economic boom that coincided with Democrat Bill Clinton's presidency. Past experience and the theory of retrospective voting held that this should have ensured a comfortable victory for Al Gore, his Democrat successor. Various explanations have been offered to account for Gore's failure, but Gerald Pomper makes

the persuasive case that the Gore campaign ignored the retrospective voting tendencies of the American electorate. By choosing to concentrate upon the future, rather that the past economy, Gore allowed Bush to fight him on level ground. As Pomper wrote: 'In theoretical terms, the vice-president turned the election away from an advantageous retrospective evaluation of the past eight years to an uncertain prospective choice based on future expectations' (Pomper et al., 2001, p. 142).

If the economy provides the main issue context of presidential elections, that does not mean that other issues are irrelevant. Foreign policy has sometimes been very important to the outcome of elections, even if it seemed to have disappeared in 1996 and 2000. And since 1968 a cluster of issues, sometimes referred to simply as 'the social issue' or 'values', has been of continuing, though variable influence. The social issue brings into electoral play attitudes on matters such as abortion, affirmative action for racial minorities and women, the death penalty, gay rights, and the place of religion in public life.

As we saw in the Introduction, by the election of 2000, these issues had to a significant degree divided the electorate into 'Red' and 'Blue' America. This means that many voters are deeply committed to one party or the other because of the values they represent, and consequently that their votes are determined long before the election campaign begins. President Bush in 2004 certainly benefited from a large number of evangelical Christian voters who came out to vote for him because of his support for their conservative social values.

Beyond the policy issues that determine the outcome of presidential elections, there is also the matter of the personal characteristics of the candidates. We should not be surprised that personal character is important in presidential elections, since the voters are choosing an individual, rather than a party. The president, moreover, represents

Figure 3.3 President George W. Bush is pleased to receive the endorsement of the organisation Rolling Thunder, a group of motorcycle-riding veterans, in his bid for re-election in 2004.

Source: © Empics

the nation as 'head of state', as well as being expected to provide able political leadership.

Precisely how much influence personal character has in elections is difficult to assess. Some presidential candidates, such as Ronald Reagan, are so well liked by a majority of voters that they are forgiven for unpopular policies. Reagan was dubbed 'the Teflon President', because the public seemed unwilling to attach blame to him for his administration's faults. George Bush, on the other hand, won in 1988 and lost in 1992 without his character being of major importance in either election, while although Bill Clinton was not particularly well liked in 1996, he was better liked than his opponent, Bob Dole (Pomper *et al.*, 1997, p. 193).

In 2000, on the other hand, Al Gore not only failed to benefit from the economic issue, he also suffered from the character flaws the public perceived in President Clinton. While Clinton was widely regarded as an able president, his morality in the wake of the Lewinsky and other scandals was less respected. This could not help but tarnish his Democrat successor and create a mood for change.

In 2004, the Bush campaign damaged his Democratic opponent by attacking his character and leadership qualities. Although George W. Bush had avoided service in the Vietnam War and John Kerry was a decorated veteran of that war, the Bush campaign and its allies alleged that Kerry's military record was exaggerated, even untruthful. Kerry was also hurt by being portrayed as someone who flip-flopped on various issues, including the war in Iraq.

In short, while any presidential election may have distinctive features, voters are usually mostly concerned with the economy and associated issues, and with the character of the candidates they must choose from.

Congressional elections

Divided government in modern America

When the framers of the Constitution opted for different procedures for electing the president, the House of Representatives and the Senate, they created the possibility of divided party control of the federal government. In other words, in today's terms, it is possible for the Republicans to control the presidency but for the Democrats to control the Congress, and vice versa. This clearly presents problems of governance, since the president is expected to provide policy *leadership*, but only the Congress can actually *pass* the legislation necessary to implement his policies.

Despite the obvious problems created by divided government, this situation has become the rule rather than the exception in contemporary America. Even when the president's party controls both chambers of Congress, the narrow majorities it enjoys there may make party government difficult.

Two things stand out in Table 3.5. First, out of the twenty-three elections involved, ten resulted in fully divided control of the presidency and the Congress. On a further three occasions under President Reagan, one chamber of the Congress was controlled by the non-presidential party. Divided government is thus very much a political reality in the United States. President George W. Bush first had Republican control in the Senate and then saw it disappear when one member of the party defected. Even when the Republicans consolidated their control in the 2002 elections, they only had a two-seat majority over the opposition.

Secondly, until 1994, the pattern of divided government was for a Republican president to be faced with a Democratic Congress. However, the 1994, 1996 and 1998 elections saw President Clinton become the first Democratic president to be faced with a Republican Congress since President Truman (1946–48).

The reasons for divided government are uncertain. For the moment, it is enough to note that American voters clearly have different political criteria for choosing a president from those which determine their choice of senator or representative.

We have seen that economic, foreign policy and social issues, as well as character, can all influence the vote for the president. What then are the different factors which appear to operate in congressional elections?

Table 3.5 Divided party control of the federal government, 1960–2004

Election year[a]	President	Senate majority	House majority
1960	**Kennedy (Dem.)**	**Dem.**	**Dem.**
1962		Dem.	Dem.
1964	**Johnson (Dem.)**	**Dem.**	**Dem.**
1966		Dem.	Dem.
1968	**Nixon (Rep.)**	**Dem.**	**Dem.**
1970		Dem.	Dem.
1972	**Nixon (Rep.)**	**Dem.**	**Dem.**
1974	Ford (Rep.)[b]	Dem.	Dem.
1976	**Carter (Dem.)**	**Dem.**	**Dem.**
1978		Dem.	Dem.
1980	**Reagan (Rep.)**	**Rep.**	**Dem.**
1982		Rep.	Dem.
1984	**Reagan (Rep.)**	**Rep.**	**Dem.**
1986		Dem.	Dem.
1988	**Bush (Rep.)**	**Dem.**	**Dem.**
1990		Dem.	Dem.
1992	**Clinton (Dem.)**	**Dem.**	**Dem.**
1994		Rep.	Rep.
1996	**Clinton (Dem.)**	**Rep.**	**Rep.**
1998		Rep.	Rep.
2000	**Bush (Rep.)**	**Dem./Rep.[c]**	**Rep.**
2002		Rep.	Rep.
2004	**Bush (Rep.)**	**Rep.**	**Rep.**

[a] Bold type indicates presidential election year, light type indicates mid-term elections
[b] President Nixon resigned in August 1974 over the Watergate scandal and was replaced by Vice-President Gerald Ford
[c] After the November 2000 election, the Democrats and Republicans each had 50 seats. Until May, the Vice-President's casting vote gave control to the Republicans. In May 2002, Republican Senator James Jeffords changed his status to Independent and caucused with the Democrats, giving them a 50–49–1 majority. The November 2002 elections saw the Republicans regain a 50–48–2 majority.

Constituency service

Beyond anything else, voters in congressional elections value the local and personal services rendered by their representatives and senators. If a member of Congress is perceived as having served the constituency well, he or she will almost certainly be re-elected. The notion of constituency service includes, for example, ensuring that a slice of federal job or construction schemes, or grants for education and social services, are brought back home to the member's district or state. Representatives, in particular, may also act as a kind of ombudsman, intervening with government bureaucracy to help constituents secure benefits or disentangle them from red tape.

Senators have a higher profile than representatives and may be more associated with national political issues. Occasionally such associations can hurt them. This was the case in 1978: a strong conservative wind was blowing that year and, partly as a result, a number of well-known liberal Democrat senators lost their seats. On the whole, however, the same golden rule applies to Senate elections as to the House: those who serve their constituents well can expect to gain re-election, regardless of party affiliation or ideological disposition.

Incumbency advantage

Sitting members of Congress are well placed to ensure that the benefits of federal largesse reach their constituents. Not only do they draft the legislation concerned, but they benefit from congressional perks which enable them to publicise the good they have done. For example, they exploit the 'franking privilege', which gives them free use of the US Mail to send letters to constituents, including mass mailings detailing members' achievements and local appearances. Although there are rules against using the franking privilege for blatant electioneering, Philip Davies points out that Representative Dennis Hastert (R – Illinois) managed forty-eight references to himself in just four pages, and that Senator Dan Coats (R – Indiana), newly appointed to fill Vice-President Dan Quayle's seat in 1989, spent $1.8 million on franked mail to 'make himself better known to his constituents'. Total spending on Senate and House use of the franking privilege in 1990 reached some $106 million (Davies, 1992, pp. 157–8).

Challengers to incumbents also suffer in other ways. Members of Congress use not only the franking privilege, but also cheap facilities for making video films to circulate back home. Thus, in 1988, the House recording studio charged members $42 for twenty minutes' studio time, when this would have cost challengers over $500 (Pomper *et al.*, 1989, p. 158).

Above all, incumbent members of Congress benefit from their ability to attract far greater campaign donations from interest groups than do their challengers (see Chapter 6).

Until the 1990s, the result of these advantages was high incumbency re-election rates: thus members of the House of Representatives seeking re-election had a success rate of well over 90 per cent in all but the most exceptional years (Bailey, 1989, p. 34).

The three elections from 1992 to 1996 saw a significant increase in the number of House incumbents being defeated. The 1992 election saw twenty-four incumbents defeated, bringing the percentage down to 86 per cent. Then in 1994, the year of the 'Republican Revolution', thirty-five incumbents, all Democrats, were ousted. Yet 1996 saw the figure drop back to twenty-one, all but three of them Republicans.

Before these recent elections, Ross Baker noted that in House elections the term 'incumbency advantage' often seemed an understatement, and that 'incumbency franchise' would be more accurate (Pomper *et al.*, 1993, p. 158). The 1990s may have brought a greater degree of uncertainty to the iron grip on power of House incumbents, but they nevertheless still enjoy many important advantages over their challengers. For that reason, incumbency re-election rates are unlikely to fall much below 90 per cent on a regular basis. In 2004, according to the Center for Responsive Politics, fully 98.3 per cent of House incumbents were re-elected.

Incumbency re-election rates for the Senate are historically neither as high, nor as consistent as those for the House. Since the 1960s, the rate has varied from 55 per cent to 96 per cent, with the average around 80 per cent (Bailey, 1989, p. 34; *National Journal*, 7 November 1992, p. 2555). As noted above, senators are more identified with national issues than representatives, and the larger size of their constituencies means they do not have quite the same personal identification with their voters as do House members. Paradoxically, however, the Senate has not mirrored the House experience in the 1990s of an increase in the number of incumbents defeated. Just one incumbent senator was defeated in 1996 and only two in 1994. The Senate incumbency re-election rate in 2004 was 90 per cent.

It is clear that congressional elections have no necessary connection with presidential elections today. Neither President Clinton in 1992 and 1996, nor President Bush in 2000 and 2004, had any presidential 'coat-tails' which benefited their parties in Congress. And since the Second World War, only twice has the capture of the White House by the out-party been accompanied by a similar breakthrough in the congressional elections: President Eisenhower in 1952 (House and Senate) and President Reagan in 1980 (Senate only).

Thus, what Ross Baker said of the 1988 elections is substantially true of most others in contemporary American politics: 'In terms of the outcome . . . the presidential and congressional contests might have taken place in different countries' (Pomper *et al.*, 1989, p. 153).

Voting behaviour

The franchise

The right of citizens to vote for their leaders lies at the heart of the democratic political process. Indeed, in assessing the democratic quality of any political system, one of the first questions to be asked is 'who is entitled to vote?'

As in most western democracies, the franchise in the United States has been greatly expanded since the eighteenth century. Early property and religious requirements imposed by some states had largely disappeared by the 1830s. Yet two great historical struggles for the right to vote remained: the enfranchisement of blacks and of women.

The struggle to enfranchise women dates back to at least the 1840s, but it was only with the passage of the Nineteenth Amendment to the Constitution in 1920 that the goal was achieved.

Box 3.2

Constitutional milestones in the expansion of the franchise

1787 The Constitution leaves it to the individual states to determine who is qualified to vote.

1870 The Fifteenth Amendment is ratified, making it unconstitutional to deprive a person of the right to vote on grounds of race or colour.

1913 The Seventeenth Amendment is ratified, requiring the direct election of US senators.

1920 The Nineteenth Amendment is ratified, making it unconstitutional to deprive a person of the right to vote on grounds of sex.

1964 The Twenty-fourth Amendment is ratified, outlawing the imposition of a poll tax as a qualification for voting in federal elections.

1971 The Twenty-sixth Amendment is ratified, lowering the voting age for both federal and state elections from 21 to 18 years.

In terms of possessing the legal right to vote, African-Americans were successful much earlier than women. Following the abolition of slavery after the Civil War, the Fifteenth Amendment to the Constitution was ratified in 1870. This declares that, 'The right of citizens of the United States to vote shall not be denied or abridged by the United States or by any State on account of race, color, or previous condition of servitude.'

Despite this categorical assertion, many southern states proceeded to disenfranchise blacks by a variety of devices. For example, a 'literacy test' was often used, whereby would-be voters were required to read and explain a written passage, such as part of the Constitution, before being permitted to vote. With little or no education for African-Americans at the time, it was relatively easy for white election officials to deem them unqualified.

It was not until the great civil rights movement of the 1950s and 1960s that the legal right of African-Americans to vote became a practical reality in the South. With the passage of the Voting Rights Act of 1965, the federal government was empowered to take over the administration of elections in any state where racial discrimination in voting rights was detected. It is now safe to say that in the United States, with a few exceptions such as the imprisoned and the insane, all citizens over the age of 18 can vote – if they want to.

Non-voting

Despite the constant rhetorical celebration of America's democracy and these heroic struggles to extend the franchise, many Americans do not appear to value the right to vote. Thus, 'With each expansion of suffrage, the percentage of those eligible who do vote has actually declined' (Wayne, 1996, p. 71). This, together with other factors, has resulted in the United States having a lower voter turnout than almost any comparable democracy. Whereas countries such as Germany and Sweden experience around 90 per cent turnout, and until recently Britain around 75 per cent, only rarely do more than 60 per cent of eligible Americans turn out to vote in presidential elections. In the mid-term congressional elections, the figures are significantly lower still, with rarely more than four out of ten eligible voters casting a ballot.

The relative lack of interest in elections by American voters is clearly unhealthy. For many Americans, voting is their primary, if not sole, means of participation in the political process. Those who do not vote, therefore, may play no role at all in the democratic process. When the proportion of such non-voters nears 50 per cent, one may reasonably ask if there is not a malaise affecting popular democracy in the United States.

Another problem created by low voter turnout concerns the mandate to govern that any president

---

Box 3.3

Measuring the turnout

The traditional method of measuring turnout in the United States is to ask how many people of voting age actually voted in the election. More recently, some scholars have challenged the validity of this measure, arguing that the Voting Age Population (VAP) includes a significant number of people who are not entitled to vote: non-citizens, convicted felons and prison inmates, for example. Instead, it is argued, a more accurate measurement can be based on the Voting-Eligible Population (VEP) which includes only those who are entitled to vote. Although the argument is technically more complicated than this, it is logical to count as non-voters only those who could have voted if they wanted to. We can see from the graph the difference it makes when we measure turnout by VEP rather than the traditional VAP. Whichever measure is used, the figures remain low compared with most other advanced societies. However, the much-discussed decline since the 1960s does not hold water when VEP is used. The decline on the VAP measure is explained by a rise in the number of ineligible voters in the VAP, rather than a decline in voting among those who could vote if they chose to do so.

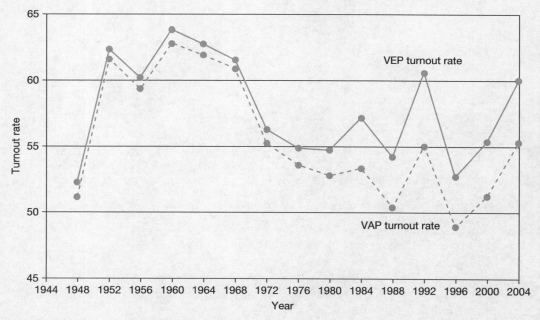

Presidential turnout rates for Voting Age Population (VAP) and Eligible Population (VEP), 1948–2004.

Source: McDonald, 2004

can claim. Consider the position of President Ronald Reagan, the clear winner of the 1984 election, having taken 59 per cent of the popular vote. Once we take into account the fact that the turnout that year was 57.2 per cent, we see that President Reagan was supported by just one-third of those eligible to vote. The Reagan 'landslide' looks far from impressive from this perspective.

It is hardly surprising, then, that there have been many studies which have attempted to identify the causes of this worrying phenomenon. Arthur Hadley found evidence to contradict the widespread belief that the typical non-voter was a figure whom he dubbed 'Boobus Americanus' (Hadley, 1978). This stereotype was poor, ill-educated, disproportionately southern, female and black. While some non-voters in Hadley's study did correspond to stereotype, many did not. Ruy Teixeira pointed out that a decline in the number of such stereotypical non-voters in the period since 1960 was to be

expected: educational levels have risen, southern blacks become freer to vote, and both women and blacks have become more equal citizens to white males in important respects (Teixeira, 1987). There must therefore be other reasons for low turnout in addition to the traditional ones of poverty and lack of education.

Another factor often cited in such studies is the relative difficulty of voter registration in some states. This is exacerbated by the fact that Americans are an unusually and increasingly mobile people, who move state frequently and therefore must re-register frequently under unfamiliar state laws. Unlike in Britain, where government actively solicits citizens to register by sending forms to their homes, many states require individuals to take the initiative, usually by visiting the local registration office. The extra effort thus required undoubtedly deters some eligible voters. Yet as Hadley pointed out, turnout has been falling even in states where registration is

Figure 3.4 Voter turnout was sharply up in the 2004 presidential elections, causing long delays at polling stations.
Source: © Empics

easiest. Moreover, the introduction of the 'motor voter' law in 1993 did not prevent a drop in the 1996 turnout over 1992.

Underpinning all these contributory factors is what researchers call the issue of *political efficacy*. 'The basic idea of political efficacy is that it taps the extent to which an individual feels that he or she has any power over governmental actions' (Teixeira, 1987, pp. 18–19). In other words, political efficacy concerns the degree to which potential voters believe there is any point in voting. Those who, for one reason or another, believe it makes no difference to them who wins the election will obviously be less likely to vote. On the basis of the turnout figures quoted above, then, some 40–50 per cent of eligible voters in the United States believe elections are in essence unimportant to them, if not wholly meaningless. By definition, this constitutes a crisis of American democracy.

Even if the VEP scholars are right and there is a 'myth of the vanishing voter', there are still large numbers who do not vote. In 2004, when there was a concerted effort by both major parties to get their supporters out, and when the election was predicted to be both close and critical, only six out of ten voters made the effort to use their franchise. Given the historic barriers to voting that have been removed, it is hard to avoid the conclusion that a very large minority of Americans simply do not think it is worth the effort.

The voters

We now come to one of the most important and interesting questions about voting behaviour in the United States: what factors determine which voters support which candidates? This is a complex question, which must take into account a variety of cultural, ideological and socio-economic factors.

In Europe, for example, we expect social class to be the most powerful, though not the sole, determinant of the way people vote. And while the notion of social class is of some use in analysing voting behaviour in the United States, the greater heterogeneity of American society by comparison with Europe brings many other factors into play. Race, region and religion, for example, are more varied in the United States than in most European societies, and American historical and cultural experience is different from European in significant ways. Table 3.6 shows the results of an analysis of the 2004 voters. What does it tell us about the motivations of voters and the appeal of the parties to different socio-economic groups?

Social class and socio-economic status

We noted above that in European societies, social class is expected to be a major determinant of the way people vote. Yet, for historical reasons, class is a difficult concept to employ in the context of the United States. Initially, divisions of class were far less marked in the United States than in, say, Great Britain. To this was added a greater degree of social mobility and an unwillingness on the part of many Americans to define themselves in terms of traditional classes.

Yet many of the characteristics associated with social class – income, education, occupation – *do* significantly affect the way Americans vote. Academics refer jointly to these factors as 'socioeconomic status' (SES).

As the portrait of the electorate in 2004 shows, income is an excellent guide to explaining the way that Americans vote. Quite simply, the higher the family income, the more likely are the adult members to vote Republican. Of course, this does not mean that all wealthy people vote Republican and all poor people vote Democrat. Thus, George W. Bush won 36 per cent of the votes of the poorest group, while John Kerry won 35 per cent of the richest group.

Educational attainment is one of the keys to gaining a well-paid job, but the trend is not as clear as it is with income. For example, the groups most inclined to vote for John Kerry were the least and the most educated. The relatively high proportion of postgraduates who vote Democrat is perhaps explained by the fact that this group includes a large number of teachers, social workers and other similar professionals who tend to hold values which incline them to support the party of the 'have-nots'. More generally, it may be that education has a

Table 3.6 Portrait of the electorate, 2004

	Bush %	Kerry %		Bush %	Kerry %
Gender			**Education**		
Male (46%)	55	44	No high school (4%)	49	50
Female (54%)	48	51	HS graduate (22%)	52	47
			Some college (32%)	54	46
Race and gender			College graduate (26%)	52	46
White men (36%)	62	37	Postgraduate study (16%)	44	55
White women (51%)	55	44	**Party identification**		
Non-white men (10%)	30	67	Democrat (37%)	11	89
Non-white women (12%)	24	75	Republican (37%)	93	6
			Independent (26%)	48	49
Race					
White (77%)	58	41	**Ideology**		
African-American (11%)	11	88	Liberal (21%)	13	85
Latino (8%)	44	53	Moderate (45%)	45	54
Asian (2%)	44	56	Conservative (34%)	84	15
Other (2%)	40	54			
			Religion		
Age			Protestant (54%)	59	40
18–29 (17%)	45	54	Catholic (27%)	52	47
30–44 (29%)	53	46	Jewish (3%)	25	74
45–59 (30%)	51	48	Other (7%)	23	74
60+ (24%)	54	46	None (10%)	31	67
Vote by region			**White Evangelical/Born Again**		
Northeast (22%)	43	56	Yes (23%)	78	21
Midwest (26%)	51	48	No (77%)	43	56
South (32%)	58	42			
West (20%)	49	50	**Church attendance**		
			More than weekly (16%)	64	35
Vote by size of community			Weekly (26%)	58	41
Big cities (13%)	39	60	Monthly (14%)	50	49
Smaller cities (19%)	49	49	A few times a year (28%)	45	54
Suburbs (45%)	52	47	Never (15%)	36	62
Small towns (8%)	50	48			
Rural (16%)	59	40	**Ever served in the military?**		
			Yes (18%)	57	41
Income			No (82%)	49	50
Under $15,000 (8%)	36	63			
$15–30,000 (15%)	42	57	**Marital status**		
$30–50,000 (22%)	49	50	Married (63%)	57	42
$50–75,000 (23%)	56	43	Unmarried (37%)	40	58
$75–100,000 (14%)	55	45			
$100–150,000 (11%)	57	42	**Most important issue (chosen from list of 7 topics)**		
$150–200,000 (4%)	58	42	Taxes (5%)	57	43
$200,000+ (3%)	63	35	Education (4%)	26	73
			Iraq (15%)	26	73
Union member in household?			Terrorism (19%)	86	14
Yes (24%)	40	59	Economy/jobs (20%)	18	80
No (76%)	55	44	Moral values (22%)	80	18
			Health care (8%)	23	77
Full-time worker?			**Is the US going in the right direction?**		
Yes (60%)	53	45	Yes (49%)	89	10
No (40%)	51	49	No (46%)	12	86

Table 3.6 continued

	Bush %	Kerry %		Bush %	Kerry %
National economy			**Opinion of John Kerry**		
Excellent (4%)	89	11	Favourable (47%)	9	90
Good (43%)	87	13	Unfavourable (51%)	92	7
Not good (35%)	26	72	**Most important quality of candidate**		
Poor (17%)	6	92	Cares about people (9%)	24	75
Sexual orientation: Are you gay, lesbian or bisexual?			Religious faith (8%)	91	8
Yes (4%)	23	77	Honest/trustworthy (11%)	70	29
No (96%)	53	46	Strong leader (17%)	87	12
			Intelligent (7%)	9	91
Policy towards same-sex couples			Will bring change (24%)	5	95
Legally marry (25%)	22	77	Clear stand on issues (17%)	79	20
Civil unions (35%)	52	47			
No legal recognition (37%)	70	29	**Compared to four years ago, is the US safer from terrorism?**		
Abortion should be . . .			Safer (54%)	79	20
Always legal (21%)	25	73	Less safe (41%)	14	85
Mostly legal (34%)	38	61			
Mostly illegal (26%)	73	26	**Decision to go to war in Iraq**		
Always illegal (16%)	77	22	Strongly approve (29%)	94	6
			Somewhat approve (23%)	75	24
Gun owner in household?			Somewhat disapprove (15%)	25	73
Yes (41%)	63	36	Strongly disapprove (31%)	5	94
No (59%)	43	57			
How President Bush is handling his job			**How are things going for the US in Iraq?**		
Strongly approve (33%)	94	5	Very well (11%)	91	8
Somewhat approve (20%)	83	15	Somewhat well (34%)	90	9
Somewhat disapprove (12%)	18	80	Somewhat badly (20%)	36	63
Strongly disapprove (34%)	2	97	Very badly (33%)	6	93
Opinion of George W. Bush			**Has the war in Iraq made the US more secure?**		
Favourable (53%)	94	6	Yes (46%)	90	10
Unfavourable (46%)	4	94	No (52%)	19	80

Source: www.cnn.com/Election/2004

liberalising effect on some issues and this moderates the effect of income differences.

Other studies reveal that a higher job status means a tendency to vote Republican. Those whose occupations are classed as professional/business are more Republican than those classed as white collar, and those classed as white-collar workers are more Republican than blue-collar workers (Polsby and Wildavsky, 1995, pp. 303–5; Pomper *et al.*, 1989, p. 133).

Thus, socio-economic status provides a good guide to voting behaviour in the United States. Nevertheless other factors must come into play too.

Ideology

While American political parties are not as clearly defined by ideology as British parties, it is reasonable to describe the Democrats as a moderate-liberal party and the Republicans as a conservative party. A voter's ideological leanings may therefore signal his or her voting behaviour. Quite predictably, the 2004 voting data show that those who classify themselves as liberals are strongly Democrat, and those who classify themselves as conservatives are strongly Republican. It is worth emphasising, however, that the largest ideological group are those who call themselves moderates, and their vote is less predictable.

Sex and age

It is not difficult to understand why wealthy conservatives vote Republican, given that party's tendency in the twentieth-first century to favour low taxes, unfettered free enterprise and traditional morality. Similarly, lower-income, blue-collar workers have a natural affinity with a Democratic party that has championed labour union rights, the welfare state and government regulation of employers. Or to take another example, voters from ethnic minority groups logically gravitate towards the Democratic party, which has led the fight for civil rights.

It is not quite so clear, however, why men should be more Republican than women, or why unmarried voters should be more Democratic than married ones. Here we must speculate more than usual. A gender gap of some kind has been present in most elections since 1952. In 1952, 1956 and 1960, women preferred Republicans more than men did. The next three elections all but saw this gender gap disappear, only for it to reassert itself in the election of 1976. Beginning in 1980, however, the gender gap reversed itself: women were now clearly more favourable to Democrats than were men. In 2004, women voters favoured John Kerry by three points, but men favoured George W. Bush by eleven points.

Why should there be any gender gap at all, and why should the direction of the gap have changed in the 1980s? The answer to the first question may lie in biological and/or cultural factors. Men are seen as more aggressive than women and this may be reflected in attitudes towards certain policies, such as defence and law and order. The answer to the second might be connected to a change in emphasis in the agenda of issues in the 1980s. In particular, the Republican party under Ronald Reagan and the New Right called for a vast increase in military expenditure, perhaps thereby increasing its attraction for men. The Republicans simultaneously called for a return to 'traditional' or 'family' values, which was seen by some as a threat to gender equality and abortion rights: this may have caused a slippage of women's votes to the Democrats.

Perhaps the issue of family values also explains the tendency of married people, with their more conventional lifestyles, to vote disproportionately for the Republican party.

Is it possible to identify a typical Democratic or Republican voter? Yes, but some caution is required. The various groupings in 2004 cut across each other: for example, better-off voters lean towards the Republicans, while women lean towards the Democrats. It remains a matter of conjecture, then, which way a well-off woman will vote. When we take into account all the other factors which can affect voting behaviour, the permutations make generalisations difficult.

Nevertheless, on the evidence of recent elections, a wealthy, Protestant, married, southern white male, with a college degree, is very likely to vote Republican. Conversely, an unmarried, black, female union member of modest financial means, and without a high-school diploma, is very likely to vote Democrat.

We must remember, however, that voting behaviour, like most aspects of politics, is a dynamic phenomenon. Historically, group voting tendencies have changed. In each election, parties and candidates must seek to renew their bonds with their traditional supporters and attempt to woo those who are not. Whatever the failings of American voters, politicians may pay a high price for taking them for granted.

Chapter summary

The complex system of elections in the United States has its origins in the Founding Fathers' desire to base the federal government upon popular sovereignty, without instituting a fully-fledged democracy or simple majoritarianism. It also reflects their need to mollify the states, particularly the less populous of them, who feared an overweening federal government. Developments since 1787 have increased the democratic qualities of the American electoral system, both by expanding the franchise and by making more federal politicians directly rather than indirectly elected. Nevertheless, the electorate's faith in the federal government, as measured by the low numbers of those actually voting, is worrying. This raises questions about the mandate and representativeness of those who win federal office. It is ironic that a system which gives voters several modes of democratic representation at the federal level, should engender such low levels of popular enthusiasm and electoral participation.

Discussion points

1. Why did the framers of the Constitution establish different electoral systems for the presidency, the Senate and the House of Representatives?

2. What are the advantages and disadvantages of imposing term limits on federal office-holders?

3. Is it important that so few Americans exercise their right to vote?

4. What are the main determinants of voting behaviour in presidential elections?

5. Are American presidential campaigns too long?

Further reading

Books providing a general introduction to elections and voting behaviour include W. Flanigan and N. Zingale, *Political Behavior of the American Electorate* (10th edn, Washington, DC: CQ Press, 2003); J. Jackson and W. Crotty, *The Politics of Presidential Selection* (New York: HarperCollins, 1996). For an analysis of the 2004 elections, see M. Nelson, *The Elections of 2004* (Washington, DC: CQ Press, 2005). On congressional elections, see P. Herrnson, *Congressional Elections: Campaigning at Home and in Washington* (4th edn, Washington, DC: CQ Press, 2003).

Websites

http://www.lib.umich.edu
http://www.archives.gov/federal_register/electoral_college/
http://usinfo.state.gov/dhr/democracy/elections.html

References

Bailey, C. (1989) *The US Congress* (Oxford: Basil Blackwell).

Cook, R. (1991) 'New primaries, new rules mark road to nomination', *CQ Weekly Report*, 7 September, pp. 2411–16.

Davies, P. (1992) *Elections USA* (Manchester: Manchester University Press).

Hadley, A. (1978) *The Empty Polling Booth* (Englewood Cliffs, NJ: Prentice Hall).

Jackson, J. and Crotty, W. (1996) *The Politics of Presidential Selection* (New York: HarperCollins).

McDonald, M. (2004) 'Up, up and away! Voter participation in the 2004 presidential election', *The Forum*, vol. 2, no. 4, article 4.

McDonald, M. and Popkin, S. (2001) 'The myth of the vanishing voter', *American Political Science Review*, vol. 95, no. 4, pp. 963–74.

Polsby, N. and Wildavsky, A. (1995) *Presidential Elections: Strategies and Structures of American Politics* (Chatham, NJ: Chatham House).

Pomper, G. *et al.* (1989) *The Elections of 1988: Reports and interpretations* (Chatham, NJ: Chatham House).

Pomper, G., Arterton, F., Baker, R., Burnham, W., Frankovic, K., Hersey, M., and McWilliams, W. (1993) *The Election of 1992* (Chatham, NJ: Chatham House).

Pomper, G., Burnham, W., Corrado, A., Hershey, M., Just, M., Keefer, S., McWilliams, W. and Mayer, W. (1997) *The Elections of 1996: Reports and Interpretations* (Chatham, NJ: Chatham House).

Pomper, G. *et al.* (2001) *The Elections of 2000: Reports and Interpretations* (Chatham, NJ: Chatham House).

Teixeira, R. (1987) *Why Americans Don't Vote* (New York: Greenwood).

Wayne, S. (1996) *The Road to the White House* (New York: St Martin's Press).

Chapter 4

Political parties, interest groups and money

Political parties and interest groups are both prominent features of American politics. They differ in key respects. Most obviously parties try to get their candidates elected into office, while interest groups do not have their own candidates and concentrate on influencing whichever party's candidates are in power. Nevertheless, their functions blur at times and even conflict, particularly when it comes to raising the huge sums of money required to fund election campaigns. In this chapter, we will look at parties, interest groups and campaign finance in turn. We will examine the power of parties and interest groups and the extent to which they enhance or undermine democratic government in the United States.

Origins and history of American political parties

Anti-party feeling and the Constitution

The Founding Fathers took a dim view of political parties. They regarded parties as selfish factions which sought to use government power to satisfy their own desires while neglecting the legitimate interests of other citizens. If such a faction commanded the support of a majority of citizens, a political party might even institute tyranny. In short, parties were viewed as divisive at a time when the country's greatest need was unity.

Yet by the end of George Washington's presidency in 1797, the United States possessed its first party system, pitching the Federalists against the Jeffersonian Republicans. In his farewell address, Washington warned the country against 'the spirit of faction' that had arisen, but to no avail. In 1800, there occurred the first presidential election fought along clear party lines. What then were the forces which compelled the emergence of political parties?

The first party system

First, and by far the most important, was the simple fact that Americans were divided by their own self-interests and the public policies linked to them. Although free of the extreme class and ideological divisions of Europe, the United States was not without economic, sectional and political rivalries. Thus, economic activity in the South consisted mainly of agriculture, while that of the Northeast was geared to shipping, banking and commerce. From these differences arose competing views of what constituted good government.

The independent farmers of the South had little need for an active federal government to support their agricultural economy and, therefore, tended to take the view that 'the government governs best that governs least'. Those engaged in commerce, however, required the national government to introduce protective tariffs for American manufacturing and to help establish the creditworthiness of American business. Logically enough, these interests called for an expansive role for the federal government.

Given the fundamental nature of these issues, it comes as no surprise that they quickly emerged as political conflicts. President Washington's Treasury secretary, Alexander Hamilton, presented Congress with a set of proposals in 1790–91 designed to promote commerce and, along with it, the power of the federal government. Those who supported him were dubbed the Federalists, the name that had first been used to describe the proponents of the Constitution of 1787.

Ironically, the opposition to Hamilton's policies in Congress was led by James Madison, a former Federalist himself and, of course, the opponent of party politics. Along with Thomas Jefferson and others, he saw in Hamilton's policies the threat of a return to autocratic, even monarchic, government as a centralising authority sought to promote the interests of the rich at the expense of 'the common man'. Seeing themselves as the guardians of the American republic, they took the name Republicans. As they increasingly gathered around Jefferson's presidential efforts, they became known as Jeffersonian Republicans.

The split between Federalists and Jeffersonian Republicans was not solely the product of economic self-interest and domestic policy. Political philosophy and foreign affairs intervened in respect of American policy towards the Anglo-French war of the 1790s, which followed the French Revolution of 1789. The more aristocratic Federalists supported the British, while the Republicans leaned towards the French.

The second main reason for the rise of political parties in the United States was that which is common to all democracies: the need to organise for competitive elections. While the Jeffersonian Republican party began as a Congressional opposition to a Federalist presidency, the aim of the movement quickly became the capture of the presidency itself. This required not merely organisation in Congress, but also in the country at large.

Republican congressmen therefore began to form Republican clubs at the state and district level. For the election of 1800, Jefferson drew up a party platform designed not merely to ensure his own election to the presidency, but also to produce a Republican majority in Congress.

This brings us to a third reason for the rise and persistence of parties in the United States. The very separation of powers which was designed to inhibit the growth of parties, paradoxically makes them a necessity. Fragmentation of political power invites an organisational network which can bring institutions together for the purpose of advancing particular policies. The best way of producing such institutional coalitions is a party which can offer candidates for each of the institutions in question. Party, then, can supply the glue which holds a fragmented political system together.

This is not to say that the Founding Fathers failed altogether in their goal of avoiding party growth. For a while they did not succeed in containing the spirit of faction, they did help to ensure that American political parties are relatively weak.

Changes in party systems

The United States has witnessed the evolution of several party systems, but the two great contemporary parties, the Democrats and the Republicans, have dominated the scene since 1856.

Box 4.1

Party systems in American history

1793–1816	Federalist v. Jeffersonian Republican
1816–1828	No party system: 'Era of Good Feelings'
1828–1856	Democrat v. National Republican/Whig
1856–1932	Democrat v. Republican: pre-New Deal system
1932–present day	Democrat v. Republican: New Deal system

The Democratic party

The Democratic party arose in 1828 in conjunction with the presidential candidacy of General Andrew Jackson, the military hero who had defeated the British at the Battle of New Orleans in 1815. The Democratic campaign concentrated heavily on promoting Jackson as a personality. However, it tapped important new sources of electoral support, such as recently enfranchised lower-class voters, particularly in the West, and Irish and German immigrant voters in the cities of the North.

These voters resented what they saw as their opponents' bias towards the interests of the rich, the banks and the corporations, and they enthusiastically bought the image of Jackson as the champion of 'the common man'. The Democrats eventually succeeded in building the first mass, popular party in the United States. However, unlike today, the Democrats at that time believed that the interests of lower-class Americans were best served by opposing the growth of government power, especially federal government power. They feared that the wealthy were intent on using the federal government not merely to enrich themselves at the expense of other Americans, but also to encroach upon the autonomy of the states' governments.

This philosophy of Jacksonian Democracy embodied themes which have been an ever-present feature of party politics in the United States. In particular, the philosophy is *populist* in its distrust of the combination of federal government power and the economic power of the banks, corporations and the rich. It is *egalitarian* in its belief not in equality, but in equality of opportunity – the right of the 'have-nots' to improve themselves without having to battle against artificial barriers designed to keep them in their place. Its *anti-elitism* is not radical in the sense that it is anti-capitalist: rather, it celebrates the form of capitalism represented in the American dream, a capitalism which creates individual wealth but does not entrench privilege.

The Republican party

The Republican party evolved out of an earlier party, the Whigs. The Whig belief in promoting national economic development through federal government activity attracted the support of many whose economic self-interest was bound up with manufacturing. Most importantly, this included the growing number of white labourers in the country. Unlike farmers, their prosperity was enhanced by tariffs which protected American manufacturing from its overseas competitors. Unlike southerners, they also had good reason to oppose the spread of slavery throughout the country. Since slave labour was inevitably cheaper than free labour, slavery, if allowed to spread, would undercut the opportunities available to white labourers in the North and West.

Anti-slavery sentiment found its expression in a number of third parties, such as the Liberty party, the Free Soil party, and the American party or 'Know Nothing party'. However, it was the Republican party, founded in 1854, which was able to combine anti-slavery with other policies and produce a viable electoral alternative to the Democrats.

The Republicans' anti-slavery policy should not be confused with abolitionism or a belief in racial equality. The Republicans did not propose to end slavery in the United States, but rather to confine it to the states where it already existed. Moreover, most Republicans did not believe in equality of the races. While many accepted that slavery was morally wrong, few advocated racial integration. Indeed, where Republicans acquired sufficient power, as in Kansas, they banned all blacks, free or slave, from entering the state.

The Republicans' anti-slavery position thus married a moral principle with the self-interest of northern and western white labourers. And the more the Democrats thundered about slave-owners' rights and 'states' rights', the more the Republicans benefited from pro-Union sentiment and resentment of 'southern arrogance' in the North and West.

However, the Republicans were not a single-issue party. They campaigned for the protective tariff and free homesteads in the West for white settlers. Moreover, in nominating Abraham Lincoln for the presidency in 1860, the party chose a moderate on the slavery issue and a westerner, rather than a northern radical, such as Senator Seward from New York. The aim was to appeal to the northern and western labourers, without frightening them with radical racial policies. It worked: without capturing a single electoral college vote in the South, or even campaigning there, Lincoln won the presidency with just 39 per cent of the popular vote. As Wilfred Binkley said, 'The successful drive to capture the labor vote was the key to Lincoln's election' (Binkley, 1947, p. 230).

Two-party politics since the Civil War

Outwardly, the party system has not changed since the Civil War (1861–65). The Democrats and Republicans have remained the only parties with a realistic chance of capturing the Congress or the presidency, although there have been occasional serious third party candidates. As we saw in Chapter 3, third parties are inhibited by the electoral system. Equally important in perpetuating the Democratic/Republican rivalry, however, has been the flexibility of these two parties. Although both have been at times closely identified with particular principles, these have rarely been permitted to stand in the way of policy reorientations deemed necessary for electoral success. In other words, the Democratic and Republican parties have survived because they have been willing to change in response to a changing society. Two features of the parties have greatly facilitated this flexibility: ideological pragmatism and coalition politics.

Ideology and party

The two major American political parties occupy a very narrow ideological space. Both are (and always have been) utterly committed to the preservation of capitalism and constitutional democracy, as indeed have most parties which have appeared on the American scene. Thus, the United States differs strikingly from European democracies in its failure to produce a major political party committed to some form of socialism or of authoritarianism.

The Progressive era

During the Progressive era (1900–17), however, the clamour for the reform of industrial-urban society became so great that *both* Republicans and Democrats moved to adopt Progressive policies. Each party succeeded in capturing the presidency with a Progressive nominee – Theodore Roosevelt (Republican, 1901–9) and Woodrow Wilson (Democrat, 1913–21).

Progressive Democrats and Republicans were responsible for enacting valuable reforms at the federal and state level. However, their leadership of their respective parties lasted only as long as the public mood demanded reform. In the 1920s, both parties reverted to conservatism, leaving their Progressive wings isolated. The two main parties had thus ridden the Progressive wave while it was electorally expedient to do so, but had not become radicalised in the process. Yet during this critical period, they had become sufficiently reformist to persuade the electorate that a genuinely radical third party was unnecessary. This flexibility within an ideologically conservative framework has allowed both Democratic and Republican parties to marginalise radical and third party movements.

The New Deal Democratic party

The greatest success of such flexibility undoubtedly came with the New Deal of the 1930s. An unprecedented seven-year period of economic expansion and prosperity had come to an abrupt, catastrophic end with the Wall Street crash of October 1929. President Hoover responded to the collapse of the stock market and the ensuing loss of business confidence with orthodox economic measures, including cutting government spending and raising taxes. This only made matters worse and helped to cause the Great Depression. By the time of the next presidential election, in November 1932, the economy and social fabric of the country were in deep crisis. Unemployment nationally had reached 25 per cent, but in many cities it was over 50 per cent or higher.

Worse still, there was little or no welfare provision for the unemployed and their families. Some states did offer support, but even the most generous states could not begin to cope with the scale of social distress. President Hoover refused to countenance any provision of welfare by the federal government. He had once referred to Britain's dole system as 'the English disease', believing that welfare would undermine the American tradition of economic self-reliance.

The Democratic candidate in 1932, Governor Franklin D. Roosevelt of New York, was also generally orthodox in his economic faith in American capitalism. However, unlike Hoover, he was a pragmatist rather than an ideologue and was prepared to experiment with ways to restore the American economy to health. Moreover, if he was to become only the second Democrat president in the last forty years, he needed to offer the electorate something different from Hoover's rigidity.

Roosevelt therefore turned flexibility and pragmatism into the main planks of his electoral platform. In one speech, for example, he said: 'The country needs, and unless I mistake its temper, demands bold, persistent experimentation. It is sensible to take a method and try it. If it fails, admit it frankly and try another. But above all, try something.'

Roosevelt won the election by a large majority. Having won the election on a promise of flexibility and pragmatism, he proceeded to govern accordingly. Eschewing Hoover's restraint, he threw the energies of the federal government into attempts to solve the major problems of the Great Depression. Moreover, he cared little for whether policy solutions came from the left or the right of the political spectrum. For rather than search for ideological consistency, Roosevelt sought to provide practical help for those who needed it. Roosevelt's 'New Deal' was aimed primarily at helping the underdog – the unemployed, the impoverished farmer, the homeless – but it did so by strengthening banking, manufacturing and landowning interests as well.

So successful was this new philosophy of government activism that Roosevelt was re-elected by a landslide in 1936 and went on to win two further elections. Equally important, his party had discovered a new recipe for electoral success. As we noted above, the Democrats had always been the party of limited government and states' rights. With the electoral triumph of the New Deal, however, the Democrats became the party of federal government activism. From now on, the Democrats would argue that the federal government must take responsibility for the economic health of the country and the social well-being of its people. Government regulation of the economy, expansion of the welfare state and continuing social reform became the paramount policies of the 'new' Democratic party.

This transformation of the Democratic party left the Republicans electorally stranded for decades. Since its inception in 1854, the Republican party had identified itself with promotion of the national economy, prosperity and social improvement. However, by allowing the Democrats to seize the initiative during the Great Depression, the Republicans were left with the choice of either opposing the new Democratic creed or adopting a 'me-too' approach. Thus, for years to come, the Republicans found themselves offering the electorate either an unacceptable alternative to New Deal liberalism or no real alternative at all.

Coalition politics

Roosevelt's brand of pragmatic politics was greatly aided by the fact that American political parties have never been ideologically based. That is to say that although parties have advanced particular principles, it is not necessarily those principles which unite the different elements within parties. Thus, in the second half of the nineteenth century, for example, the Democrats' main electoral bases were southerners and the immigrants of the northern cities. These two groups had little in common other than their dislike of the Republican party. Southerners disliked the Republicans because of the Civil War: many immigrants, particularly Catholics, disliked the nativist and pietist tendencies of the Republicans. In that sense, party coalitions were based upon the principle that the enemy of my enemy is my friend. Different groups came together under a party banner in order to share the spoils of victory and to deny those spoils to the common enemy.

In a country as heterogeneous as the United States, attempts to enforce ideological conformity on the party usually end in electoral disaster or worse, as the southern Democrats discovered when they tried to impose a pro-slavery policy on the party before the Civil War. The secret of a successful governing party coalition, then, is to be able to reward one element of the party without causing too much offence to another.

Party realignment

The New Deal enabled the Democrats to initiate what political scientists call a 'partisan realignment'. The notion of partisan realignment views American electoral history in cyclical terms. It argues that one party dominates elections for both the presidency and the Congress – and often state elections, too – for several decades. It dominates the political agenda and normally can rely upon a majority of the electorate to support it. Then, because new issues arise that cut across previous party loyalties, a *critical election* occurs which transfers dominance to the opposition party.

Box 4.2

Critical elections and partisan realignment

1. **Election of Andrew Jackson (D) as president, 1828**

   Dominance of Democratic party, 1828–60
   Years in control of:

Presidency	24
Senate	28
House	24

2. **Election of William McKinley (R) as president, 1896**

   Dominance of Republican party, 1896–1932
   Years in control of:

Presidency	28
Senate	30
House	26

3. **Election of Franklin D. Roosevelt (D) as president, 1932**

   Dominance of Democratic party, 1932–68
   Years in control of:

Presidency	28
Senate	32
House	32

Until the contemporary electoral era cast doubt upon it, realignment theory seemed a useful way of understanding changes in the fortunes of the main political parties.

Party dealignment since 1968

In the period since 1968, the cyclical pattern described above has become less clear. While the Democrat ascendancy has come to an end, it is still not certain that a Republican ascendancy has replaced it. To be sure, President George W. Bush won two successive elections in 2000 and 2004 and the Republican party captured the Congress, too. However, the margins of victory in both presidential elections were so narrow that it is unconvincing to describe them as constituting a realignment. Rather, the Republican party has a slight but persistent edge over the Democratic party.

One explanation of the post-1994 election era is that of the 'no majority realignment', proposed by Everett Ladd. He argues that the old realignment theory still works as far as its philosophical/political dimensions are concerned. In other words, a philosophical realignment has indeed taken place since 1968, just as it has done with each major realignment. In this case, the philosophical realignment consists of a marked shift to the right, based upon a growing scepticism about the effectiveness of centralised government (Ladd, 1997, p. 5).

This philosophical realignment, however, has not been matched by a party realignment. According to Ladd: 'the chief reason no party has majority status is that large segments of the electorate are abandoning firm partisan ties' (Ladd, 1997, p. 13). Traditional realignment presupposes the existence of parties which are strong enough to exert comprehensive control of the electoral environment. Yet, in recent decades, the argument goes, American parties have actually been in decline in this respect, losing their grip on voters and politicians alike. This view, however, has been challenged by what appears to be a resurgence in party identification since the 1990s.

Party decline?

Until the 1990s, there was wide agreement that political parties were of declining significance in American politics. Since the 1960s, social, technological and institutional changes had undermined the importance of parties in their two main spheres of operation: elections and government.

Prior to the 1960s, parties could fairly claim to represent the views and interests of the great mass of Americans. As a result, parties not only dominated the electoral process, but also provided a reasonably effective means of ensuring cooperation between different offices of government. There then followed a sharp decline in many aspects of party influence, leading many analysts to write the obituary for the American party system. However, parties have made a determined effort to regain some of their lost influence. While this has not been successful in all respects, parties are no longer in danger of extinction and they play a significant, though not dominant, role in both the electoral process and government.

Partisan identification

Whether partisan identification in the United States is in decline depends in part upon how it is measured. The most common method is to ask voters whether they consider themselves to be Democrats, Republicans or Independents. Some studies also distinguish between 'strong' and 'weak' Democrats and Republicans (McSweeney and Zvesper, 1991, p. 143).

The general picture obtained by such data suggests that after a marked dip in the 1970s, partisan identification has almost recovered to the high levels of the 1950s. This is especially true when those who describe themselves as leaning towards one party or the other are counted as party identifiers. In a 2004 exit poll, 37 per cent of those asked described themselves as Democrats and exactly the same number described themselves as Republicans. Just 26 per cent described themselves as Independents.

Table 4.1 Party identification, selected presidential years, 1952–2000

Party identification	1952 (%)	1964 (%)	1980 (%)	1984 (%)	1988 (%)	1992 (%)	1996 (%)	2000 (%)
Strong Democrat	22	27	18	18	17	18	19	19
Weak Democrat	25	25	23	22	18	18	20	15
Independent Democrat	10	9	11	10	12	14	14	15
Independent-Independent	6	8	13	6	11	12	8	12
Independent Republican	7	6	10	13	13	12	11	13
Weak Republican	14	14	14	15	14	14	15	12
Strong Republican	14	11	9	14	14	11	13	12
Apolitical	3	1	2	2	1	1	1	1

Note: Columns may not add to 100 because of rounding
Source: Center for Political Studies, University of Michigan

These figures tell us only how people think of themselves, rather than how they actually vote. A more reliable guide to party loyalty may be obtained by comparing the figures on self-identification with the actual votes cast by these identifiers in elections. By measuring the number of 'deserters' or split-ticket voters, we can see how much hold the party label has on voting behaviour. Studies indicate that split-ticket voting surged in the period 1956–84, but has since been in steady decline. Thus, whereas in 1984, 43.9 per cent of congressional districts were carried by the presidential candidate of one party but the House candidate of the other party, this figure fell to 25.5 per cent in 1996 and to 20.0 per cent in 2000 (Keefe and Hetherington, 2003, p. 225).

In general, then, we can say that about one-quarter of the American electorate do not identify themselves with one of the two main parties. Moreover, even among those who do identify, from one-fifth to one-quarter do not stay loyal to their party. As a result, there is a large body of voters to whom party is meaningless. This group may switch votes from one election to the next, making sustained periods of electoral dominance difficult to achieve.

Nevertheless, the puzzle remains as to why, after a period of decline, party identification has recovered. After all, as we shall see below, campaigns remain candidate-centred, and primary elections rather than party officials still dominate the candidate selection process. The answer, according to many, lies in the increased ideological polarisation of the political parties from the 1980s onwards. As the Republican party in Washington became more uniformly conservative and the Democrat party more uniformly liberal, partisan conflict in Congress sharpened. And, 'in a world characterized by significant cleavages between the parties, who wins and who loses matters a great deal. In short, greater partisan differences in Washington have created a more partisan public' (Keefe and Hetherington, 2003, p. 180).

Nominating candidates

As we saw in Chapter 3, the proliferation of primary elections has all but ended party influence in the selection of candidates for office. All those who call themselves a Democrat (or a Republican) are entitled to enter a party primary, provided the technical requirements have been fulfilled. And given that candidates these days are largely independent of the party in terms of finance and organisation, they are free to pursue their own electoral strategy regardless of party wishes.

It is even possible for successful primary candidates to be so at odds with the party that the party feels obliged to disown them. Such was the case with David Duke, a former Grand Wizard of the Ku Klux Klan, who won the Republican Senate primary in Louisiana in 1990. President George Bush and the National Republican Party urged voters not to support Duke in the primary and publicly denied that Duke was a 'real' Republican.

Financing elections

Although we deal with campaign finance in detail later in this chapter, it is important to note at this point the changing role of parties in financing elections. In the 1970s, a series of reforms eliminated parties as a significant source of direct campaign donations. In the 1980 congressional elections, parties contributed just 4 per cent of total donations to House candidates and 2 per cent to Senate candidates (Malbin, 1984, p. 20).

However, in the 1990s, parties began to exploit so-called soft money donations. Rather than giving money directly to particular candidates, parties were allowed to spend money on 'party-building' activities: these originally included voter registration drives, get-the-vote-out drives and generic campaign buttons. The parties, however, collected vast sums and increasingly used them for generic advertising at federal and state level. Although not officially coordinated with individual campaigns, they clearly were designed to help party candidates win elections. In the 1992 elections, parties spent some $80 million in soft money; by 2000, the figure was $300 million (Magleby and Monson, 2004, p. 45).

There was a widespread belief that soft money expenditure was being used to circumvent the reforms of the 1970s, and in 2002, Congress passed the Bipartisan Campaign Reform Act. The 2002 Act did succeed in curbing soft money expenditures by *parties*, but a loophole was found to allow soft money expenditures to continue through the use of so-called 527 groups. Named after the tax code which exempted them from the 2002 contribution limits, these highly partisan groups spent huge amounts of soft money. The largest of these, America Coming Together, was dedicated to the defeat of George W. Bush. According to the Federal Election Commission, by January 2005 the group had spent $76,270,931 on the 2004 campaign. It is not yet clear what control the parties had over 527 groups. If the level of control proves to be substantial, then parties will remain significant players in campaign finance. If not, then this is one more area where parties will have lost influence relative to interest groups.

Campaign services and organisation

As well as a partially revitalised role in funding elections, the parties have also become more energetic in providing their candidates with various services. Thus, 'along with increased funding, the national parties have provided help for their candidates in campaign planning, polling, and the production of campaign advertisements, including experiments in generic national ads for congressional candidates' (Caesar, 1990, p. 121).

Nevertheless, campaigns are resolutely candidate-centred and candidate-controlled. Candidates have their own strategists, media consultants, pollsters and managers. Moreover, not only has the rise in non-party sources of finance stimulated this independence, but the development of the electronic media has eliminated much of the parties' previous role in communicating with the voters.

Thus the revitalisation of the parties in the electoral process since the 1980s should not be exaggerated. Links between candidates and parties are stronger than they were in the 1970s, but in the key elements of nominations, finance, organisation and communication, parties play, at best, a secondary role.

Party government

We noted above that one reason why parties developed in the United States was the need to coordinate the activities of different office-holders. There are two particularly important facets to this function today: coordination between different members of Congress and coordination between Congress and the president. An examination of both these relationships yields yet further evidence of the problematic nature of party unity.

Party unity in Congress

Members of Congress are much more independent of party control than, say, their British counterparts. In the first place, since senators and representatives do not owe their election to the party whose label they wear, they do not feel bound to follow party policy. This is particularly true where the party line is unpopular with the member's constituents.

Secondly, and largely as a result of members' electoral independence, party discipline in Congress is weak. There *are* designated party leaders in Congress, including whips; Congress is also organised on party lines and party members do meet in caucus to try to develop strategies and policies that will unite the party. Nevertheless, there is little the party can do to force unwilling members to conform to party wishes. Parties do not possess the power of ultimate sanction: deselection of disloyal members. Moreover, members of Congress value their own independence and are therefore content to allow a similar autonomy to their colleagues. Leaders in Congress can offer inducements to members to support the party line, such as help in getting the best committee assignments, but they have less to mete out as punishment. As Senator Tom Daschle (D – South Dakota), the former co-chair of the Senate Democratic Policy Committee, put it: a Senate leader trying to influence a colleague's vote has 'a bushel full of carrots and a few twigs' (*CQ Almanac*, 1992, p. 22-B).

Thirdly, as noted above, American political parties are broad coalitions of diverse interests. As a result, one wing of a party may be fiercely opposed on certain policies to another wing. This produced a situation in the twentieth century whereby the conservative southern wing of the Democratic party formed an informal coalition with the Republicans to defeat certain legislation proposed by their northern Democrat colleagues. This so-called Conservative Coalition was, for example, responsible for defeating all meaningful attempts at civil rights reform in the 1950s and was invaluable to President Reagan in his efforts to foster a 'conservative revolution' in the early 1980s (Keefe and Ogul, 1993, p. 292).

As the South has largely realigned and become a Republican stronghold, the Conservative Coalition is no longer as significant as it once was. Nevertheless, it may still play an important role on occasion. Thus, when Bill Clinton's presidency was on the line in August 1993 over his budget proposals, the Coalition almost defeated him. Despite a Democratic majority of eighty-two in the House, the president's proposals were approved by a margin of just two votes, and a Senate Democratic majority of eight resulted in a tie in the Senate, with the budget being passed only on the casting vote of the speaker, Vice-President Al Gore. In short, conservative members of the Democratic party were not only prepared to defeat Clinton's budget, but also willing to see their votes cripple, even destroy, his presidency. And in 2004, retiring Georgia Democratic Senator Zell Miller demonstrated his loyalty to the party by appearing on the platform of the Republican nominating convention and endorsing George W. Bush.

Even aside from the Conservative Coalition, party unity is generally low in the Congress compared with, say, parliamentary parties in Britain. Take, for example, the frequency of party unity votes in the Congress. The definition of such votes is hardly a stringent one – it is simply when the majority of one party in the House or Senate votes against a majority of the other party. Although the number of such votes rose significantly in the 1990s to levels of 65 per cent, they fell back again in the first two years of George W. Bush's presidency to below 50 per cent (Keefe and Hetherington, 2003, p. 148). In short, while most members of Congress prefer to vote in line with their party, they do not feel obliged to do so. Thus, while the Republican leadership in Congress opposed the Bipartisan Campaign Reform Act of 2002, many Republicans voted in favour of it simply because it was popular with their constituents.

Party unity: Congress and president

A second measure of party unity in government can be gained by examining the frequency with which members of Congress vote in support of a president of their own party. Since the 1950s, presidents have on average been able to count on the support of their fellow party members in 72 per cent of House votes and 76 per cent of Senate votes (McSweeney and Zvesper, 1991, p. 168; *Congressional Quarterly*, various years).

Thus in the 1997 session of Congress, the average House Democrat backed President Clinton in 71 per cent of the votes on which he took a clear position. This was about the same as in the previous year. By contrast, the average House Republican supported the President in 30 per cent of votes, down from 38 per cent the previous year (*Congressional Quarterly*, 3 January 1997, p. 17). President George W. Bush achieved a very high success rate in his first two years in office, showing that party unity can be very strong when members of Congress so wish. However, as the historical variations in support for the president demonstrate, such unity can never be taken for granted.

The historical data suggest that party policy and party discipline are important but not necessarily controlling factors in congressional behaviour. In fact, negotiation and compromise in pursuit of consensus across party lines remains a notable feature of Congress. This is true despite attempts by both parties in the wake of the Republican capture of the House and Senate in 1994 to develop clearer party positions and coherence. The markedly increased partisanship of 1994–96 may have pleased more ideologically pure politicians, but it seemed to turn the voters off. The message of the 1996 elections seemed to be that the public expected a Democrat president and a Republican Congress to overcome partisan differences and work together for the good of the country. This, of course, is precisely what the constitutional scheme of separation of powers and checks and balances was intended to promote. As Representative David Skaggs (D – Colorado) commented in 1997: 'We all have to go back to school on a regular basis to remember that this is not a parliamentary system, and the Constitution essentially drives a consensus approach to government in the country (*Congressional Quarterly*, 3 January 1998, p. 18).

Interest groups

Whereas parties have always been quite weak in American politics, interest groups (or pressure groups) have always been strong. The diversity of American society has encouraged Americans to make full use of their freedom to petition the government, a right guaranteed by the First Amendment to the Constitution. With the huge growth in government activity since the New Deal of the 1930s, the importance of representing one's group interests in politics has become paramount. Nevertheless, interest-group activity is the subject of considerable controversy. On the one hand, it is argued that such groups perform a legitimate and valuable representative function. On the other, it is alleged that interest groups subvert democracy by making government the pawn of the rich and well organised.

Definitions and origins

An interest or pressure group is an association of individuals or organisations that band together to defend or advance the particular interests they have in common. Those may range from shared business interests and professional status, through common ethnic origins and religion, to shared public policy and ideological convictions. There are literally thousands of interest groups in the United States. While they can be categorised as shown in Table 4.2, it is worth remembering that a group might well encompass the attributes of more than one category. Many, if not most, for example, have an ideological orientation, even if their principal goal is representing the particular interests of a profession or advancing a particular issue.

The United States has always been fertile soil for interest group formation. In 1835, the great French observer of American politics, Alexis de Tocqueville, wrote: 'Americans of all ages, all conditions, and all dispositions constantly form associations. Wherever at the head of some new undertaking you see the government in France, or a man of rank in England, in the United States you will be sure to find an association' (Tocqueville, 1956, p. 198).

The prevalence of interest groups in American political life is due to four broad factors. First, the sheer diversity of American society has spawned numerous ethnic, social, economic and issue groups.

Table 4.2 Typology of interest groups

Business/trade	Agriculture	Unions	Professional	Single issue	Ideological	Group rights	Public interest
American Business Conference	American Farm Bureau Federation	American Federation of Labor–Congress of Industrial Organisations (AFL–CIO)	American Medical Association	National Abortion and Reproductive Rights Action League	American Conservative Union	National Association for the Advancement of Colored People (NAACP)	Common Cause
National Association of Manufacturers	National Farmers Union	United Auto Workers	National Education Association	Mothers Against Drunk Driving	People for the American Way	National Organization for Women	Friends of the Earth
National Automobile Dealers Association	Associated Milk Producers, Inc.	International Association of Machinists and Aerospace Workers	Association of American Universities	National Rifle Association	Christian Voice	American Association of Retired Persons	Children's Defense Fund
					American Civil Liberties Union		

Secondly, as we have already seen, weak parties have failed to fulfil the representative needs of the American people. Thirdly, the fragmented and decentralised structure of American government means that there are numerous points of access to the policy-making process that groups can readily exploit. Fourthly, and particularly true since the 1930s, the rapid expansion of governmental activity means that more and more groups have found their interests affected by public policy.

More recently, the 1960s and 1970s witnessed an 'advocacy explosion' (Berry, 1989, p. 42). Several particular factors contributed to this. Among the most important were the new burst of government programmes associated with President Lyndon B. Johnson's Great Society, the rise of many new divisive political issues (such as race and gender, the Vietnam War and lifestyle issues), and the simple fact that, as some interest groups became prominent, other groups formed in imitation (Cigler and Loomis, 1991).

Furthermore, a little-known variant of the interest group – the political action committee (PAC) – proliferated astonishingly in the 1970s and 1980s, stimulated by new campaign finance laws. Most recently of all, as noted above, there has been an explosion of '527 groups' as a response to the Bipartisan Campaign Reform Act of 2002.

Not surprisingly, the exponential growth of interest groups since the 1960s appeared to eclipse the representative functions of political parties. Moreover, because interest groups conduct much of their activity away from the public view, in the corridors of Congress or the federal bureaucracy, there developed a heightened anxiety over whether representation by interest group was good for American democracy.

Interest group functions

There are, it is said, five principal functions of interest groups: representation, citizen participation, public education, agenda-building and programme monitoring (Berry, 1989, pp. 4–5). The last four, however, are really aspects of the central task of self-interest representation.

Interest groups, like parties, are representative institutions, but their aims and methods are not the same. Most importantly, interest groups do not put forward candidates for elected office. Although some interest groups do try to influence electoral outcomes, most concentrate on representing their members' interests in the policy-making process. This means lobbying not only elected politicians but also those who wield power in the bureaucracy and the judiciary.

Interest group methods

Public campaigning

Interest groups operate in a variety of ways. One means of influencing the policy-making process is to stir up public opinion, in the hope that this will put legislators under pressure. One of the oldest forms of interest-group activity in this respect is the public march. This can be very successful, as when a host of civil rights groups got together to organise the 1963 'March on Washington'. The march, coming after almost a decade of public campaigning to end racial segregation, was designed to put pressure on President Kennedy and Congress to take action on the pending civil rights bill. Whatever the precise role of the March in producing the Civil Rights Act of 1964, there can be little doubt that it was a moving spectacle that won converts to the cause.

Public demonstrations can, however, prove counter-productive. Thus, anti-abortion groups organise an annual protest outside the Supreme Court to commemorate the day of the historic 1973 *Roe* decision, which announced a new constitutional right to abortion. When that right seemed threatened in the 1980s, pro-abortion groups began holding counter-demonstrations on the same day.

Another related form of public campaigning is direct action. Here, too, anti-abortion groups have been prominent. For example, Operation Rescue specialises in trying to block access to clinics where abortions are performed. Its members hope that their activities – and their frequent arrest by the police – will stimulate the conscience of judges, legislators and the public and result in a ban on abortions.

Other forms of public campaigning include newspaper and television advertising. In the early 1990s, for example, the National Rifle Association (NRA) produced television advertisements featuring the veteran Hollywood star Charlton Heston as part of its ultimately unsuccessful campaign against the Brady Bill. The legislation aimed only to improve checks on would-be gun purchasers, but the NRA opposes virtually all gun legislation.

Less spectacular, but potentially effective nevertheless, is direct mailing of group members and likely sympathisers. Taking advantage of computerised mailing systems, interest groups can quickly identify and mobilise members on behalf of a particular campaign. During the intense fight over ratification of the Panama Canal Treaties in 1978, conservative groups mailed an estimated 7–9 million letters to members of the public (Berry, 1989, p. 60).

However, although the above strategems for mobilising members and the general public are often employed, the oldest and still most effective activity of interest groups is lobbying.

Lobbying and lobbyists

The most desirable method of influencing policy-makers is through direct contact with them. For that reason, the more affluent and powerful interest groups maintain a permanent office in Washington and employ professional lobbyists to act on their behalf.

These lobbyists may be committed activists in the groups they represent, but these days are increasingly likely to be neutral 'guns for hire' – experts in the legislative process, who sell their skills to those who can afford them. Thus, in 1993, the top lobbying firm of Patton, Boggs and Blow was working to obtain government money to save jobs at Chrysler, supporting a bill to make it easier for the homeless to vote, and fighting a constitutional amendment that would ban flag-burning. In the past, it had also represented Baby Doc Duvalier, the Haitian dictator, and the scandal-ridden Bank of Credit and Commerce International. The firm's most prominent lobbyist, Tommy Boggs, once said: 'We basically pick our customers by taking the first one who comes in the door' (*The Economist*, 27 February 1993, p. 56). The typical working day of a professional lobbyist is described in Box 4.3.

Lobbyists have often acquired their detailed knowledge of the policy-making process from having worked in the federal government – as legislators or legislative assistants, bureaucrats or presidential advisers. Such experience can be invaluable, not merely for the expertise acquired but also for the personal contacts and relationships established over the years. Thus, when Senators

Box 4.3

A day in the life of a lobbyist

This is how the Washington lobbyist for a professional association describes his typical day:

'I am one of those people who gets to work no later than 7.45. The first hour is spent reading the papers – the *Washington Post*, *Wall Street Journal*, and *New York Times*, trade association publications, and the *Congressional Record* from the prior day. Each of these plays into my need to plan the activities for the current day. The next activity is meeting with the staff for a brief period to check the work plans for any changes. There is then one or more hearings on the Hill in the morning. After lunch, I usually meet with committee staff or use that time to lobby specific members of Congress. I'm usually back by 4.00 to meet with the staff to check on what's happened while I was gone and if we are on top of the work planned for the day. About 5.30 I usually go to some reception or fund-raiser to represent our group. These settings give me an opportunity to swap stories and position with members and other lobbyists who are concerned with the same issues as we are. I usually get home for dinner about 8.00.'

Source: Extract from Berry, 1989, pp. 77–8

Russell Long and Paul Laxalt retired in 1986 their services were sought by many Washington law firms which represent clients before government agencies. Both eventually joined Finley, Kumble at salaries of $800,000 a year (Berry, 1989, p. 86).

This so-called revolving door phenomenon has been criticised as unethical, and measures have been taken to try to limit it. In 1978, Congress passed the Ethics in Government Act which forbade certain former executive branch officials from lobbying their previous government agencies within a year of leaving them. In 1989, Congress applied a similar restriction on former legislators and legislative staff. Nevertheless, continuing scandals did little to reassure the public that these measures were sufficient. When President Clinton took office in 1993, therefore, his first executive order extended the one-year limit to five on all top executive branch officials, and banned them from lobbying on behalf of foreign governments and parties for ever.

The revolving door problem is just one of several aspects of lobbying that have given cause for concern in recent years. For example, the first attempt to monitor the activity of lobbyists came with the Regulation of Lobbying Act of 1946. Under this, all people hired principally for the task of lobbying Congress were required to register with the House or Senate. Its terms, however, are easily evaded. According to Senator Carl Levin, who introduced more demanding (but unsuccessful) legislation in 1992, around 70 per cent of Washington lobbyists are not registered under the 1946 Act (*CQ Almanac*, 1992, p. 79).

If all that lobbyists did was to act as the eyes and ears of their organisations and try to convert policy-makers to their members' point of view, their activities would be largely uncontroversial. However, what transforms the perspective on interest groups is money – the money they give to legislators in the form of electoral campaign donations. Immediately, then, the suspicion arises that lobbying Congress involves a form of bribery: interest groups enable legislators to get re-elected by financing their campaigns, and legislators in return listen to the pleadings of interest groups and advance their interests through the nation's policy. This suspicion is at the heart of the controversy over interest groups in American politics.

Campaign finance

Interest groups, and particularly business corporations, have always tried to buy favours from legislators by giving them money: hence Will Rogers' satirical comment that 'Our Congress is the best that money can buy!' Bribery and corruption were especially rife in the late nineteenth century and the first attempt at reform came with the passage of the Tillman Act in 1907. This banned business corporations from making direct contributions to federal election campaigns.

Nevertheless, the flow of illegal funds continued and it was only when the Watergate scandal broke in 1973, with its revelations of slush funds, huge personal donations and laundered money, that more determined action was taken (Sabato, 1985, p. 4). In 1974, Congress amended the Federal Election Campaign Act (FECA) of 1971 in ways that were to transform, but not necessarily improve, the funding of federal elections.

In an attempt to lower the cost of elections and to reduce the power of rich individuals and organisations, Congress enacted three major reforms. First, it provided public funds for presidential elections. Secondly, it set strict ceilings on the amount of money that any person or group could give to a candidate for the presidency or Congress. Thirdly, it limited the overall amount of money that could be spent on congressional elections.

The limits on spending were quickly challenged in the courts as an unconstitutional restriction on free speech. In *Buckley* v. *Valeo* (1976), the Supreme Court upheld the restrictions on personal and group donations to candidates, but struck down those which limited expenditures independent of particular candidates and the amount that candidates could spend out of their own pockets, except for presidential candidates who accepted public funds.

Presidential elections

The campaign finance reform legislation of the 1970s largely ended the controversy over rich-individual and interest-group donations to presidential candidates. In the pre-nomination phase, candidates may seek donations from both, though these are strictly limited to a maximum of $2,000

from an individual and $5,000 from a group. Such limits do not prevent huge sums being raised and spent. In 2004, both George W. Bush and John Kerry accepted public funding of $74.6 million each for their post-nomination campaign. But they turned down public funding for the pre-nomination phase, thus freeing themselves to raise as much as they could. Bush raised some £290 million and John Kerry $250 million. Indeed, the presidential election of 2004 was by far the most expensive election in American history. Total expenditures were $717.9 million, more than double the figure for the 2000 election, which was $343.1 million.

Congressional elections

Unlike for presidential elections, the reforms of the 1970s failed to provide public funding for congressional elections. Several reasons lie behind this and subsequent refusals to introduce public funding. Republicans, in particular, tend to believe that using so much taxpayers' money is simply wrong.

Nevertheless, the subject keeps forcing itself back onto the agenda for one simple reason: the widespread public belief that interest-group donations to congressional candidates mean that Congress represents interest groups rather than the public. This situation was, if anything, exacerbated by the 1970s' reforms. As with presidential elections, individual and group donations to candidates were subjected to limits. Individuals could donate up to $1,000 for each phase of an election, with a maximum to all candidates of $25,000 per year. Groups could give up to $5,000 to one candidate for each phase of an election, with no overall maximum.

With large donations now eliminated, the key to raising campaign funds became soliciting money from as many groups and individuals as possible. It was in this context that political action committees (PACs) came into their own.

Political action committees

Political action committees are a form of interest group which exist for the sole purpose of raising

Table 4.3 Growth of political action committees, selected years, 1974–2000

Year	Corporate	Labour	Trade, membership, health	Independent	Cooperative	Corporation without stock	Total
1974[a]	89	201	318				608
1976[a]	433	224	489				1,146
1978	785	217	453	162	12	24	1,653
1980	1,206	297	576	374	42	56	2,551
1982	1,469	380	649	723	47	103	3,371
1984	1,682	394	698	1,053	52	130	4,009
1986	1,906	417	789	1,270	57	157	4,596
1988	2,008	401	848	1,345	61	169	4,832
1990	1,972	372	801	1,321	60	151	4,677
1992	1,930	372	835	1,376	61	153	4,727
1994	1,875	371	852	1,318	56	149	4,621
1996	1,836	358	896	1,259	45	134	4,528
1998	1,821	353	921	1,326	45	133	4,599
2000	1,725	350	900	1,362	41	121	4,499

[a] For 1974 and 1976 the data for trade, membership, and health PACs include independent, cooperative, and corporation-without-stock PACs. On 24 November 1975, the FEC issued its 'SUNPAC' advisory opinion. On 11 May 1976, FECA (Public Law 94-283) was enacted. All data are from the end of the year indicated.
Source: Federal Election Commission, press release, 25 January 2001: http://fecweb1.fec.gov/press/012501/count.htm

campaign funds. Although they have been in existence since the 1940s, they were rare before the passage of the 1974 FECA amendments. Thus, in 1972, there were just 113 PACs registered with the government. The 1974 amendments, however, stimulated a rapid growth in their number, with the total settling down in the 1990s at around 4,000. Although each PAC was limited in how much it could give to a candidate, there was no limit on how many PACs could make a donation. Logically enough, then, the number of groups proliferated.

Most of these new PACs have been created by business corporations: in 1995 there were 1,670 corporate PACs, compared with 334 labour union PACs and 804 PACs sponsored by trade and professional associations (Hrebener, 1997, p. 198). Moreover, although labour unions are prominent in the list of the biggest donors, collectively business easily outspends labour and other groups in campaign donations. In the 1993/94 election cycle, business outspent labour by some $70 million to $42 million. In the 1995/96 cycle, the gap widened dramatically as business gave $147 million compared with labour's $49 million (Center for Responsive Politics website: http://www.crp.org/, 1998).

A further spur to PAC growth has been the rapidly rising cost of running an election campaign for Congress. In particular, the increasing use of expensive television slots contributed to the escalation. By 2004, the total cost of congressional elections was a staggering $1 billion. There was a considerable variation in the costs of individual elections. A notable case was the Senate race in South Dakota, where the Republicans mounted a successful bid to defeat the Democrat Senate leader, Tom Daschle. Together, the two main candidates spent some $36 million on winning the Senate seat of one of the least populous states in the Union.

Soft money

The 1990s witnessed an explosion of so-called soft money donations. These evaded the campaign finance laws by giving money to parties for general expenditures not directly associated with particular candidates. The result was that soft money accounted for 48 per cent of funds raised by the parties in 2001, compared with just 17 per cent ten years earlier. Widely viewed as subverting

Table 4.4 Highest spenders in congressional elections, 2004

House candidates	Amount spent ($)	Senate candidates	Amount spent ($)
Hastert, Dennis (R)[a] (Illinois District 14)	4,739,045	Hull, Blair (D) (Illinois Senate)	28,927,114
Frost, Martin (D)[a] (Texas District 32)	4,641,675	Specter, Arlen (R)[a] (Pennsylvania Senate)	20,058,902
Schwartz, Allyson (D) (Pennsylvania District 13)	4,530,790	Daschle, Tom (D)[a] (South Dakota Senate)	19,739,259
Sessions, Pete (R)[a] (Texas District 32)	4,401,618	Schumer, Charles E. (D)[a]	15,084,370
Herseth, Stephanie (D)[a] (South Dakota District 01)	3,984,681	Boxer, Barbara (D)[a] (California Senate)	14,252,368
Menendez, Robert (D)[a] (New Jersey District 13)	3,875,576	Obama, Barack (D) (Illinois Senate)	14,143,166
Streusand, Benjamin Earl (R) (Texas District 10)	3,607,176	Thune, John (R) (South Dakota Senate)	14,126,941
Blunt, Roy (R)[a] (Missouri District 07)	3,431,390	Bowles, Erskine B (D) (North Carolina Senate)	13,276,538
Harris, Katherine (R)[a] (Florida District 13)	3,410,405	Burr, Richard (R) (North Carolina Senate)	12,786,603
Wilson, Heather (R)[a] (New Mexico District 01)	3,328,561	Martinez, Mel (R) (Florida Senate)	12,198,941

[a] Incumbents running for re-election in 2004

Source: Based on data released by the Federal Election Commission (FEC) on 4 January 2005

the purposes of the original campaign for finance reform, there was an irresistible call for soft money donations to be brought under control. In 2002, Congress passed the Bipartisan Campaign Reform Act (or McCain–Feingold Act, as it was frequently referred to). The Act banned soft money donations but permitted an increase in hard money donations from $1,000 per federal candidate to $2,000. Many interest groups and some politicians opposed the new restrictions and mounted a constitutional challenge. In the case of *McConnell* v. *FEC* (2003), however, the Supreme Court upheld the main portions of the legislation. It remains to be seen exactly what effect the Act will have. Over the years, interest groups and PACs have shown themselves to be adept at getting ever-increasing sums of money to politicians they wish to influence. And as long as candidates display an almost insatiable thirst for campaign finance, interest groups will find one way or another to satisfy their needs.

527 groups

Indeed, the 2004 elections witnessed the rise to prominence of so-called 527 groups, named after the Internal Revenue Service code relating to their tax-exempt status. Because they are not explicitly linked to particular candidates or parties, they were able to raise and spend millions of dollars

during the election. Most of the major 527s were liberal groups, such as America Coming Together (ACT), an organisation backed by billionaire George Soros, which set out to defeat George W. Bush. ACT spent over $76 million on the election. The group which probably received the most attention, however, was Swift Boat Veterans and POWs for Truth. The group was dedicated to attacking the Democratic candidate, John Kerry, who, they alleged, had misrepresented his own war service in Vietnam and falsely accused other US servicemen of war crimes. They spent over $22 million on this cause and most commentators believe they did serious damage to their target.

Influence of interest groups and PACs

Closer examination of campaign contributions to congressional candidates sheds considerable light on the motivations behind them.

The first point to note is that not all interest groups have as their primary aim the election of a candidate who shares their political viewpoint. True, ideological groups give overwhelmingly to candidates who champion their preferred policies;

Table 4.5 Election campaign contributions and expenditures, 2004

Party	No. of candidates	Total raised ($)	Total spent ($)	Total cash on hand ($)	Total from PACs ($)	Total from individuals ($)
House:						
All	1,213	688,465,438	621,688,941	180,473,817	231,311,207	391,898,770
Dem.	554	299,328,052	271,378,673	83,342,517	102,627,281	175,418,524
Rep.	608	387,359,688	348,589,871	96,485,854	128,513,769	215,279,707
Senate:						
All	188	474,586,313	469,653,593	63,375,214	67,321,250	314,239,492
Dem.	77	235,848,427	236,147,563	33,675,129	29,790,133	158,998,233
Rep.	93	237,382,035	232,843,570	29,013,807	37,515,565	154,782,195
President:						
All	15	862,997,556	810,928,348	49,417,620	3,688,379	627,500,068
Dem.	10	489,813,172	465,197,402	24,636,999	782,112	351,763,133
Rep.	1	366,554,535	339,280,603	24,595,515	2,903,767	271,634,244

Source: Based on data released by the FEC on 4 January 2005

and labour unions give funds almost exclusively to Democrats. Thus, in the 2003–4 cycle, one of the largest union donors, the International Brotherhood of Electrical Workers, gave a total of just over $2.3 million and 96 per cent went to Democrats. The American Medical Association (AMA) gave 80 per cent of its $2 million to Republicans, while Wal-Mart Stores gave 78 per cent of its $1.6 million to Republicans. Other groups, however, take a more pragmatic approach. They want to influence whichever party or candidate succeeds and they spread their money accordingly. Thus, the National Association of Realtors split their $3.8 million in donations 47 per cent to Democrats and 52 per cent to Republicans. The American Dental Association split their $1.5 million 40 per cent to Democrats and 60 per cent to Republicans.

A second notable feature of PAC donations is that they are not necessarily intended to affect the outcome of the elections concerned. Large amounts of money are given to candidates whose victory is a foregone conclusion, but whose position makes them enormously powerful. Take, for example, Republican Speaker of the House, Dennis Hastert, who represents the 14th district in Illinois. Hastert won his 2002 race with 74 per cent of the vote. Nevertheless, in 2004 he still received almost $2 million in PAC donations, 90 per cent of it from business groups. Hastert was re-elected with 69 per cent of the vote (Center for Responsive Politics). Quite simply, many recipients of PAC largesse do not need the money in order to win.

What most PACs – especially corporate PACs – want, therefore, is less to influence elections than to cultivate and influence those who make policy between elections. This is reinforced by the fact that, on average, those with most influence in policy-making – committee chairpersons – get 20 per cent more in PAC donations than ordinary House members (Stern, 1988, pp. 5–6). Further support for this view comes from the fact that PACs target their money on incumbents who sit on the committees that deal with legislation most likely to affect their group.

Access or votes?

Lobbyists for interest groups readily concede that they expect something in return for their money, but categorically deny that they are engaged in simple vote-buying. Instead, they hope to obtain access to those who write the nation's legislation. In this way, they are at least assured that policy-makers listen to their side of a policy debate before any action is taken. Lobbyists are aware that legislators are kept extremely busy by the demands of their job and that they have only a limited amount of time to devote to any one issue. If lobbyists get the opportunity to present a legislator with information and a point of view on the issue, there is a good chance that this will influence his thinking. As one lobbyist put it: 'I know what it means to put in a call to a legislator and get a call back and not to get a call back. And if that $500 is going to increase my chances of getting a call back, that is a heck of a lot, because frequently all it takes is the opportunity to talk to a legislator 10 or 15 minutes to make your case. He may not have ten or fifteen minutes to hear the other side' (Sabato, 1985, p. 127).

If a lobbyist can build up a long-term working relationship with a legislator, by providing expert and accurate information, he can acquire the status of a valued and trusted adviser. It may even reach the point where, when a relevant issue arises, it is the legislator who contacts the lobbyist to request information (Berry, 1989, p. 84).

The essence of this view of pressure-group activity is that influence is only exerted where the legislator receives an informed briefing by a lobbyist and is convinced by it. Donations to campaign funds facilitate the likelihood of that briefing taking place, but they do not buy, or even attempt to buy, legislators' votes.

Although this argument may raise eyebrows given the large sums of money involved, there is evidence to support it. In the first place, even a generous PAC is only one factor in determining a legislator's vote. Party loyalty or personal ideology may be pulling in a contrary direction. Above all, however, a member of Congress will pay the closest attention to what her constituents think on a subject. She is unlikely to risk alienating her voters in order to please a PAC who gave her $5,000.

Moreover, a number of academic studies tend to support the view that legislators do not sell their votes to generous interest groups. By comparing legislators' votes on bills with the campaign donations received from interested groups, the studies have concluded that while money certainly does buy access, at best it only influences votes

at the margins – when legislators have no strong inclinations or contrary pressures being exerted on them (Wright, 1990; Evans, 'PAC Contributions and Roll-call voting: Conditional Power', in Cigler and Loomis, 1991).

It is also important to remember that a mere correlation of votes with donations does not establish an unambiguous relationship of cause and effect. Quite sensibly, interest groups try to reinforce the position of those whom they know are already sympathetic to their views. In other words, money may follow the voting inclinations and behaviour of legislators, rather than determine them.

Nevertheless, there is other evidence that contradicts this limited view of the influence of campaign finance. In the first place, some members of Congress openly acknowledge that it is difficult to resist the pressure to vote in line with groups who have contributed money. As Representative John Bryant said, 'Anytime someone, whether a person or a PAC, gives you a large sum of money, you can't help but feel the need to give them extra attention, whether it is access to your time or, subconsciously, the obligation to vote with them.' Representative (now Senator) Barbara Mikulski put it less gently: 'I fear we could become a coin-operated Congress. Instead of two bits, you put in $2,500 and pull out a vote' (Sabato, 1985, p. 126).

We noted above that a mere correlation between votes and campaign donations is not enough to establish a clear causal relationship. Nevertheless, some analyses of voting and donations do produce the strong implication that money has determined votes.

Philip Stern's analysis of the lobbying campaign by the National Automobile Dealers Association (NADA) to defeat the 'lemon law' is a case in point. The lemon law was a regulation issued by the Federal Trade Commission requiring second-hand car dealers to inform prospective customers of any flaws in a car of which they were aware. In the early 1980s, NADA campaigned to have Congress veto the regulation. This campaign included making donations to over half the members of Congress and which totalled over $1 million. The larger the donation, the more likely a member is to vote against the lemon law.

Table 4.6 Campaign donations and the 'lemon law' vote in the House of Representatives, 1982

Amount received from NADA PAC, 1979–82	Percentage of House members voting against the 'lemon law' in 1982
More than $4,000	90.2
$1,000–3,000	88.3
$1–1,000	68.0
0	34.2

Source: Stern, 1988, p. 45

Interest groups and the public good

Policy

It may be argued that, on balance, interest groups make a valuable contribution to the development of good public policies. As a powerful representative force, their activities help to keep politicians in touch with the needs and demands of different social groups. If one measure of good public policy is its responsiveness and acceptability to the people at large, then interest groups may plausibly be said to be a positive element in the political system.

Yet there are many who claim that interest groups distort the policy-making process and are a prime cause of many of the policy problems which the United States has faced in recent years.

Iron triangles

One such line of criticism is that interest groups have formed a mutually regarding and mutually rewarding relationship with two other political institutions: congressional committees and sub-committees, and the bureaucratic agencies which correspond to the same policy areas. These three-way relationships are known as iron triangles.

The most famous (or infamous) of these iron triangles has been that concerned with national defence. As far back as 1961, President Eisenhower took the opportunity of his farewell address to warn the country of the dangers posed by what he termed 'the military–industrial complex'. The three points of the triangle here are arms manufacturers, the government defence establishment, including the armed forces and Defense Department, and members of Congress who represent constituencies whose economies are defence-oriented. All three have a vested interest in ever larger defence expenditures. The arms manufacturers reap profits from such outlays; the government defence establishment acquires more power, and members of Congress earn the votes of constituents who gain jobs in the defence plants.

What is missing, as Eisenhower tried to point out, is any concept of the national interest. And the danger is that the iron triangle will cause greater expenditure on arms than the nation needs or can afford. Although the military–industrial complex provides a dramatic example of an iron triangle, similar relationships can be seen to exist right across the range of policy areas (Levine and Thurber, 'Reagan and the intergovernmental lobby', in Cigler and Loomis, 1991).

Indeed, in his farewell address in 1989, President Reagan blamed 'special interests' and iron triangles for Americas massive annual budget deficits. They prevented their favourite expenditures from being cut and effectively shut off debate on alternative policies that might be harmful to them, although beneficial to the nation.

Democracy

Finally we come to the most fundamental question of all: are interest groups compatible with democracy? As with most aspects of the interest group debate, opinion remains divided on this.

We have already noted that interest groups can be seen as performing a valuable and legitimate representative function. Indeed, at one time, so-called 'pluralist' political theorists argued that interest groups positively advanced democratic values. They believed that since all interests in society could be organised into groups, and because these groups would compete with each other and then compromise, the end-product of interest group activity would mirror the nation's demands as a whole (Truman, 1971).

Figure 4.1 The military-industrial complex: US military power defending the oil industry rather than the national interest.
Source: © Kirk Anderson

Pluralist theorists acknowledged the fact that not all interest groups were equal, with corporate groups, for example, having far greater financial resources than others. Nevertheless, it was argued that interest group resources were not cumulative: that is, no one type of group possessed an advantage in all resources. Thus, while corporate groups had an advantage in money, labour or civil rights groups had an advantage in numbers (Dahl, 1961).

The principal critics of the pluralist view have been elite theorists on both the political left and right (Mills, 1956; Dye, 1995). They stress the cooperation that occurs between privileged interest groups, especially those from the corporate sector, and other government elites. They deny that this political network is equally open to all-comers, especially groups who lack the financial clout to 'buy themselves a seat at the table'.

Those who defend the role of interest groups today concede some of the arguments made by the critics. Not only is there a real inequality among interest groups in terms of resources, but they are not even internally democratic. They tend to be run by a handful of full-time leaders who rarely consult their members on policy issues (Berry, 1989, p. 66).

Nevertheless the sheer number of interest groups tends to support the view that they perform a valuable representative function. They are a vehicle for putting new issues on the public agenda and for encouraging Americans to participate in a small way in their own government. And for all that Americans lambaste the power of special interests in general, they tend to value the role of the groups that represent *them* (Berry, 1989, p. 8).

For both good and ill, therefore, interest groups will remain a powerful force in American politics.

They will continue to organise and represent significant sections of the community, and they will continue to provide the financial fuel for congressional elections. This in turn means that they will continue to have a privileged claim on the attention of policy-makers and a privileged opportunity to place private interest at the heart of public policy.

Chapter summary

In combination with a fragmented system of government, the heterogeneous nature of American society has given rise to an impulse to form both parties and interest groups. As government has grown in its responsibilities and campaign expenditures have rocketed, the activities of interest groups have greatly expanded. Parties, on the other hand, have been weakened by rule changes, such as those which encouraged primary elections and those which limited the parties' ability to make direct financial contributions to election campaigns. These changes have made elected politicians less dependent on their parties and have brought them into closer relationships with interest groups. Nevertheless, parties and interest groups cooperate on issues and on elections and perhaps are best viewed less as rivals and more as two equally central and valuable agencies of representation. This does not mean that parties, and especially interest groups, do not harm democratic politics in some respects. As a result, there will be continued efforts to refine campaign finance and lobbying laws to try to ensure that parties and interest groups do not abuse their privileged positions within American politics.

Discussion points

1. To what extent and why are political parties in decline?

2. What are the advantages and disadvantages of weak party discipline in the federal government?

3. Why are interest groups so numerous in the United States?

4. How plausible is the argument that interest-group money buys access but not votes?

5. Do interest groups impair or enhance American representative democracy?

Further reading

Interest groups
Excellent introductions to this subject include R. Shaiko *et al.*, *The Interest Group Connection: Electioneering, Lobbying and Policymaking in Washington* (2nd edn, Washington, DC: CQ Press, 2004); R. Hrebener, *Interest Group Politics in America* (3rd edn, New York: Sharpe, 1997); A. Cigler and B. Loomis, *Interest Group Politics* (6th edn, Washington, DC: CQ Press, 2002).

Parties
One of the most accessible but authoritative books on this subject is W. Keefe and J. Hetherington, *Parties, Politics and Public Policy in America* (9th edn, Washington, DC: CQ Press, 2003). Another which encompasses the relationship of parties to interest groups is R. Benedict, M. Burbank and J. Hrebenar, *Political Parties, Interest Groups and Political Campaigns* (Boulder, Colo.: Westview, 1999).

Websites

http://www.opensecrets.org
http://www.democrats.org/
http://www.rnc.org/
http://www.politics1.com/parties.htm
http://www.fec.gov

References

Berry, J. (1989) *The Interest Group Society* (2nd edn, Glenview, Ill.: Scott, Foresman/Little, Brown).

Binkley, W. (1947) *American Political Parties: Their Natural History* (New York: Knopf).

Caesar, J. (1990) 'Political parties – declining, stabilizing, or resurging?' in King, A. (ed.) *The New American Political System* (2nd edn, Washington, DC: American Enterprise Institute).

Cigler, A. and Loomis, B. (1991) *Interest Group Politics* (3rd edn, Washington, DC: CQ Press).

Dahl, R. (1961) *Who Governs?* (New Haven, Conn.: Yale University Press).

Dye, T. (1995) *Who's Running America? The Clinton Years* (6th edn, Englewood Cliffs, NJ: Prentice Hall).

Hrebenar, R. (1997) *Interest Group Politics in America* (3rd edn, New York: Sharpe).

Keefe, W. and Hetherington, J. (2003) *Parties, Politics and Public Policy in America* (9th edn, Washington, DC: CQ Press).

Keefe, W. and Ogul, M. (1993) *The American Legislative Process* (8th edn, Hemel Hempstead: Prentice Hall International).

Ladd, E. (1997) '1996 elections: the "no majority" realignment continues', *Political Science Quarterly* (Spring), pp. 1–28.

Magleby, D. and Monson, J. (eds) (2004) *The Last Hurrah: Soft Money and Issue Advocacy in the 2002 Congressional Elections* (Washington, DC: Brookings Institute).

Malbin, M. (ed.) (1984) *Money and Politics in the United States: Financing Elections in the 1980s* (Chatham, NJ: Chatham House).

McSweeney, D. and Zvesper, J. (1991) *American Political Parties* (London: Routledge).

Mills, C. (1956) *The Power Elite* (Oxford: Oxford University Press).

Sabato, L. (1985) *PAC Power: Inside the World of Political Action Committees* (New York: Norton).

Stern, P. (1988) *The Best Congress Money Can Buy* (New York: Pantheon).

Tocqueville, A. de (1956) *Democracy in America* (New York: Mentor), first published 1835.

Truman, D. (1971) *The Governmental Process* (2nd edn, New York: Knopf).

Wright, J. (1990) 'Contributions, lobbying and committee voting in the United States House of Representatives', *American Political Science Review*, vol. 84, pp. 417–38.

Chapter 5

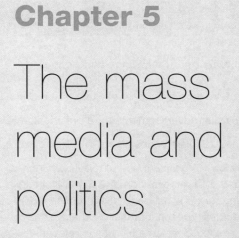

The mass media and politics

This chapter analyses the impact of the media, especially television, on elections and politics in general. American politics without television is unthinkable. Not only do voters gain most of their knowledge about politics from television, but candidates gear their campaigns almost entirely to the demands of this particular medium. Moreover, presidents regard the media as a critical element in the art of political persuasion. Unsurprisingly, then, great controversy surrounds the power of the media in politics.

Gerry Rafshoon, a leading media consultant in American politics, tells an amusing story from the 1952 presidential election. Political television was still in its infancy. The Democrats decided for the first time to give their candidate, Adlai Stevenson, a television adviser – a man called Bill Wilson. Stevenson had been introduced to Wilson at the Democratic Convention yet, weeks into the campaign, the candidate had not once called upon his new assistant for advice. Finally, however, in a hotel at a campaign stop, Wilson received a call to come up to Stevenson's suite. Excited at the prospect of getting down to work at last, Wilson hurried to the candidate's room. Stevenson greeted him by pointing to the television in the corner and saying, 'Ah yes, the television man. Can you fix that thing? I can't get a picture' (White and McCarthy, 1985).

A few elections further on, however, no candidate or campaign would be so naive or ignorant about the enormous potential for the use of television in elections. Today, according to one expert, 'Media coverage is the very lifeblood of politics because it shapes the perceptions that form the reality on which political action is based. Media do more than depict the political environment; they *are* the political environment' (Graber, 1989, p. 238).

Box 5.1

Key dates in the history of television and politics

1947   First live television broadcast of State of the Union address (President Truman).

1952   First television advertisements for a presidential candidate.

First use of television consultants in campaigns.

First politically significant use of television. Vice-presidential candidate Richard Nixon is threatened with removal from the Republican ticket, after allegations that he had used a secret slush fund for personal gain. Nixon decides to appeal to the public through television. He makes the 'Checkers' speech, confessing that he had received one gift: his children had been given a little dog called Checkers. His children loved the dog and Nixon vowed that they were going to keep him, whatever the critics said. He then asks viewers to contact Republican headquarters if they want him to stay on the ticket. Viewers respond positively and Nixon is saved.

1960   First televised presidential debate, between John F. Kennedy and Richard Nixon.

1961   President Kennedy gives first live televised presidential press conference.

1963   Network television news programmes extended to 30 minutes.

1964   First controversial political advertisement on television: the 'Daisy Commercial' on behalf of President Johnson. Without mentioning his opponent by name, the advertisement implies that Barry Goldwater could launch a nuclear war, if elected.

1965   US involvement in Vietnam leads to first 'televised war'.

1968   Richard Nixon turns to television advertising specialists to change his negative image: they create the 'new Nixon'.

The American press

When we speak of the media we mean television, radio, newspapers and magazines. Although television is undoubtedly the pre-eminent form of the media in the United States, this does not mean that the others are not important. Although the *New York Times* newspaper, for example, is seen by far fewer people than network television, it is both read and taken very seriously by the political elite.

As in most democracies, the written press in the United States is privately owned. However, three characteristics distinguish it from the press in, say, Great Britain.

Circulation

First, virtually all newspapers are local rather than national publications. Most importantly, the circulation of even the 'quality press' (*New York Times*, *LA Times* and *Washington Post*, for example) is substantially limited to the city or region of origin. This means that there is a very large number of daily newspapers in total in the United States: according to the Newspaper Association of America, in 2003 there were 1,456 daily newspapers and 917 Sunday newspapers published in the United States. On the other hand, precisely because they are restricted in area of circulation, there is far less competition between papers than there is in, say, Britain. Some

Table 5.1 Leading print media in the United States, 2005

Newspapers	Largest reported circulation
USA Today	2,665,815
Wall Street Journal	2,106,774
New York Times	1,680,583
Los Angeles Times	1,292,274
Washington Post	1,007,487

Source: Audit Bureau of Circulations, 2005

cities do have more than one newspaper: thus New York has the *Wall Street Journal*, the *New York Times*, the *Daily News* and the *Post*; and Chicago has the *Tribune* and the *Sun-Times*. Most cities, however, have only one of any significance.

Censorship

The second distinguishing aspect is that the American press is much less subject to legal restraint than the British press. This is due in large part to the protection provided by the First Amendment to the Constitution, which provides that 'Congress shall make no law ... abridging the freedom of speech, or of the press'. Although originally the amendment restricted only the federal legislature, the Supreme Court has applied it to state legislatures as well since 1931 (*Near* v. *Minnesota*).

Moreover, the Court has generally interpreted the First Amendment in a fashion that makes it difficult to gag the press. In 1964, in the case of *New York Times Co.* v. *Sullivan*, the Court held that a newspaper could not be convicted of libel merely because it published a false story. It was further necessary to prove that the story had been published with actual malice: that is, that the paper knew it was false. This makes it extremely difficult for public officials to intimidate the press with threats of libel suits.

Even where national security is involved, the Court has granted the press wide latitude. Thus, in *New York Times* v. *United States* (1971), the Court permitted the *Times* to go ahead with publication of the so-called Pentagon Papers, a leaked Defense Department secret history of government policy-making on the Vietnam War. The Court held that publication could only be prevented in situations where it would otherwise create immediate and irreparable harm to the nation.

The Supreme Court has also interpreted the First Amendment to give strong protection to political satire. A notable case in this regard occurred in 1988, in *Flynt* v. *Falwell*. The Reverend Jerry Falwell, the leader of the Moral Majority, a politically conservative Christian group, had been parodied in the most lewd manner by the scurrilous, pornographic magazine *Hustler*. The magazine was owned by Larry Flynt, and Falwell sued him for libel. Despite the fact that the parody contained utterly and maliciously false statements about Falwell's sex life, the Supreme Court ruled unanimously that he could not seek damages from Flynt. They reasoned that since no one could have taken *Hustler*'s portrayal of the reverend's sex life seriously, Falwell could not have been libelled.

These decisions on the First Amendment pay testament to Americans' belief that a free press is indispensable to open and democratic government. They help to ensure that the press, and indeed other media, can speak with a powerful voice in American politics, both by challenging official versions of the truth and by exposing the wrongdoing of government.

Objective journalism

The third distinctive feature of the American press is that, despite the opportunities for irresponsible bias that local exclusivity and First Amendment freedoms create, the major newspapers are far less overtly partisan than those in, say, Britain. The journalistic profession in the United States is imbued with a norm of 'factual reporting' and political 'objectivity'. One writer described this norm as follows:

Objectivity rules contain two primary requirements. *Depersonalisation* demands that reporters refrain from inserting into the news their own ideological or substantive evaluations of officials, ideas, or groups. *Balance* aims for neutrality. It requires that reporters present the views of legitimate spokespersons of the conflicting sides in any significant dispute, and provide both sides with roughly equivalent attention.

Entman, 1989, p. 30

Another analyst likened the model of objective journalists to that of medical doctors: 'white-coated specialists describing pathologies as if through microscopes' (Diamond, 1980, p. 235).

Total objectivity is clearly not possible, since the very selection of the items that constitute the news involves judgements which are in part subjective. As we shall see below, many politicians and academics do believe that the American media are politically biased. Nevertheless, it remains true that American newspapers are generally much less inclined to play the role of cheerleader for a politician or political party than are their British counterparts.

Television

Television is by far the most important medium in American politics. Not only do most Americans get the bulk of their information about politics from television, but they trust it more than any other medium. Adult Americans spend a lot of time watching television. The US Census Bureau projects that during 2006, Americans aged 18 and over will watch some 1,679 hours of television, that is, approaching 5 hours per day. The most significant trend in relation to this is the growing share of the cable and satellite channels, which by 2006 is projected to be 53 per cent of all television viewing.

Unsurprisingly, very few of these hours are spent watching news or other programmes about politics. Most Americans watch television as a leisure activity and seek entertainment, not political enlightenment from their television sets. Furthermore, even the main political programmes, such as the prime-time network news, actually convey little information compared with a newspaper. As Robert Spero pointed out: 'The word-count of a half-hour news programme would not fill up much more than one column of one page of the *New York Times*' (Spero, 1980, p. 177).

That said, television is critical to most Americans' knowledge of political affairs. If we take as an example the sources from which Americans gain knowledge of presidential elections, we find a clear predominance of television.

Table 5.2 Voters' Main Sources of Campaign News

Source	1992 (%)	1996 (%)	2000 (%)
Television	82	72	70
Newspapers	57	60	39
Radio	12	19	15
Internet	–	3	11
Magazines	9	11	4

Source: Graber, 2002, p. 246

Moreover, according to a Pew Research Center report of June 2000, television remains the most credible source of political news. The cable network CNN received the highest believability ratings, but the network broadcasters, such as NBC and CBS, were not that far behind.

The reliance of the American public upon television for political information, together with the importance attached to television by politicians themselves, raises several critical questions about the power of television in American politics. Who owns and runs television stations? How does television cover political news? Is television coverage of politics biased? And, perhaps most important of all, how much impact does television have on viewers' political opinions and behaviour? Each of these questions is examined in turn below.

Television ownership and control

Ownership of television in the United States is in private, commercial hands. There is no equivalent of the BBC. There is a small non-commercial television channel (Public Broadcasting Service – PBS) supported financially by a mixture of grants and viewer subscriptions. PBS audiences are very small, however, with a quality political programme such as the MacNeil/Lehrer *NewsHour* attracting about 1 per cent of the nation's viewers.

Television broadcasting is thus largely the preserve of private business, and especially of the four main network television companies – the Columbia Broadcasting System (CBS), the American Broadcasting Company (ABC), the National Broadcasting Company (NBC) and the Fox Broadcasting System

(FBS) – and, as noted above, cable and satellite stations. The four main corporations sell their programmes to the hundreds of local television stations across the country and are estimated to dominate the programming for about one-third of the nation's television households (Graber, 1989, p. 45). They are also responsible for producing the main national evening news programmes.

American television companies are, in many respects, just like any other business enterprise. They are owned by even larger corporations or by rich tycoons and the main task of the executives who run them is to make profits. Like other businesses, television companies seek to expand their markets, something which may involve buying up other broadcasting companies.

Here, however, there is a degree of governmental regulation. Broadcasting licences are issued by the Federal Communications Commission (FCC), the members of which are appointed by the president, subject to approval by the Senate. In order to ensure that no owner or television company acquires too much media power, the FCC limits the number of media outlets that any one company can own. There is, however, a constant debate over ownership caps, with the FCC coming under considerable pressure from large corporations and their political allies to relax the regulations. The Telecommunications Act of 1996 and subsequent revisions of regulations by the FCC have allowed for a much greater concentration of corporate ownership. A handful of corporations, including AOL Time Warner, Viacom and the News Corporation, now dominate television and other media outlets. Although there has been fierce criticism of this process of consolidation, a deal agreed by President George W. Bush and the Congress in 2003 allowed a further increase that permitted Viacom and the News Corporation to keep all their stations. Whether these commercial developments have any significance for media coverage of politics, however, is the subject of much debate.

Television coverage of politics

The principal way that a television corporation seeks to maximise its profits is to increase the number of viewers who tune into its programmes. The more viewers who watch a programme, the more the television company can charge advertisers who wish to reach that audience. Inevitably, then, virtually all television programmes, including news and current affairs programmes, are designed to pull in the largest audience possible. This has significant consequences for the way in which politics is packaged for television.

Television is a visual medium that most people watch for entertainment. These are two of the principal factors which constrain the coverage of politics on television. Most viewers want visual images which entertain them, whether they are watching an election campaign item or a report of urban rioting. The main ingredients of visual entertainment are movement, drama, emotion and conflict.

Because Americans are relatively uninterested in politics and television therefore devotes relatively little time to it, news items must also be brief and simplified. Finally, because the aim of the company is to maximise its audience, news items should not unnecessarily antagonise any section of the viewing public.

One can immediately see that such constraints raise considerable problems for television coverage of the complex issues which lie at the heart of American politics – the budget deficit, health care, civil rights and foreign affairs, for example. Television takes these important political issues and, in rendering them palatable for viewers, distorts them. Distortion should not be confused with bias: while the latter slants coverage towards a particular political viewpoint, distortion involves misrepresenting events in order to meet journalistic needs.

The result of meeting these needs, say critics, is a diet of trivialised, simplified, emotion-laden items which do little or nothing to develop an informed public. An example of this occurred in the early summer of 1993, when President Clinton went to California as part of his campaign to build political support for his budget proposal. The main story to arise from that tour, however, was not whether the president's plan was a good one, or even whether he had sold the plan well; rather, it was the fact that while aboard *Air Force One* at Los Angeles

Airport, waiting to take off for Washington, he had his hair cut by a fashionable stylist. Since all airport traffic is routinely halted when *Air Force One* is in the vicinity, the president's haircut caused a long delay to other travellers. Moreover, the haircut cost $200. The president was pilloried for his alleged indifference to other travellers and his vanity. Moreover, it later emerged that most, if not all of the story, was actually untrue.

The story, however, was entertaining, simple to tell and amenable to visual representation by pictures of the president's hair, *Air Force One* and the backlog of air traffic at the airport. On the other hand, its political significance is minuscule, except for the irony that it showed Clinton, a master of the political arts, as having been naive about the ability of the media to turn a trivial episode into one that is politically damaging.

On a more serious matter, television coverage of the Vietnam War has frequently been attacked for distorting the nature of the conflict. Television allegedly concentrated on dramatic scenes involving combat, destruction and refugees, even though such scenes were comparatively rare and not typical of the realities of life in South Vietnam. The simple fact is, however, that combat is emotionally and visually exciting, while peasants peacefully tending their rice-paddies is not.

Television bias

As well as being accused of distortion, journalists covering the Vietnam War were also accused of straightforward political bias. Robert Elegant, for example, claimed that many journalists were opposed to the war on political grounds and therefore their reports were negative and damaging to the American cause (Elegant, 1981).

Although the Vietnam War is an outstanding illustration, accusations of political bias in television and press reporting are routine in American politics. Politicians are notoriously thin-skinned and they are quick to attribute media criticism of their actions or policies to political bias. Richard Nixon made such accusations an ongoing feature of his political career. When defeated for the governorship of California in 1962, just two years after he lost the

presidential election to John F. Kennedy, Nixon retired from politics, telling journalists at a press conference that, 'You won't have me to kick around any more.'

Even after his successful comeback in the presidential election of 1968, Nixon was convinced that the media were out to get him. Among other things, he had his vice-president, Spiro T. Agnew, conduct an aggressive public campaign accusing the media of liberal bias. The names of many journalists also featured on President Nixon's secret Political Enemies List that was discovered during the Watergate scandal.

Beyond Richard Nixon's personal feelings, however, it is almost a staple of conservative politics in the United States to accuse the media of liberal bias. At first glance, this may seem an unconvincing allegation. Most obviously, as already noted, television is a commercial business and one would expect those who run it to share the pro-business values of much of the rest of corporate America. Indeed, it is on precisely these lines that the left usually accuses the media of *conservative* bias.

Nevertheless, the allegation of liberal bias is not altogether without foundation. Most obviously, the four major television networks are based in New York city, the centre of American liberal culture. Moreover, those who work in television are part of an intellectual and cultural liberalism which is strong among the artistic and entertainments community (Dye, 1995; Graber, 1989).

There is also some empirical evidence to support this view. Those who work in television, as opposed to the actual owners of television companies, are far more likely to identify themselves as Democrats or Independents, than as Republicans. One study of executive media personnel in the 1980s found that 33 per cent were Democrats, 58 per cent were Independents and just 9 per cent were Republicans. This led Doris Graber to conclude that 'owners of prominent media hire Democrats and liberal Independents to operate their media properties, although they themselves usually share the Republican leanings of the big business community' (Graber, 1989, p. 62).

Allegations of bias are easy to make and there is clearly some truth to them. Few seriously doubt that Fox News is conservative and supportive of President George W. Bush, while other stations lean towards the liberal side of politics. On the other hand, other factors can be mistaken for bias. Take the CBS scandal of 2004/5, which resulted in the retirement of superstar news anchorman Dan Rather and the firing of several top executives at CBS. The scandal stemmed from a CBS news report in September 2004, claiming that George W. Bush had received preferential treatment during the Vietnam War era by being admitted to the Texas National Guard. Not only did this mean that Bush did not have to serve in Vietnam, but CBS further claimed that he did not fulfil even his obligations to the National Guard. The basis of the CBS story was some newly discovered documents of the era. When the story was challenged, however, CBS were unable to demonstrate the authenticity of the documents or the truth of the allegations. Many conservatives believed that Rather and the CBS team had been motivated by their political opposition to Bush. An enquiry that reported in early 2005 dismissed this charge and found instead that CBS had been so determined to beat its rivals and be the first to run the story, that it neglected its usual procedures for verifying the facts.

It is one thing, then, to identify media personnel as liberal, but quite another to show that their political persuasion results in slanted news coverage. Thomas Dye believes that the liberal bias of the media is most strongly reflected in the actual selection of items that are included in the news:

Topics selected weeks in advance for coverage reflect, or create . . . current liberal issues: concern for poor and blacks, women's liberation, opposition to defense spending, and the CIA, ecology, migrant farm labor, tax loopholes and Indian rights and, for nearly two years, Watergate.

Dye, 1995, p. 107

This argument is countered by journalists who claim that television news coverage mirrors society and the public's concerns. This view is buttressed by the point made earlier that, ultimately, television news is an entertainment designed to attract as many viewers as possible, in order to maximise advertising revenue. Content, like other aspects of journalistic coverage, is constrained by the need to please the maximum number of viewers. Any programme which ignored this, and instead pursued an agenda of issues that interested only liberals, would soon fall behind in the ratings war.

The liberal bias of the media certainly did not spare President Clinton when he became embroiled in yet another sexual scandal in 1998. Despite the fact that conservative groups had been using such scandal to undermine the Clinton presidency from its inception in 1993, liberal newspapers like the *Washington Post* took the lead in exposing the president's alleged intimate relationship with a White House employee. Moreover, broadcast and print media alike repeated unsubstantiated stories, sometimes from anonymous sources, in their rush to beat their competitors with 'breaking news'.

A further factor which undermines the theory of liberal bias in the American media is the simple fact that reporters are heavily dependent upon government for stories and information. Daniel Hallin disputed the myth of liberal bias in reporting on the Vietnam War by showing that government was not only the major source of information relayed by the media, but also that such information was reported largely unchallenged (Hallin, 1986). What was true of Vietnam coverage is also true of political news in general (Graber, 1989, p. 78). If there is any structural bias in media coverage of politics, it is bias in favour of the government of the day, whatever its political colour.

Impact of television

There is a passionate debate in most countries about the impact of television on people's attitudes and behaviour. It is typically argued that exposure to a heavy diet of explicit television violence or sex leads to antisocial or criminal behaviour in viewers. Evidence to support this is said to be the number of criminal offenders who cite television programmes as the inspiration to their crime.

On the other hand, it can be plausibly argued that television does not cause violence in people, but rather that people prone to violence are attracted to programmes which portray it graphically. Thus the causal relationship between television and behaviour is in dispute.

The same debate exists in regard to television's coverage of politics. Don Hewitt, the executive producer of the popular politics programme *60 Minutes*, tells of a woman who told him that television violence was to blame for John Hinckley's attempt to assassinate President Reagan in 1981. Hewitt responded by asking her how much television John Wilkes Booth had watched before assassinating Abraham Lincoln (White and McCarthy, 1985).

Social scientists have, of course, investigated the impact of television on political behaviour, especially voting behaviour. These studies have failed to produce any evidence that what people see on television affects the way they vote: 'the persistent finding of almost three decades of research has been that the mass media have minimal effects in changing voters' attitudes' (Arterton, 1984, p. 4).

As another analyst pointed out, this conclusion presents us with something of a paradox: 'The public believes that the media have an important impact on the conduct of politics and on public thinking. Politicians act and behave on the basis of the same assumption. But many studies conducted by social scientists fail to show substantial impact' (Graber, 1989, p. 12).

These findings are troubling because common sense tells us that if Americans get most of their political information from television, and if they place a great deal of faith in the reliability of that information, then surely they *must* be influenced by television.

Selective attention

Here as elsewhere, however, common sense may not be right, for media researchers agree that human beings are adept at controlling what information they accept. The most important phenomenon in this respect is selective perception, also known as selective exposure or *selective attention*. Quite simply, viewers will screen out political messages which make them psychologically uncomfortable by contradicting their existing beliefs. Selective attention is thus a defence mechanism against disturbing political information. It can take a variety

of forms in practice: the television can be turned off or the channel switched; or the viewer can 'challenge' the unwelcome message by drawing upon different, contradictory evidence or disputing the validity of the source of the message; or the viewer may simply ignore the message.

The importance of selective attention will vary from one individual to the next. Viewers with deeply held political convictions or strong party loyalties are extremely unlikely to be affected by news or propaganda which contradicts their existing opinions. The weaker their knowledge or political beliefs, however, the less they are likely to be discomforted by new political information and the less, therefore, they are likely to invoke the defensive shield of selective attention. Consequently, this section of the population is most vulnerable to the impact of television and any political bias which operates.

It is probable, then, that the main impact of television on the substance of Americans' political beliefs stems from its power to help set the political agenda. By definition, news is what is reported in the media. Selecting newsworthy items from the mass of stories and issues available is a subjective process. However, as noted above, such judgements are likely to be guided at least as much by professional and commercial considerations as by the political bias of the television or newspaper.

It is therefore difficult to avoid the conclusion that the power of the media to influence Americans' political attitudes is frequently exaggerated by those who mistake its pervasiveness for persuasiveness. Nevertheless, as we shall now see, that very pervasiveness is a critical ingredient of the representative process.

The media and elections

Media strategy

In effect, elections take place on television in the United States. Since most Americans get most of their political information from television, candidates for office spend most of their time, effort and money on developing an effective media strategy. To be successful, the first thing they need is exposure: they need to be seen on television as often as possible. The second major condition of a successful media strategy is that this exposure must cast the candidate in a positive light.

Fulfilling both of these demands can be problematic. Take, for example, the relatively unknown politician in a large field of primary candidates. This politician needs to do something that brings favourable publicity onto herself, but the media will prefer to concentrate their attention upon the front-runners in the election. Moreover, those front-runners are likely to be better financed than she is and therefore able to buy more advertising time on television.

The front-runners too, however, may face difficulties in presenting themselves to the public via television. The most obvious problem that may arise is that the media may cover them *too* closely and expose things that they would rather keep hidden. Such was the experience of Senator Gary Hart, the leading candidate for the Democratic party presidential nomination in 1988. When rumours began to circulate about Hart's extramarital affair with model Donna Rice, Hart denied them and challenged the media to produce proof. In hindsight, this was a foolish act of bravado, as evidence soon showed the rumours to be true. The Hart campaign never recovered.

There are ultimately two kinds of media attention with which a candidate has to deal. First there are those situations in which the initiative and control are mainly with the candidate. Most important here are the candidate's public image which he tries to promote and the television advertisements about himself which he pays to have broadcast.

Candidate image

How a candidate looks on television is crucial to his overall strategy of establishing his image in the minds of the electorate. The most basic aspect of this is literally the physical appearance of the candidate. Academics and political consultants agree that it is becoming increasingly difficult for physically unattractive candidates to get elected.

They also agree that even great politicians from the past who were not physically blessed, such as Abraham Lincoln, would find it difficult today to pursue a successful political career. Professor Larry Sabato believes that, in effect, candidates are now pre-selected by physical appearance, with their model being the good-looking television presenters: 'We've had a convergence among three types of people. Anchor-persons on television, politicians and game-show hosts all look very much alike today. And that's the effect of television' (Rees, 1992).

The most famous example of the impact of the physical appearance of candidates on television occurred during the 1960 presidential election. In the first televised debate between John Kennedy and Richard Nixon, viewers were presented with a strong contrast between the two candidates. Kennedy was tanned, youthful and dressed in a dark suit which gave him a crisp outline against the pale studio background. Nixon was pale following a recent illness, perspiring and had a dark 'five o'clock shadow'; he also wore a light grey suit which merged his figure with the background. Analysis later showed that those who heard the debate on radio believed that Nixon had won, but those who had watched on television thought Kennedy had won.

Candidate image depends upon more than raw physical appearance, however. Politicians present themselves so as visually to symbolise their character and politics. Jimmy Carter, for example, both as candidate in 1976 and then president, would sometimes dress casually on television in order to try to project an image of being an informal, approachable 'man of the people'.

On the other hand, during the 1980 presidential election, when Carter was under severe public pressure from perceived domestic and foreign policy failures, he sought to emphasise his presidential character by adopting a 'Rose Garden strategy'. This is when an incumbent president invites the cameras in to witness him signing important bills or meeting foreign dignitaries in presidential surroundings, such as the White House Rose Garden. The object is to appeal to the respect that the voters hold for the office, in the hope that this will compensate for any lack of respect for the man or his policies.

Figure 5.1 In the first 2004 presidential debate President George W. Bush reacted with impatience to his opponent's criticisms. This counted against Bush as it was deemed 'conduct unbecoming'. Source: © Ron Sachs/Corbis

The 2004 presidential election provided some interesting insights into the image issue. President George W. Bush chose a strategy that presented him as clear and determined in his ideas and policies. It was less important whether people actually agreed with those ideas and policies. What counted was clarity, not content. This strategy was reinforced by the attacks on his opponent, Senator John Kerry, for being indecisive and 'flip-flopping' on issues.

Political advertisements

Undoubtedly the main opportunity for a candidate to define himself with the public is the paid television advertisement. Here the candidate, or rather his television consultant, has almost total control over the presentation.

Advertisements may try to establish a candidate's position on certain policy issues, but they are more likely to try to project his image and character. As with commercial advertising, political advertisements seek to entertain and to produce a favourable response to the 'product-candidate', by evoking an emotional rather than a rational response. Thus advertisements have very little to do with conveying information upon which a viewer can base a reasoned voting decision. Rather, advertisements try to make the viewer like the candidate for other, even irrational, reasons. Advertisements hope to make viewers prefer a candidate for the same reasons that they prefer a news presenter or game-show host.

Not surprisingly, then, political advertisements have come in for a great deal of criticism for their failure to convey the kind of information that rational voting requires. Critics claim that political advertisements either present false information about candidates or no information at all.

Robert Spero's analysis of political advertisements by presidential candidates adds weight to these criticisms (Spero, 1980). He discovered that these advertisements regularly violated the codes of truthfulness that regulate commercial advertising. They contained both demonstrable lies and seriously misleading statements. Thus, in 1976, the Jimmy Carter campaign ran commercials proclaiming their candidate to be a peanut farmer and a political outsider who started out on his quest for the presidency with no organisation, no influential contacts and no money. In fact, Carter was a millionaire owner of a peanut-processing corporation, who had put his campaign organisation into place some three years before the election. He had also served on the Trilateral Commission, where he had established good contacts with leading politicians, academics and businesspeople.

Nevertheless, while such distortion of the truth may be morally reprehensible, it is not clear that it seriously misleads many voters. As Doris Graber says: 'Commercials are perceiver-determined. People see in them pretty much what they want to see – attractive images for their favourite candidates and unattractive ones for their opponents (Graber, 1989, p. 196). As with political news, then, viewers are very good at screening out information which contradicts their existing beliefs, while accepting that which confirms them.

What advertisements can achieve, however, is a crystallisation of a latent feeling that the viewer has about a candidate. This is particularly important in the case of negative advertising, an increasingly common and controversial feature of American election campaigns.

Negative advertising

In terms of political impact, it seems more profitable to attack your opponent than to promote yourself. Typically, campaign consultants will interview a selected panel of voters to find out what they dislike most about the opposing candidate. Advertisements are then produced which attack the opponent on these issues, often in a crude, vicious and misleading manner. At their worst, they attack an opponent's character or distort his or her political record or position.

The first major negative political advertisement was Tony Schwartz's 'Daisy Commercial', screened on behalf of President Johnson during the 1964 presidential campaign. It depicted a little girl counting as she pulls the petals off a flower. Suddenly a male voice is superimposed, counting down from ten to one as if in preparation for a rocket launch. The camera zooms into the eye of the girl, and as the voice reaches zero, a nuclear explosion is heard and the mushroom cloud appears. President Johnson's voice is now heard warning of the dangers of nuclear war.

His opponent, Barry Goldwater, is never mentioned in the commercial. However, the right-wing Goldwater had a well-deserved reputation as a hard-line anti-communist, and the daisy commercial played on this to suggest that, if elected, he might be willing to risk a nuclear war. The commercial was scaremongering but its effectiveness depended upon the fact that Goldwater's extremism was already an issue in the public's perception. It was thus a classic example of the power of advertising to sharpen and define an opponent's negative characteristics.

By the late 1980s, negative advertising had become a regular feature of elections at all levels of office and even of primary elections. For example, the 1990 Democratic primary for governor of Texas featured a Jim Mattox advertisement accusing Ann Richards of having used drugs; and a Richards advertisement mentioning an earlier indictment of Mattox for bribery, even though he had been acquitted (Davies, 1992, p. 95).

The 1988 presidential election was particularly noted for the use of negative advertising by Republicans against the Democratic candidate, Governor Michael Dukakis of Massachusetts. In particular, they played on the fact that a convicted murderer in Massachusetts, Willie Horton, had committed rape while out of prison on a weekend pass. Although many states had such furlough systems, Dukakis was attacked for being 'soft on crime'. Other advertisements attacked him for being unpatriotic, because he had vetoed a state bill requiring schoolchildren to begin the day by reciting the Pledge of Allegiance. The advertisements failed to mention that the bill was clearly unconstitutional under well-known Supreme Court decisions.

Such advertising may lower the tone of elections and increase the cynicism of the public about politics and politicians in general. Candidates are also aware that the public condemns negative advertising and this may have helped both the Clinton and Dole campaigns in 1996 decide to avoid the worst excesses of character attacks on their opponent. The Clinton campaign concentrated on so-called comparative advertisements, which criticise the opponent's record (Just, 1997, pp. 92–3). This may still be thought of as negative in the sense that it does not concentrate on the candidate's own virtues, but it is also entirely legitimate in a contest between two individuals presenting two different programmes for the public's endorsement.

Ultimately, however, negative advertising can have a significant effect on voter choice. It seems that it is more effective to focus on your opponent's negative features than merely to emphasise your own positive features. In other words, it is sometimes more effective to play on the electorate's fears than on its hopes. This is nothing new in electoral politics. It becomes a problem, however, when it is so widespread that voters are presented with a campaign which is almost wholly negative in tone. The danger is that it will simply turn people off politics altogether. However, the evidence of the

2004 presidential campaign suggests otherwise. There was a sharp rise in voter turnout, despite the fact that much of the advertising was negative. A classic example was the advertisement broadcast on behalf of the so-called Swift Boat Veterans, attacking the Vietnam War record of Senator John Kerry. Although a supposedly independent group, it was later discovered that they had been advised by some who were working for the Bush campaign. The allegations made by the advertisement were dubious where they were not simply wrong. Yet the media, despite its supposedly liberal, anti-Bush bias, took up the allegations without thoroughly checking them. As a result, Kerry experienced several difficult weeks trying to put the story right, and perhaps never quite recovered his image as the patriotic veteran.

Candidates versus the media

Whereas candidates can control the advertisements that are screened on behalf of their campaign, they are much more vulnerable when it comes to news coverage of elections. Here the supposedly adversarial relationship of politicians and the media comes into play. Candidates want only favourable coverage, while the media wants the truth as they see it, though the truth must be packaged to meet their commercial demands.

Although the media has claimed its victims in the past, as we saw with Gary Hart above, candidates are becoming increasingly adept at manipulating the needs of the media for their own purposes. If television requires pictures, excitement and statements that can be condensed into simple language in a few sentences, then that is what politicians give them.

As a result, American elections are now governed by the 'soundbite' and the 'photo-opportunity'. In fact, campaigning amounts to creating as many opportunities as possible to have the cameras photographing the candidate in attractive settings, and to produce the telling, short phrase that will be broadcast on that evening's news programmes. Thus, in the 1996 campaign, the average length of a candidate quote on the evening news was 8.2 seconds (Just, 1997, p. 98).

Local news coverage is very important in a country the size of and as diverse as the United States, so candidates are given a manic schedule of trips to different parts of the country, spending only enough time in each to provide the media with what they need. As Christopher Arterton argued, 'If a candidate spends one hour in a city, he is likely to receive the same amount of news coverage of that visit as he would during a four-hour or eight-hour stop in the same location. Thus, modern presidential candidates are kept continually on the move by

Figure 5.2 Ronald Reagan addressing a crowd against the backdrop of New York harbour and the Statue of Liberty.
Source: © Bettmann/Corbis

their desire for local news coverage. The scheduler's goal is to set up appearances in three or four major news markets each day' (Arterton, 1984, p. 13).

These appearances are carefully planned, even choreographed, to produce good visuals. Enthusiastic supporters are strategically placed to demonstrate that the candidate is popular. A site may be chosen to produce a positive response from the viewers – for example, Ronald Reagan addressing a crowd against the backdrop of New York harbour and the Statue of Liberty. Or again, the candidate might be filmed eating spaghetti at an Italian-American social in order to identify himself with that particular section of the electorate. None of these images tells the voters much about the candidate's policies, but they are appealing and entertaining.

Soundbites fulfil the media's need for simplification and drama at the expense of detailed policy statements. Vice-President George Bush's most famous statement about his economic policies was the endlessly repeated 'Read my lips – no new taxes'. Unfortunately, this soundbite returned to haunt him as president when he *did* agree to raise taxes, but at least Bush's slogan purported to say something about policy. In 1992, the Clinton soundbite that took the media's fancy was a sentimental reference to his birthplace that was supposed to rekindle belief in the American dream: 'I still believe in a town called Hope.'

Candidate control of media reporting of elections was taken to extremes by Michael Deaver, Ronald Reagan's media adviser, in the 1984 election. Because Reagan was always liable to make a gaffe when questioned by reporters, Deaver permitted just one press conference with the president during the entire campaign. However, he did supply endless attractive photo-opportunities which the media felt bound to broadcast.

In 1992, the presidential candidates found new ways to bypass the rigours of media interrogation. Instead of reaching the public through interviews with 'heavyweight' political journalists, they appeared instead on popular television programmes, like the *Larry King Show*, *Phil Donahue* and *Arsenio Hall* and the rock music station MTV. Here candidates were not in danger of being confronted with difficult questions and they could also provide good photo-opportunities, as when Bill Clinton donned dark glasses and played the saxophone. Ross Perot went even further, simply buying media time to broadcast his own thirty-minute specials.

Even when candidates cannot hide from the political media, they are not without means of trying to ensure that coverage is favourable. All campaigns employ spin doctors whose job it is to move among the media after, say, a televised debate or primary election, trying to persuade them that their candidate was the victor. Bill Clinton's team provided an excellent illustration of this in the 1992 presidential election. In the key New Hampshire primary, Clinton was beaten by Paul Tsongas. Nevertheless, the Clinton team claimed victory by arguing that because the campaign had been hit so badly by sex scandals, his second place was truly remarkable. They even persuaded the media to adopt their description of Clinton as 'The Comeback Kid'.

Moreover, for reasons that are not always clear, some candidates and politicians seem to get away with serial gaffes. President Reagan usually joked his way out of such difficulties, but President George W. Bush lacked Reagan's easy charm. Nevertheless, despite often garbling his words and creating a well-publicised list of 'Bushisms', a sufficient number of voters were willing to discount his verbal frailties and elect him president in both 2000 and 2004.

Chapter summary

Ideally, the media should communicate the kind of political information that the electorate needs in order to make rational voting decisions. Voters should know what policies the candidates propose and what the effect of those policies is likely to be. Voters should also be informed about the past record of politicians and the kind of government they propose to run.

Clearly, however, current media presentation of politics falls far short of these goals. Politicians seem increasingly able to package themselves for television in ways that make them attractive figures, without revealing much about their true selves or their policies. Media personnel may try to penetrate the politicians' veneer, but even when successful they provide mostly a simplistic, trivial and perhaps distorted picture.

It is not clear, however, how much of the blame for this should be laid at the door of the media. For any citizen who wishes to be well informed *can* find newspapers, magazines and television programmes that provide serious and detailed coverage of politics. If the average voter wanted such coverage, then popular print and broadcast media would provide it, for commercial reasons if nothing else. Most Americans, however, appear to value entertainment more than real politics and that, therefore, is what both politicians and the media seek to give them.

Discussion points

1. Does media coverage of politics give viewers the information they need?

2. How biased is media coverage of politics?

3. How important is 'image' in elections?

4. Is negative advertising harmful to the political process?

Further reading

An excellent introduction to this subject is Doris Graber, *Mass Media and American Politics* (6th edn, Washington, DC: CQ Press, 2002). See also Graber's *Media Power in Politics* (4th edn, Washington, DC: CQ Press, 2000). A good discussion of the impact of television on the political process is Robert Entman, *Democracy Without Citizens: Media and the Decay of American Politics* (New York: Oxford University Press, 1989). A useful chapter on the structure of American media can be found in Thomas Dye, *Who's Running America?* (6th edn, Englewood Cliffs, NJ: Prentice Hall, 1995). For an analysis of the media

campaign in the 2000 election, see G. Pomper *et al.*, *The Elections of 2000: Reports and Interpretations* (Chatham, NJ: Chatham House, 2001); for the 2004 election see M. Nelson, *The Elections of 2004* (Washington, DC: CQ Press, 2005). For a sophisticated analysis of the power of the media in politics, see Daniel Hallin, *The 'Uncensored War': The Media and Vietnam* (New York: Oxford University Press, 1986).

References

Arterton, F. (1984) *Media Politics* (Lexington, Mass.: Lexington Books).

Davies, P. (1992) *Elections USA* (Manchester: Manchester University Press).

Diamond, E. (1980) *Good News, Bad News* (Cambridge, Mass.: MIT Press).

Dye, T. (1995) *Who's Running America?* (6th edn, Englewood Cliffs, NJ: Prentice Hall).

Elegant, R. (1981) 'How to lose a war', *Encounter*, August, pp. 73–90.

Entman, R. (1989) *Democracy Without Citizens: Media and the Decay of American Politics* (New York: Oxford University Press).

Graber, D. (1989) *Mass Media and American Politics* (3rd edn, Washington, DC: CQ Press).

Graber, D. (2002) *Mass Media and American Politics* (6th edn, Washington, DC: CQ Press).

Hallin, D. (1986) *The 'Uncensored War': The Media and Vietnam* (New York: Oxford University Press).

Just, M. (1997) 'Candidate strategies and the media campaign', in Pomper, G. *et al.*, *The Election of 1996: Reports and Interpretations* (Chatham, NJ: Chatham House).

Rees, L. (1992) 'We have ways of making you think' (BBC2, broadcast 1992).

Spero, R. (1980) *The Duping of the American Voter: Dishonesty and Deception in Presidential Television Advertising* (New York: Lippincott & Crowell).

White, T. and McCarthy, L. (1985) 'Television and the presidency' (BBC2, broadcast 1985).

Chapter 6

The presidency and the executive branch

The presidency of the United States is often referred to as the most powerful office in the world. In truth the executive is but one branch in American constitutional government, and the presidents who occupy the leading office in this branch face considerable complications in turning their executive agenda into deliverable policy. The Constitution provides the president with the tools of office, and the office-holders use these tools with differing skills, and in differing contexts. The office has certainly taken a central role in national and international perceptions of American government, and this perception itself adds to the authority that it has gained over the centuries. The president still faces a complex situation, having at all times to negotiate major initiatives with the members of the US Congress.

The executive branch of the federal government includes a vast array of experts organised into departments and agencies. Their purpose is to serve the government, and especially the president, by providing specialist knowledge to policy-makers and by administering national laws and policies. The executive branch of the United States government employs almost 2.7 million men and women, that is, approximately one in fifty of all Americans in work (*Statistical Abstract of the United States, 2004–5*). This is a remarkable number of government employees for a nation which prides itself on its individualism and its belief in limited government. Nevertheless, the phenomenal growth in the size and range of the federal bureaucracy is no aberration. Rather, it has been a logical response to the increasing complexity of American society and the unrelenting growth in federal government responsibilities.

The constitutional debate

The members of the US Constitutional Convention debated long and hard about the form that the nation's executive should take. There was little enthusiasm for a system that might replace George III with a home-grown executive that might prove equally threatening, but there were concerns that the new nation should have an executive leadership capable of acting decisively in the nation's interest when necessary. Thomas Cronin (1989) points out that at least sixty votes were taken by the authors of the US Constitution on the method of election of the executive, eligibility to hold the office, and the length and number of terms of office.

These issues impacted upon each other as the delegates searched for a form that would produce a relatively autonomous and energetic executive; not too dependent on, or in league with, the legislature, but checked from having absolute power; con-

nected to the consent of the governed, but without the potential to rule through the mob; and with the qualities that would be respected in an executive. The final form was agreed only days before the Convention ended. The president of the United States would serve for four years, would be eligible for re-election, and would be selected through a new invention – the electoral college.

The electoral college

The authors of the US Constitution heard arguments for various forms of presidential selection. The individual states, and especially the small states, had reservations about an executive elected

Figure 6.1 In 2004, Senator John F. Kerry (Democrat – Massachusetts), seen here compaigning with rock star Bruce Springsteen, won more votes for the presidency than any previous Democratic candidate, but could not overtake incumbent President Bush.

Source: © Jim Young/Reuters/Corbis

by any process that might erode the identity of individual states. Small states in particular ran the risk of having their interests overlooked in any presidential election process that did not include a specific role for states.

The electoral college addresses some of these concerns. Electors, chosen by the states, in their turn choose the president. The number of electors is equal to the total congressional representation of each state. This system, which has remained fundamentally the same for over two centuries, expressly recognises the place of the states in American national government.

The number of electors is equal to the number of US representatives (a distribution based on population), plus the number of US senators (two per state). By the Twenty-third Amendment to the Constitution (1961) the federal district of Washington, DC (which is not part of any state) was allocated three electoral college votes. The inclusion of two votes per state regardless of size has the most impact on the states with small populations. Almost all states have adopted the practice of awarding all of their electoral college votes to the candidate who leads in the state's popular vote. The total number of electoral college votes nationwide is 538. Victory in the presidential election requires a candidate to collect an absolute majority, or at least 270, of these votes. If no candidate receives an absolute majority, the Constitution describes a method for the House of Representatives to choose from the leading candidates.

When public support for the leading candidates is very close, there is potential for the electoral college results, totalled from all the states, not to favour the candidate who has been supported by most individual voters. This is what happened in 2000. George W. Bush took many more of the small states than Al Gore. In all Bush took thirty states, to Gore's twenty states (plus Washington, DC). The popular vote favoured Gore by about 0.5 per cent of the total. But Bush's support was distributed between enough states to give him 271 electoral college votes – just exceeding the necessary absolute majority in the electoral college, enough to make him the next president of the United States. There were concerns that a similar problem could arise

in 2004. Any possible crisis was avoided when President George W. Bush achieved both a popular vote lead of 3 per cent and gained a majority in the electoral college, but there were some anxious hours before the state of Ohio fell firmly into the Republican column. A modest shift of votes in that one state would have left Bush firmly ahead in the total popular vote, but would have given the presidency to Democrat John Kerry on electoral college votes.

A national office

The presidency holds a special place with American citizens, whose respect for the office often provides the foundation for admiration of the office-holder. The president and vice-president are the only office-holders in the US government that are elected nationally. While the contemporary electoral college is built firmly on the eighteenth-century constitutional foundations of the USA, the presidential election process has adapted to the contemporary context of the twenty-first century. The choice of the national executive leadership is one political event in which every eligible citizen of the United States can take part.

The election process puts the president at the centre of the national political process, and the modern media coverage of elections, and of the policy process, often gives same impression, but it is not clear that the Constitution was written with this aim in mind.

The US Constitution does not make the executive branch its first concern. It moves on to this branch in Article II, after devoting the first Article of the Constitution to the legislative branch. It may be that the authors of the Constitution felt that the legislature, and especially the US House of Representatives, which was in the early days the only directly elected part of the national government, would be the most dynamic element of national government. In fact it was clear quite quickly that the presidency had great potential to establish a clear leadership role in national government.

Figure 6.2 The annual State of the Union address is just one of the responsibilities that put the president at the centre of the public's perception of politics.

Source: © Brooks Kraft/Corbis

Presidential centrality: commander-in-chief

Article II of the Constitution opens: 'The executive power shall be vested in a President', then proceeds to list and describe elements of the office. These constitutional grants of power and authority to the president have been said by some analysts to give the appearance of establishing a set of institutionalised presidential 'chiefdoms' putting the president at the centre of US government. The most clearly mentioned of these constitutional roles is commander-in-chief of the armed forces.

The significance of the commander-in-chief role is never more evident than in times of international stress, and has a clear and strong relevance at the beginning of the twenty-first century. The president's commander-in-chief power has been most tested during major combats, such as the War of 1812, the American Civil War, the World Wars, the Vietnam War, the Gulf War, and most recently the post-September 11th, 2001, engagements with Afghanistan and Iraq.

Through much of the second half of the twentieth century the USA and the USSR were seen as superpowers maintaining an uneasy international balance. The implosion of the USSR has left just one international superpower, and while Russian defence spending still leaves it in the same league as the United Kingdom, Japan, France or Germany, none of them come close to the USA, where the annual defence budget is now double that of all these other countries combined.

As commander-in-chief the president leads an armed force of almost 1.5 million. There are also many civilian personnel involved, and the Department of Defense is the largest executive department, with almost 640,000 employees. These non-uniformed government defence workers make up about 40 per cent of the total government employment in all fifteen executive departments within the executive branch.

The commander-in-chief power is not without controversy. During the American Civil War, for example, President Abraham Lincoln announced the suspension of habeas corpus, and ordered the use of military courts for some cases. In *Ex parte Milligan*, a case conveniently left undecided until after the conflict was finished, the Supreme Court ruled against the late president's actions. The court's decision liberated Lambdin Milligan from prison, and established precedent aimed to protect citizens' civil liberties in wartime.

A century after the *Milligan* case the USA was again at war, this time against communist foes in Southeast Asia. The conduct of the war by successive administrations disturbed the US Congress enough that in 1973 it overrode the veto of President Richard Nixon to pass the War Powers Resolution, requiring consultation with Congress on troop deployments. While presidents have on occasion taken the debate on military actions to Congress, they have generally indicated their willingness to ignore the apparent limitations of war power legislation, citing the need for effective and decisive executive action in times of crisis.

The significance of these issues has re-emerged at the start of the twenty-first century, as President George W. Bush led the United States into what he termed a 'war on terror'. Reacting after the September 11th terrorist outrages on the United States, President Bush has led his country, and some allies, into attacks on Afghanistan and Iraq. The United States chose to hold captives taken in Afghanistan at a detention camp in Cuba, and indicated that it saw these prisoners as outside the scope of the Geneva Convention, and as subject to US military law. Domestically, a new executive department of Homeland Security was established, and actions taken which some criticised as contrary to American traditions of individual rights. There is no doubt that the authority of the commander-in-chief to take these actions will be fought out in the American federal courts.

Presidential centrality: chief diplomat

The diplomatic centrality of the president appears quite clear in the Constitution. The president receives ambassadors, thereby recognising other nations and their leaders, and, with the advice and consent of the US Senate, the president appoints ambassadors from the United States, and makes treaties with foreign nations.

The constraint of being checked by a legislative chamber, though, is not inconsiderable, especially as treaties have to be agreed by a two-thirds majority of senators. Perhaps the executive calamity most recalled is that afforded to President Woodrow Wilson after the First World War. Welcomed in Europe as a saviour, Wilson led the negotiations for a post-war League of Nations, only to find on his return to Washington that he could not negotiate his own international plan through the US Senate.

Presidents may reinterpret existing treaties to suit their administration's strategic aims more closely, and they can end treaties without congressional sanction, but they must find a way to work with Senate in order to establish new treaties. Executive agreements, though, do provide one alternative mechanism for a more independent conduct of some diplomacy. Actions based on the broad constitutional statement of the president's executive power, and on interpretations of existing legislation, have been used by many presidents. These are usually, though not always, quite tightly constrained agreements.

In spite of repeated congressional attempts to limit presidential use of the executive agreement it has become a substantial tool for any administration wishing to use the president's centrality in foreign and diplomatic policy to its full extent. The president is head of state, and this is exhibited no more clearly than in the conduct of foreign affairs, where the executive can make strategic use of the office's diplomatic and commander-in-chief powers with international consequences. As the post-Cold War USA has emerged to occupy a position without international equal in terms of power and authority, the president's foreign affairs leadership roles have acquired ever increasing significance both internationally and in terms of the domestic prestige associated with the position of world leadership.

Presidential centrality: chief legislator

It is perhaps stretching a point to claim this title for the president, but it cannot be ignored that the office brings with it a defined legislative role. The State of the Union address has become a key annual feature of any administration, giving the president a clear and unchallenged opportunity to present the administration's achievements in the best possible light, as well as the chance to recommend to the Congress those measures which the administration would like to see enacted.

Skilfully used, the State of the Union address can act as an important part of the agenda-setting that any ambitious president will want to see as part of the administration's activity. Passing this executive wish list into legislation, however, will still take a great deal more than sending a presidential message.

Congress is the legislative branch, and its members guard that privilege jealously. Even when Congress is controlled by members of the president's own political party, they cannot be relied on to respond unquestioningly to the executive prompt. The executive branch has to liaise carefully with members of Congress to make sure that the major elements of its legislative agenda pass relatively unhindered through the system. Congress will take account of many cues. For example, a president with a substantial and recent election mandate is likely to have an advantage in dealing with Congress; a president with skilful liaison aides and whose message is clear and accompanied by helpful evidence and documentation will have improved chances for success.

Negotiation with Congress takes many forms, and probably the most used constitutional legislative power afforded to the president is the power to veto legislation. In fact, very little legislation is vetoed, and both the executive and Congress recognise this as a heavy-handed tool in the process, but the threat of presidential veto can have the effect of concentrating the minds of everyone interested in passing legislation, thereby contributing to compromise legislation being designed.

Certainly the president is a serious player in the legislative process, even if the institutional structure limits and encumbers the executive's freedom as a player in the law-making process.

Limited powers and presidential personality

While the institutional 'chiefdoms' that make up the role of chief executive are solidly founded in the Constitution, the powers granted are not huge, and it is clear that the accompanying checks and balances constrain even further the power of the presidency. Still it is not uncommon for the presidency of the USA to be referred to as the most powerful political office not just in America but in the world. There are clearly elements other than the defined constitutional parameters of the office that contribute to the perception of the presidency as having such potential for power.

One of the most influential analyses of the presidency, by the late Richard Neustadt, was based originally on his first-hand observations of the presidencies of the mid-twentieth century. Neustadt (1990) concluded that the limited and constrained authority granted to the president in the Constitution did not aggregate to very much presidential power. Other resources for presidential power exist, said Neustadt, and the personal political skills of the president in mobilising these resources goes a long way to accounting for the success or failure of a particular administration.

Key to Neustadt's perception of presidential potential were the forces of modernisation in twentieth-century America. In part the shift was a reflection of the course of history. It had been observed before that in times of crisis, such as war, the nation demanded centralised leadership, and that the president was the natural focus of national authority from which the citizenry expected that leadership to emanate. Two World Wars, the Great Depression, the Cold War, the War in Southeast Asia, the collapse of the communist hegemony, together put a series of intense demands on the federal executive through most of the twentieth century. The policy leadership provided was not uncontested, but always placed the executive at the very centre of the action and the debate.

Presidential centrality: the media

The death of former President Ronald Reagan, in June 2004, prompted a host of commentators to recall the impact of his 1981–89 occupancy of the White House. Repeated through much of this coverage was reference to Reagan's reputation as the 'Great Communicator', a shared term of commemoration that emphasised the way the growth of electronic media has transformed the public and political relations role of the president.

Administrations have taken media relations seriously for many years. Well before the advent of the electronic media successive presidential administrations had on occasion suffered from adversarial press coverage, and benefited from supportive reporting. President Theodore Roosevelt was an active campaigner for his policies, and believed that press dissemination of his energetic and well-constructed speeches could act to maintain his proposals high on the public agenda, even to the extent of appealing directly to the public in an attempt to influence the congressional receptiveness to presidential initiatives. Roosevelt's belief that the presidency was a 'bully pulpit' for ideas has become one of the received wisdoms of executive life.

In the twentieth century radio, and then television, became the major sources of public news consumption, but some elements of the press remained important, with a few major newspapers finding new roles through investigative and in-depth reporting that could influence the news agenda of the other news formats. President Woodrow Wilson was the first to use occasional formal press conferences as a way of channelling and guiding media coverage

of the presidency, but the electronic news media had an immediacy that forced administrations into a much more continuous, varied and active media management style by the twenty-first century.

Within the White House the Press Office and the Office of Communications work constantly with representatives from all the reporting media in an effort to gain favourable coverage, and to limit the damage caused by negative coverage, of the administration. A level of activity has developed that might previously have been expected only in election years, as presidents have moved towards adopting a strategy of 'permanent campaign' to maintain political and public engagement with their agenda, and to minimise the diversions that might be caused by political scandal or criticism.

Certainly presidents appear to have some genuine advantages in their attempt to manage their position in the mediation of American politics. The executive, led by a single figure and with concentrated resources, is easier to cover than the legislature. The presidential election campaign provides a foundation of knowledge about the administration that has been projected through a high-expenditure media-based campaign. The presidency has an iconic place in US politics that gives its occupants a media advantage – it is just more likely that what a president does can be classified as news. There is nonetheless a tension in the relationship between commentators and those being commented on. The journalists want access to potential stories to be as free as possible, while the subjects of the limelight would prefer to have as much control as possible over the message that will be projected to the public. Therefore, while the presidency may have an advantage in attracting attention, it also applies considerable resources to 'spin' that attention to its greatest advantage.

If the president is a central actor in American political reporting and campaigning, not all analysts agree that this translates automatically into communications success. George C. Edwards III argues that even President Reagan had little effect in changing public attitudes, but points out that presidential communication strategies can still help facilitate political success (Edwards and Davies, 2004). Presidential intervention may help a policy campaign that is already going in the right direction, and leadership that appears to move public opinion a few points on any closely fought issue is going to be significant. Successes of this kind can prove a valuable asset in the longer term by enhancing an administration's reputation for influencing public opinion and political outcomes. For all the work that goes into maintaining and developing the president's media centrality this cannot be counted on always to offer the same potential, and there are indications that media coverage of hard news, political news, and of the presidency itself, has declined in recent years.

Presidential centrality: the party

In spite of the fact that two major political parties occupy almost all the elected partisan offices in the USA, the nation is often referred to as having a weak party political system. The weakness lies not in the abilities of Democrats and Republicans to dominate the elections process, but in the relatively loose ideological affiliations that exist under the umbrellas offered by these two parties, and in the absence of sanctions with which party managers may exert authority over their elected colleagues. In effect the electoral strengths and the internal weaknesses of US political parties are opposite sides of the same coin. In such a large and diverse nation it is unlikely that two parties could dominate electoral politics so well if they did not allow for considerable internal variation, dissent and independence of action.

While the role of party leader does not necessarily appear to offer a huge resource, party loyalty may offer a president some leverage, especially if the incumbent is associated with other indications of success. A large, or surprising, electoral victory, a perceived skill in using the media to communicate with the electorate, skill in managing legislative initiatives, can all consolidate party loyalty and enhance the advantages of party leadership. But even at its weakest, party leadership still gives the president an advantage. One can really speak only of the incumbent party as having a leader at all, since there is no clearly identifiable single political leader of the party that is not in the White House.

Presidential centrality: the offices of persuasion

Presidents use formal and informal management techniques in the attempt to give their priorities an advantage in the Washington policy process. The Executive Office of the President has grown substantially since it was established in 1939, and now includes a dozen separate units, including such important elements as the National Security Council, the Council of Economic Advisors, and the Office of Management and Budget. The first two of these are small groups of key advisers on major policy areas, while the third is a large body of officials dedicated to producing annually the budget that the president will send to Congress, and which the administration hopes will dominate and set the parameters for the policy-making agenda. It is within his Executive Office that President George W. Bush established the Office of Homeland Security as part of his initial response to the attacks of September 11th, 2001. All of these units have a role in bringing together expertise to help and support efficient administration-led policy-making and implementation.

The expertise within the Executive Office and within the White House staff is closely connected to the president, and is dedicated to helping the president present a convincing policy agenda. This concentration of skills is impressive, but still presidential strategy cannot depend solely on the weight of argument and conviction that comes from these bodies of advisers. The White House must also be able to create and take advantages of policy opportunities. The transition period from the election of a new president in November into the early days of the new administration, almost three months later, is a critical period in which the ground can be laid for a successful term of office.

A speedy and well-ordered transition, in which the new administration lines up its major appointments, enters into constructive liaison with Congress, and moves rapidly towards establishing policy priorities, gives the impression that the president is hitting the ground running. The White House Office in particular will maintain the effort to bolster the president's potential in the system. Work specifically for use in promoting the president's programme in Washington will include public opinion polling and the identification and nurturing of political allies, especially if the programme faces hard challenges in the legislative process.

From the transition stage onwards the presidency will be engaged in the active pursuit of its political ends. All other things being equal, a president near the end of his term has less clout than one with a full term ahead, and a president's second term is hampered by the certain knowledge that someone else will be taking office at its end. Effective executive management of the federal bureaucracy will improve the chances that an administration's agenda will be implemented.

Table 6.1 Government departments under President Bush, 2003

Department	Number of civilian employees
State	31,402
Treasury	134,302
Defense	669,096
Justice	115,259
Interior	74,818
Agriculture	107,204
Commerce	37,330
Labor	16,296
Health and Human Services	67,240
Homeland Security	146,963
Housing and Urban Development	10,660
Transportation	89,262
Energy	15,823
Education	4,593
Veterans Affairs	226,171

Source: US Bureau of the Census, 2005

Main elements of the federal bureaucracy

The cabinet

In 2005 there were fifteen departments and their heads, or secretaries, form the core of the president's cabinet. As the number of employees in the departments indicates, cabinet secretaries are responsible for a wide number and variety of policy programmes. Indeed, along with the independent agencies and commissions (see below), the department secretaries administer some 1,400 federal programmes.

Beneath the department secretary, is an undersecretary and several assistant-secretaries. These top officials and other senior appointees, about 3,300 in total, are nominated by the president but require Senate confirmation (DiClerico, 1995, p. 165). While the president can usually rely upon getting his nominees confirmed, the Senate has developed a tendency in recent years to seize opportunities to examine nominees carefully, and occasionally to reject them, reminding incumbent presidents of the limits to their authority. While Alberto Gonzalez was appointed Attorney-General in 2005, this George W. Bush nomination was strongly opposed by some and closely examined by the Senate.

Presidential selection of cabinet secretaries

Presidents are free to nominate whomever they wish to cabinet posts. Most cabinet appointees either have strong political ties to the president's party or are respected for skills and expertise displayed outside the political arena. A president may well also take into account the likely reaction to an appointment from the main groups that deal with a particular department.

President Clinton had yet another criterion in making his cabinet appointments. In an effort to consolidate his support among diverse sections of the community, he wanted a cabinet that 'looked like America'. This translated into a policy that became known as EGG – Ethnicity, Gender and Geography. President George W. Bush continued the diversity theme. In 2005, for example, he appointed the first Asian-American woman to the cabinet, Elaine Chao, as Secretary of Labor. Similarly, Alberto Gonzalez became the first Hispanic Attorney-General.

When making cabinet appointments, then, the president combines political and practical criteria. Ideally, his appointees will obtain Senate confirmation with ease, earn the respect of those who deal with particular departments and also satisfy the president's supporters and the public at large. Of course, the president also wants his cabinet secretaries to further his goals and policies, in as far as he has any. As we shall see below, this can prove quite difficult.

The cabinet in operation

The American cabinet is a weak body in that it meets solely at the president's discretion and discusses only those topics that the president chooses to put before it. Furthermore, it has no collective responsibility for the administration's policy. 'The cabinet . . . has rarely been a source of advice upon which the president continuously relies. It exists by custom and functions by presidential initiative and is therefore largely what the chief executive chooses to make of it' (Koenig, 1996, p. 188).

President Kennedy only held six cabinet meetings in three years, while President Nixon believed that 'no [president] in his right mind submits anything to his cabinet' (Pious, 1996, p. 277). Consequently the cabinet exists collectively only to serve goals of secondary importance, such as acting as a sounding board for new ideas or for trying to coordinate public pronouncements on administration policy.

Individually, however, department secretaries can wield considerable influence over policy in their own area of competence and perhaps outside of it as well, especially when the secretary heads one of the more prestigious departments, such as State, Defense or the Treasury, or is a particularly valued adviser to the president.

Some presidents have used sub-groups of the cabinet as important policy-makers on particular clusters of issues. The Reagan administration created 'cabinet councils', each with six to eleven cabinet members, to advise in areas such as economic affairs, natural resources and environment, and food and agriculture (Whicker, 1990, p. 57). Much of their effectiveness depends upon the ability of different cabinet members to cooperate without allowing 'turf fights' and egos to get in the way.

Ultimately, however, the cabinet amounts to far less than the sum of its individual parts. Department secretaries are highly important members of the executive branch, not because they collectively devise administration policy, but because individually they are responsible for carrying out administration policy on vital matters. In that sense, they are the real heads of the federal bureaucracy.

Independent agencies and commissions

While there are only fifteen departments, there are dozens of agencies and commissions within the federal bureaucracy – 136 of them in 2005. Some of these play an enormously important role in implementing government policy and regulating key areas of public business. The Equal Employment Opportunity Commission (EEOC) has developed many of the policy guidelines which attack race and sex discrimination in employment; the Federal Reserve Board (the Fed) is a major influence in economic policy through its power to set interest rates; and the Federal Communications Commission (FCC) oversees broadcasting policy and sets national standards. Others are far more obscure, such as the American Battle Monuments Commission and the Postal Rate Commission.

The chairpersons of these agencies are appointed by the president. However, while secretaries can be sacked at will by the president, agency heads are usually appointed for a set term of office, giving them greater autonomy from the White House. Agency heads may thwart the president on policy by exploiting their independence and status.

Career civil service

The mass of the federal bureaucracy consists of career civil servants. There were some 20,000 federal employees in the 1830s, but this had more than doubled by the end of the Civil War to 53,000 and then reached 131,000 by 1884 (Garraty, 1968,

p. 253). Moreover, serious problems had emerged regarding the professionalism of these employees.

Patronage and professionalism in the civil service

It had always been understood that the main role of the federal bureaucracy was to serve the president. For that reason, the president was given the power to appoint civil servants. However, under the presidency of Andrew Jackson (1829–37), the right to appoint civil servants became a crude power of patronage, with appointees receiving their public posts as rewards for political service rather than for their skills or expert knowledge. The resulting civil service was often inefficient and corrupt.

By the late nineteenth century appointments were so thoroughly in the hands of corrupt party bosses that President Benjamin Harrison (1889–93) found himself unable even to select his own department secretaries. All the cabinet posts had been sold by the party bosses to pay election expenses.

At a lower level of the federal bureaucracy, steps had already been taken to end corruption and cronyism. In 1883, the Pendleton Act (or Civil Service Reform Act) was passed. This 'classified' certain positions within the federal bureaucracy, subjecting applicants to competitive examination. The Act also created the Civil Service Commission to oversee recruitment, thus further undermining corrupt political control. The president was empowered to place further posts within the classified category, and by the end of the century, roughly half of all federal employees were in classified positions (Garraty, 1968, pp. 257–8). The Pendleton Act was the foundation stone of the modern American civil service, bringing genuine specialist knowledge and administrative skill to prominence within the federal bureaucracy.

The qualities of bureaucracy

As in most countries, there are unflattering stereotypes of civil servants in the United States. Yet bureaucracy and civil servants bring valuable, even vital, qualities to American government. As theorists of bureaucracy have pointed out, these negative and positive attributes of bureaucrats are actually two sides of the same coin, so it is difficult to have the advantages of modern bureaucracy without the disadvantages.

The 'permanent government'

Unlike politicians who come and go, the federal bureaucracy brings a sense of permanence and continuity to American government. Many policy programmes transcend the terms of office of presidents and members of Congress and it is clearly important for those affected to know that a programme's operation is not dependent upon the whim, inexperience or ignorance of incoming politicians.

Career civil servants constitute a government store of knowledge about issues, problems and programmes. No new presidential administration, however radical in intent, would wish or be able to redesign all the federal government's major policies. The most ambitious of administrations would still depend upon the advice and assistance of the bureaucracy in formulating and implementing new policy.

Bureaucratic creativity and administrative law

The federal bureaucracy is no mere passive repository of expertise and experience. Frequently it plays a major part in legislating by filling in the details of congressional legislation. It is very common for Congress to write legislation in broad terms, leaving detailed 'guidelines' for implementation to departments and agencies. This has created a mass of 'administrative law' (as opposed to the statutory law of Congress).

Administrative law can be highly creative. For example, when Congress passed the Civil Rights Act of 1964, it failed to define what it meant by 'discrimination' on grounds of race or sex. It was therefore left to the federal bureaucracy to determine exactly what constituted discrimination and what kinds of evidence would demonstrate its existence in any particular context. In the field of race discrimination in employment, it was the Department of Labor, through its Office of Federal Contract Compliance (OFCC), that initiated a policy of affirmative action to fulfil the aims of the 1964 Act. In 1968 and 1971, the OFCC issued guidelines which established numerical goals and timetables for the greater employment of minority group members in certain jobs, and then decided that a disproportionately low employment rate of such members in any occupation was proof of discrimination. This was a radical development from what Congress had in mind when it passed the basic legislation in 1964.

Bureaucratic rationalism and neutrality

As well as bringing collective knowledge and experience to bear on problems, the federal bureaucracy is also presumed to be rational in proposing solutions. More precisely, civil servants are supposed to discount political and partisan considerations and to give advice which is politically objective and neutral. This expectation stems from the basic assumption that the federal bureaucracy is willing and able to serve political masters of differing political complexion. Even when the change from one administration to the next is unusually sharp, the federal bureaucracy is supposed to serve the new as faithfully as it served the old.

The bureaucratic ideal of political neutrality is viewed with considerable scepticism by politicians, who see political motivations in the bureaucratic resistance to policy that they may encounter. For the moment, it is sufficient to note that there is solid evidence to suggest that in the career civil service more bureaucrats have political attitudes closer to Democratic than to Republican philosophy (DiClerico, 1995, p. 166). Given that the Democratic party has traditionally favoured governmental activism, while the Republican party has not, it is perhaps logical that those who believe in governmental activism should be more likely to seek government employment than those who do not.

Controlling the federal bureaucracy

If the ideal of the bureaucracy is of a body of disinterested experts, advising the president on policy matters and faithfully carrying out his wishes, the reality is significantly different.

Presidential control of the bureaucracy

Most presidents have found dealing with the bureaucracy a frustrating aspect of their job. President Truman (1945–53) once commented that 'I thought I was the president, but when it comes to these bureaucracies, I can't make them do a damn thing'. Years later, President Carter indicated that things had not changed much: 'Before I became president, I realized and was warned that dealing with the federal bureaucracy would be one of the worst problems I would have to face. It has been even worse than I had anticipated' (DiClerico, 1995, pp. 163–4).

These were Democratic presidents experiencing difficulty in controlling the bureaucracy. It is safe to assume that Republican presidents must expend even more effort in the same task.

President Reagan entered office determined to do something to bring the bureaucracy under his control. He started at the top, making sure that his cabinet secretaries were ideologically sympathetic to his conservative goals. The Reagan White House also insisted that all secondary and tertiary positions in the departments were given only to those who had voted for Reagan, who were known Republicans and who were known conservatives (DiClerico, 1995, pp. 189–90). Moreover, President Reagan insisted that both cabinet and sub-cabinet appointees be briefed not by the permanent civil servants but by White House staff indisputably loyal to the president.

Reagan had campaigned for office proclaiming that, 'Government isn't the solution: government is the problem.' Strongly opposed to 'big government' and what he considered to be intrusive bureaucracy,

Figure 6.3 Bureaucratic rivalry: the FBI and CIA pull in opposite directions trying to promote homeland security. Source: © Steve Sack

President Reagan quickly set about reducing both the number of civil servants in domestic policy agencies and departments and the number of federal regulations.

President Reagan certainly gained increased control of the bureaucracy through making ideological sympathy and personal loyalty determining factors in appointments. In other respects though, the degree of change he wanted was limited by the fact that his appointees necessarily were often lacking in experience and competence in administration (DiClerico, 1995, p. 192).

'Presidentialising' the bureaucracy

President Reagan was merely raising to a new level the process of 'presidentialising' the bureaucracy: that is, using his appointment power to try to bring the bureaucracy under closer political control (Rourke, 1991). Why should presidents have to work so hard to ensure the loyalty of the members of their cabinet and of the sub-cabinet and permanent civil servants?

Going native

There is always the fear in the White House that political appointees will 'go native'. This means that, instead of imposing the president's agenda on the permanent bureaucracy, they come to share

the bureaucracy's outlook and start to resist the White House. This can happen where the cabinet secretary or deputy secretary disagrees with presidential policy or simply believes that the civil service has a better policy. Or going native can occur simply as a result of the fact that political appointees to the bureaucracy spend far more time in the company of civil servants than they do with senior White House personnel.

The president may use the appointments process to try to minimise this, but may also try to increase the involvement of White House staff in the departments and agencies. This can cause friction between presidential aides and civil servants, who resent interference from those they consider to lack the requisite knowledge and experience to make sound decisions.

Politicising the bureaucracy

There is a very fine line between strengthening presidential control of the bureaucracy and politicising the bureaucracy. It is possible to see President Reagan's actions as either an attempt to force the bureaucracy to follow his legitimate requests as its chief, or as an attempt to persuade the bureaucracy to become part of an ideological or partisan crusade. Equally, it is difficult to identify the line between serving an administration and abandoning the virtues of bureaucratic neutrality and professionalism.

Political versus bureaucratic values

Disputes between presidents and bureaucrats have their roots in one basic factor: the two have real differences in outlook. Presidents and their White House assistants see themselves as bearers of a democratic mandate. As democracy's champion, the president embodies what some see as the core values of democracy: responsiveness, direction and revitalisation.

The values of the modern administrative state, however, are different; here the emphasis is upon continuity, professionalism, expertise and effectiveness. All of these values may be desirable but they are not always compatible. A president will wish to demonstrate to supporters that the government can respond to their needs and can be made to perform more economically. Bureaucrats, however, may not see the drive to satisfy a particular section of the electorate as a factor in producing a rational policy response to a problem.

Moreover, if presidents and other politicians are most likely to believe that their loyalty lies with the electorate, bureaucrats will tend to identify with their department or even with a particular programme. Senior civil servants may spend twenty-five or thirty years working within the same policy area. They may acquire not merely knowledge of the subject that greatly surpasses that of politicians, but also a belief that their programmes must continue for the good of the people. In that sense, politicians and bureaucrats can have quite different visions of what constitutes 'good' public policy.

Bureaucratic political resources

The differences of values that produce tensions between the president and the bureaucracy can, as we have seen, lead to a struggle between them for control of policy. The bureaucracy is by no means without its own resources in these power struggles.

The first and most obvious weapon of the recalcitrant bureaucrat is delay. This is particularly the case in the United States, where the president may serve only four or, at most, eight years in office. By not following the spirit of the president's orders or by throwing up seemingly endless objections to proposed changes, civil servants may succeed in a waiting game with the White House.

Iron triangles

Bureaucrats can and do build alliances with other political actors. Most notably, they form mutually beneficial relationships with committees in Congress and with interest groups. These 'iron triangles' are based upon the fact that all three elements have a common interest in particular policy areas or programmes.

Congress and the bureaucracy

Congress, as well as the president, has a significant measure of control over the bureaucracy. This means that the bureaucracy must seek to satisfy its congressional master, as well as the White House.

The principal instruments of congressional control of the bureaucracy are its general legislative power and its appropriations power – the 'power of the purse'. Congress uses its legislative power to create, abolish or merge departments, to inaugurate new programmes and agencies, and to fix terms of appointment and other structural details. It is true that Congress has ceded the initiative to undertake such reorganisations to the president in recent decades, but it retains the power to veto presidential reorganisation plans and to institute its own. Following the attacks of September 11th, 2001, President George W. Bush wanted to establish a Department of Homeland Security. He got his way only after considerable discussion and compromise with members of Congress.

Congress uses its appropriations power to fund departments, agencies, programmes and civil servants. Since money is the oil that makes the machinery of government turn, the federal bureaucracy cannot afford to alienate its source in Congress.

Figure 6.4 Creating new bureaucratic structures may reassure the public that something is being done, but may prove ineffective if too complex.   Source: © Steve Sack

Congress establishes the structural and financial parameters of federal bureaucracy, and presidential control must be exercised within those constraints. From the perspective of those who work for the federal bureaucracy, the presidency is their day-to-day manager, but Congress is the manager upon whom they depend for their sheer existence.

Congress also has the right to investigate the operation of any part of the executive branch, and will normally include holding hearings and calling executive branch personnel to testify before a congressional committee. Depending on the outcome of the investigation, Congress may reward certain departments or programmes with better finance or more staff, or it may shut them down altogether. Members of congressional committees wish to ensure that programmes administered by bureaux bring benefits to their constituents back home. Most members of Congress seek membership of committees that deal with matters closest to the heart of their electorate.

The third element in the 'iron triangles' is the interest groups and their paid lobbyists. Lobbyists seek access to and influence over decisions made within the civil service. This can involve participation in the writing of administrative law or even in the appointment of particular individuals to key posts. In return, lobbyists will work to enhance the power and prestige of the bureau by testifying before Congress that it is doing a fine and important job, and by lobbying the president to the same effect.

Interest groups and Congress have a strong relationship based on the need of lobbyists to gain access to those who legislate in their areas of concern and the need of members of Congress to obtain election campaign funds from interest groups and their political action committees. Thus, bureaux, congressional committees and interest groups have tight bonds of mutual self-interest that can unite them against a president who wishes to make unwelcome changes. To put it another way, any president who tries to exercise total control over 'his' bureaucracy may soon discover a wall of resistance which is at times impossible to break down.

Issue networks

Iron triangles are accompanied by what Hugh Heclo (1978) has called issue networks. These characterise the way that policies are debated in certain areas of economic regulation, especially in cases where federal agencies (for example, the Environmental Protection Agency) have economy-wide purview rather than being restricted to a certain segment of the economy (for example, farming). Issue networks are in one sense more democratic than iron triangles: they are more open and can involve many more participants. One becomes part of an issue network simply by becoming recognised as an expert in the field, somebody who needs to be consulted.

Bureaucratic agencies involved in issue networks are subject to many pressures, and for that reason are, if anything, even less likely to be decisively influenced by either presidents or Congress. This newer pattern of policy-making thus underlines many of the doubts that had already been raised about the role of bureaucracy in the American political system. The phenomenon of issue networks can be seen as a sign that ideas do matter in public policy (Reich, 1990), but the tendency towards short-term electoral bias in members of Congress, coupled with the equally self-interested behaviour and the limited outlook of bureaucrats makes upbeat portraits of the policy-making process somewhat optimistic.

Bureaucracy and effective government

We saw earlier in the chapter that the president has many demands made upon him, but inadequate means of ensuring that he satisfies them. As chief executive, one might think that he could at least count upon the federal bureaucracy to carry out his wishes, but this is simply not the case. Just as the president must struggle to exert influence over Congress, so too the executive cannot assume that the bureaucracy will be a willing partner.

At first glance, this may seem a regrettable state of affairs. Nevertheless, there is another side to this situation. Koenig writes that

It is good for democracy but bad for an effective presidency – though by no means always for either – that the chief executive possesses a highly imperfect capacity to induce the vast officialdom of the executive branch to abide by his purposes and follow his directives.

Koenig, 1996, p. 181

Koenig has in mind that total presidential control of the bureaucracy could and sometimes does lead to presidential abuse of that power. President Nixon, for example, put pressure upon the Internal Revenue Service (IRS) and the Federal Bureau of Investigation (FBI) to aid attempts to destroy those he considered his political enemies. A civil service that believed it had no means of resisting such unconstitutional demands could easily be turned into a weapon that undermined or even destroyed democracy.

As in other aspects of American politics, then, we must look at the bureaucracy through the perspective of the separation of powers and checks and balances. Effective government and democratic responsibility require that the president should be able to direct the bureaucracy and have it cooperate with his legitimate policy initiatives. On the other hand, effective government and democratic values also require that the bureaucracy not be left wholly vulnerable to a president animated by crass and even unconstitutional motivations.

Meeting twenty-first century challenges

The coincidence of a new century being accompanied by the election of a new presidency might inevitably concentrate more than usual attention on the new incumbent. In 2000 the presidential election race was exceptionally close. Democrat Al Gore led in the national popular vote, but needed to take the marginal state of Florida to win in the electoral college. The vote in Florida was so close that only after five weeks of legal challenges and counter-challenges did the US Supreme Court confirm a Republican victory in the state, ensuring that George W. Bush would be the 43rd president of the United States. Under the circumstances it is not surprising that the new administration would come under particular scrutiny.

It was not clear that the new president could claim any kind of mandate and in his initial statements after being awarded the victory he seemed ready to reach out to a broad and bipartisan political spectrum. This appearance did not last for long, as the new president constructed an administration that drew deeply on Republicans with previous experience, and pitched his message into the Republican heartland.

Given the paper-thin Republican majorities in the US Senate and House of Representatives, Bush appeared to be taking a politically risky path. Analyses of the early period of George Bush's presidency were often not generous, though they have to be read through partisan lenses. Actions such as withdrawal from the Kyoto targets on global warming seemed rational and pragmatic to Republican supporters, but were interpreted as typical of a backward-looking isolationism that Democratic critics detected generally in the new administration's determination to move towards less international engagement. The defection from the Republican party of Vermont's Senator Jim Jeffords put the Senate back in Democrat hands only months after the 2000 election, and the Bush administration did not appear strong.

The attacks of September 11th, 2001, changed the context for the Bush administration, and probably for the US presidency in the foreseeable future. An already weak stock market plunged, wiping out years of recent gains. A US administration accused of a tendency to international disengagement unveiled a doctrine of pre-emption, launched attacks on Afghanistan, hideout of those who had launched the September 11th attacks, and on Iraq, perceived by the USA as a threat. The broad international sympathy that was felt for the first of these military reactions was not generally evident for the second. The commander-in-chief had led the country resolutely back onto the international stage, but this had been done firmly on US terms.

Figure 6.5 President George W. Bush interpreted his 2004 victory as an endorsement of a mandate for his policies and his leadership style.

Source: © Empics

On the domestic front, a series of projected budget surpluses rapidly disappeared under the pressure especially of increased security and defence expenditure. The administration's commitment to cut taxes did not waver, and the USA once again was in the counter-intuitive position of having a Republican president lead it through a period of deficit spending and increased national debt.

Strategically, the first twenty-first century presidency has been forced to work on a political landscape changed irredeemably by unexpected events. Scholars differ on the merits of the policy decisions the administration has taken, but there is a general recognition that President Bush has adopted strategies designed to maximise his potential to lead actively within the different contexts of these difficult years. For example, analysts have credited him with successfully taking his message to the public in the early, potentially shaky days of the administration. He is considered to have judged correctly the elements of political etiquette that determines inter-institutional relations during the period when Republican legislative majorities could not have been automatically assumed.

In the aftermath of the September 11th attacks, the Bush administration made its case for a 'war on terror'. Nations are changed by war, and typically in American history, the presidency has gained authority when the nation is defending itself. In this case the lack of an enemy defined by geographical position or national status creates unusual difficulties in the conduct of the war, the identification of the enemy, and the ability to define what constitutes victory and conclusion. The Bush administration appears to have expanded the president's foreign policy authority, at least initially with the general support of the American public. The lesson from history is that over time these expansions of authority will come under challenge.

In the twenty-first century, as before, the continuing power of America's presidency will rely on the ability of successive administrations simultaneously to engage with the demands of domestic and foreign policy-making in a changing political environment, and the need to negotiate with political institutions with their own long heritage and expectations of authority.

Chapter summary

The executive branch has emerged as a clear and central focus within the separated, checked and balanced federal system. The presidency and vice-presidency are the only offices in America to be elected nationally. The electoral college process can occasionally result in apparently confusing results, but was invented to meld the influences of the popular vote and the demands of the federal system. It was tested severely in 2000, but appears unlikely to be reformed in the near future. It does maintain the position of the president as central in the nation's electoral and political structure.

The centrality of the presidency has emerged in a number of parallel and mutually supporting ways. The constitutional roles assigned to the president in international affairs, legislative development and passage, and as commander-in-chief, have been developed and expanded over time, as a result both of presidential actions and the growth of the USA as a world military and economic power. Other roles outside constitutional definition, for example as a focus of national and international media attention, and as the only leader of a political party in the United States, have acted to bolster the president's central position in the American political system.

Notwithstanding the potential afforded to the executive by its constitutional and unconstitutional roles, the way in which this is operationalised has varied considerably between different presidential administrations. Presidential scholars have sought to explain the operation of presidential authority in terms of context, governmental structure, and personal skills. President Truman's comment to presidential scholar Richard Neustadt that the key to presidential power lies in the ability to persuade has generated much of the contemporary debate on the presidency.

We have seen that, despite its ideological opposition to 'big government', the United States has developed a vast federal bureaucracy. This bureaucracy brings considerable virtues to American government, especially expertise, experience, professionalism, political neutrality and continuity. However, the very size and authority of the federal bureaucracy make it difficult for the president, the supposed head of the executive branch, to control it. This is exacerbated by the ability of the bureaucracy to form alliances against the president with other political actors. The tensions that exist between the president and the bureaucracy give rise to conflicting and seemingly insoluble concerns about an ineffective presidency and an overpoliticised bureaucracy.

The early twenty-first century, with one presidential election decided in the US Supreme Court, an international and domestic agenda shifted dramatically by the attacks of September 11th, 2001, a second election decided by a clear but narrow majority, and a period of one-party leadership in the legislature and executive unusual in recent decades, presented a context both of challenges and of opportunities for the presidency.

Discussion points

1. Is the president particularly advantaged by the relationship of the media to this office?

2. With all the powers of office, does the president really also have to be a persuasive character?

3. How well has the current presidential administration managed to establish its leadership role in the federal government?

4. Are iron triangles a positive feature of American politics?

5. Is the federal bureaucracy too powerful?

Further reading

Presidential scholars offer many structures for the discussion of the presidency. Fred I. Greenstein's *The Presidential Difference: Leadership Style from FDR to George W. Bush* (2nd edn, Princeton, NJ: Princeton University Press, 2004), offers a range of six qualities that bear on presidential leadership. This list includes public communication, organisational capacity, political skill, policy vision, cognitive style, and emotional intelligence. Individual presidential qualities are also significant in James P. Pfiffner's *The Character Factor: How We Judge America's Presidents* (College Station, Tex.: Texas, A&M Press, 2004), which examines the centrality of truthfulness and lying to crises that have faced the modern presidency.

There are few books devoted solely to the bureaucracy which are appropriate at this level, but the best is Francis E. Rourke, *Bureaucracy, Politics and Public Policy* (Boston: Little, Brown, 1984). A book which deals more generally with the presidency and has excellent sections on the bureaucracy is Louis Koenig, *The Chief Executive* (6th edn, Fort Worth, Tex.: Harcourt Brace, 1996).

References

DiClerico, R. (1995) *The American President* (4th edn, Englewood Cliffs, NJ: Prentice Hall).

Cronin, T.E. (ed.) (1989) *Inventing the American Presidency* (Lawrence, Kans.: University Press of Kansas).

Edwards, G.C., III and Davies, P.J. (eds) (2004) *New Challenges for the American Presidency* (New York: Pearson Longman).

Garraty, J. (1968) *The New Commonwealth* (New York: Harper & Row).

Heclo, H. (1978) 'Issue networks and the executive establishment', in King, A. (ed.) *The New American Political System* (Washington, DC: American Enterprise Institute).

Koenig, L. (1996) *The Chief Executive* (6th edn, Fort Worth, Tex.: Harcourt Brace).

Neustadt, R. (1990) *Presidential Power and the Modern Presidents: The politics of leadership from Roosevelt to Reagan* (New York: Free Press).

Pious, R. (1996) *The Presidency* (Boston: Allyn & Bacon).

Reich, R. (ed.) (1990) *The Power of Public Ideas* (Cambridge, Mass.: Harvard University Press).

Rourke, F. (1991) 'Presidentializing the bureaucracy: from Kennedy to Reagan', in Piffner, J. (ed.) *The Managerial Presidency* (Pacific Grove: Brooks/Cole), pp. 123–4.

US Bureau of the Census (2005) *Statistical Abstract of the United States* (Washington, DC).

Whicker, M. (1990) 'Managing and organising the Reagan White House', in Hill, D., Moore, R. and Williams, P. (eds) *The Reagan Presidency* (Basingstoke: Macmillan).

Chapter 7

The Congress

Congress and the president are rivals for political power generally, and legislative power in particular. To a considerable extent, this rivalry is a 'zero-sum' game: any increase in the power of one player inevitably means a corresponding loss of power for the other. Nevertheless, as a responsible national legislature, Congress cannot simply devote itself to institutional self-preservation. It must pass laws to advance the national interest and, to do this, it needs to cooperate with the president. In this chapter, we trace the origins and development of this ambiguous relationship with the presidency and assess the contemporary balance of power between the two. We also examine the main structures, processes and procedures that determine the way that Congress works, in order to understand both the strengths and weaknesses of the national legislature.

Legislative power: the constitutional design

Legislative power is the power to pass laws. It lies, therefore, at the heart of the policy-making process and, indeed, is a central attribute of what we more generally call political power. Although the framers of the Constitution were concerned that no single institution should accrue too much political power, it is clear that they entrusted legislative power mainly to the Congress. True, the president was also given a role in the legislative process, but it was not until the twentieth century that he began to expand this role at the expense of Congress and to assume legislative leadership.

Legislative powers of Congress

Article I of the Constitution begins by stating that 'All legislative powers herein granted shall be vested in a Congress of the United States, which shall consist of a Senate and House of Representatives'. Section 8 of Article I goes on to specify the particular powers which the framers wished to transfer from state legislatures to the federal legislature. Among the most important of these *enumerated powers* are the power to levy taxes, the power to regulate both international and interstate commerce, and the power to declare war.

The framers did not intend that the new Constitution signify a general transfer of legislative power from the states to the Congress, hence the detailed specification of the matters on which Congress was entitled to pass laws. The Tenth Amendment to the Constitution (1791) reinforced the fact that the legislative ambit of Congress was strictly limited by stating that 'The powers not delegated to the United States by the Constitution . . . are reserved to the States respectively, or to the people.'

Nevertheless, the legislative range of Congress *did* expand, thanks in particular to the doctrine of *implied powers*. The seeds of this were sown in the last paragraph of Article I, Section 8 of the Constitution. This entitled Congress 'to make all laws which shall be necessary and proper for carrying into execution the foregoing powers'. However, expansive interpretation of the 'necessary and proper clause' by the Supreme Court has allowed Congress to legislate on virtually any matter it wishes.

Box 7.1

Functions of Congress

Primary ————————→ Law-making

Major ←——————→ Oversight
Political education for public
Representation

Minor ←——————→ Judicial function
Leadership selection

These are seven functions of Congress, categorised by their importance (Keefe and Ogul, 1993, p. 16). The primary and major functions are discussed in this chapter. The minor functions can be briefly summarised: the judicial function consists mainly of the role of Congress in the process of impeachment. This procedure allows for the removal of presidents and federal judges from office for 'high crimes and misdemeanours'. Rarely used, but dramatic when it is, the most significant instance of impeachment came in 1974 when President Nixon resigned after the House Judiciary Committee investigating the Watergate scandal voted to indict him on three counts. Had Nixon not resigned at that point, the Senate would have acted as the 'jury' in his impeachment trial. More recently, President Bill Clinton was impeached, though not convicted. His impeachment sparked a bitter debate about whether the president's opponents were abusing the impeachment power for partisan ends.

The leadership function is an unwritten but important contribution to political life: it allows politicians to develop their skills and reputations, with the Senate in particular often providing a launch pad for the presidency. In recent years, however, the Senate has produced vice-presidents rather than presidents. Thus, none of the last five presidents (George W. Bush, Bill Clinton, George H. Bush, Ronald Reagan and Jimmy Carter) served in the Senate, though three of their vice-presidents had done so (Al Gore, Dan Quayle and Walter Mondale).

The key Supreme Court decision came early, in *McCulloch* v. *Maryland* (1819). Here the Court decided that 'necessary and proper' meant convenient, rather than indispensable, to the exercise of an enumerated power. Subsequent Court decisions, such as those legitimating the New Deal legislation of the 1930s, recognised the political reality that national problems required national solutions, even if this meant allowing Congress to encroach upon state legislative power as conceived by the framers in 1787. Consequently, 'Nowadays, so long as Congress's actions do not violate specific constitutional rights of individuals or interfere with Constitutional powers delegated by the Constitution to the president or federal courts, there is little that Congress wants to do that it lacks constitutional authority to do' (Peltason, 1988, p. 36).

Legislative powers of the president

As we have seen, Article I of the Constitution stated that Congress was endowed with *all* legislative power. This, however, is not quite true. Congress is indeed legislatively supreme to the extent that it alone can pass a law, yet the president was given a certain degree of both influence and actual power in the legislative process.

The power given to the president was negative power, in the form of the veto, for Article I, Section 7 of the Constitution requires that all

---

Box 7.2

The Impeachment of President Clinton

President Bill Clinton (1993–2001) was the third president to be impeached by the House of Representatives. In 1868, President Andrew Johnson was impeached largely for political reasons by those in Congress who wanted a more radical reconstruction policy after the Civil War. The vote in the Senate was 35–19, meaning that Johnson survived by one vote, since the Constitution specifies a two-thirds majority is required to convict. In 1974, President Richard Nixon was impeached in a more bipartisan manner as a result of evidence suggesting he had organised a cover-up of the Watergate scandal. Nixon resigned before the Senate trial could be held, but he almost certainly would have become the only president to be removed from office by the impeachment mechanism.

President Clinton's impeachment in 1998/99 was for perjury and obstruction of justice, but was almost wholly motivated by partisan political considerations. The Constitution allows for impeachment where it can be shown that the president is guilty of 'high crimes and misdemeanours'. That phrase is vague, but is generally taken to refer to official rather than personal wrongdoing. Clinton had been hounded by arch-conservative opponents from the start of his presidency: first, for alleged corrupt financial dealings when governor of Arkansas (the Whitewater scandal) and then for alleged sexual harassment (the Paula Jones scandal). The president was wholly cleared of wrongdoing in Whitewater, and the Jones scandal was going nowhere until her lawyers learned of Clinton's relationship with a young White House employee, Monica Lewinsky. It emerged that the president had lied about his relationship with Lewinsky in a grand jury statement in the Jones investigation. It was this and associated efforts to keep his affair with Lewinsky secret that led to his impeachment.

The vote in the House was overwhelmingly partisan and public opinion polls showed that some two-thirds of Americans believed that the impeachment was driven by politics rather than law. The president was easily acquitted in the Senate: the two articles of impeachment were defeated 45–55 and 50–50.

bills passed by Congress must be signed by the president before they can become law. Moreover, it explicitly states that the president need not sign a bill if he has objections to it: instead, he can simply return the bill unsigned to Congress, stating the reasons for his veto. Congress can only override that veto by a two-thirds majority of both the Senate and the House. Mustering such a majority of both chambers is no easy matter and thus the presidential veto is a formidable weapon with which to counter the legislative power of Congress.

As well as this negative power, the president was invited by the Constitution to influence the legislative agenda of Congress. Article II, Section 3 instructs him as follows: 'He shall from time to time give to the Congress information of the state of the Union, and recommend to their consideration such measures as he shall judge necessary and expedient . . .'. As the wording of the clause suggests, it was not intended that the president recommend legislation to Congress on a routine basis. Nevertheless, it does indicate an awareness on the part of the framers that Congress might not always be capable of providing the legislative leadership that the country needs.

These avenues of presidential intrusion into the legislature's domain are, of course, applications of the principle of checks and balances. Yet while the framers intended the president to be able to check congressional legislative power, they did not intend that he should be able to usurp it, for that would have violated that other cardinal principle of the Constitution, the separation of powers. Thus, the balance struck by the Constitution was one weighted heavily in favour of congressional dominance in the legislative field: 'It is clear that the original design was intended to give Congress the legislative authority that was, in fact, the power to determine national policy' (Wayne, 1978, p. 7).

Today, however, that balance of power has been largely reversed. To be sure, the constitutional framework has barely been altered with respect to legislative power. However, historical forces, interacting with institutional capacities, have engendered a transfer of substantial legislative power from Capitol Hill to the White House.

The changing balance of legislative power

In the eighteenth and nineteenth centuries, Congress dominated the legislative process. From time to time, a strong president such as Jefferson, Jackson or Lincoln might challenge that supremacy, but most presidents readily conceded that legislation was in essence a matter for the Congress. Furthermore, demand for national legislation was limited during this period and Congress had little need to seek help from the presidency in accomplishing its constitutional duties. In the post-Civil War era, the presidency came close to being eclipsed altogether by a powerful and confident Congress.

Ironically, it was precisely at this zenith of congressional power that the socio-economic changes that were to undermine it were sweeping the nation. The Industrial Revolution eventually brought forth an unprecedented demand for national legislation. By the end of the Progressive era (1900–17), not only had a new legislative activism been generated, but the presidency had moved to centre stage of the legislative process. President Theodore Roosevelt declared his office a 'bully pulpit' from which he could spur Congress into action. The other major Progressive president, Woodrow Wilson, became the first since John Adams to deliver his State of the Union address personally before the Congress. Moreover, he personally lobbied for bills on Capitol Hill and sometimes provided his supporters there with draft legislation (Wayne, 1978, p. 15).

What the Progressive period had demonstrated was that an activist federal government required a new level of presidential energy and initiative. Not only could the president personally dramatise legislative issues in a way that a collective body like Congress could not match, but, more important still, much of the new legislation required technical expertise that members of Congress simply did not possess. This was to be found rather in the federal bureaucracy, located within the executive branch.

These indications of an emerging new balance of legislative power between Congress and president became unmistakable – and irreversible – during the Great Depression of the 1930s. With the exception of the Civil War, the Depression was the greatest domestic crisis in American history. Industry and agriculture had all but collapsed, unemployment reached 50 per cent in some areas, and welfare provision was wholly inadequate. After enduring this misery for some three years under President Herbert Hoover, the country turned to Franklin D. Roosevelt for remedial action.

Roosevelt's first one hundred days in office are rightly famous for the flood of major legislation which he sent to Congress. What is particularly striking, however, is not merely the energy and ingenuity of the president and his advisers, but the reception given by Congress to this legislative bombardment. A body which had hitherto had the reputation of moving at a snail's pace, approved radical new proposals by huge majorities in a matter of days or, sometimes, hours.

Roosevelt's New Deal saw the creation in the executive branch of many new bureaucratic agencies, such as the Securities and Exchange Commission and the Social Security Administration. Having been set up with broad grants of power, these agencies proceeded to make detailed policy decisions on a routine basis. In effect, this also entailed a transfer of policy-making power from Congress to the presidency.

Events since the 1930s have generally had the effect of enhancing the legislative dominance of the presidency. Most importantly, the emergence of the United States as a world superpower has maximised the foreign policy powers inherent in the presidency. However, in the field of domestic affairs too, the sheer volume of legislation, combined with an ever greater need for technical expertise, has also made presidential leadership the central feature of the legislative process.

Congress today: mandate and the legislative agenda

In the early autumn of 1993, the *Congressional Quarterly* looked forward to the legislative battles ahead. It noted that President Clinton was in an inherently weak position, having been elected the previous November by a plurality rather than a majority of the voters. Yet, it reported,

this fall's legislative calendar is a reminder of Clinton's power to determine what Congress fights over – even if he lacks the clout to control the outcome. Congress's agenda for the rest of the year is jammed with White House proposals on trade, health care and other domestic policies.

CQ Weekly Report, 4 September 1993, p. 2295

Even a relatively weak president, then, sets the legislative agenda of Congress. In his first term, President George W. Bush had an even weaker mandate than President Clinton, since he had actually won fewer votes than his main opponent. Nevertheless, Bush acted as if he had a mandate to lead and the Congress generally accepted this. Put another way, Congress has lost much of the capacity and will to determine the legislative priorities of the nation. This has come about for a number of reasons. First, there are causes which arise from the electoral characteristics of Congress.

Electoral factors in congressional decline

While Congress contains members from all parts of the nation, it is not, in important respects, a truly national body. Each member of Congress is elected by a discrete, local electorate. Even the two senators elected from the same state are usually chosen in different years, when issues and political moods may well be quite distinct. Moreover, those seeking election to Congress are not normally bound by a common set of policies or manifesto, or, indeed, by strong party or ideological loyalties.

All this means that congressional elections are in essence local elections, fought on local issues, with candidates offering themselves as representatives and guardians of local interests. As a result, when those elected on such a basis gather in Washington, they can scarcely claim to represent a national constituency or be in possession of a national mandate. In this sense, Congress as a whole is not much greater than the sum of its parts.

This is not to suggest that members of Congress have no concern with national issues or no idea of the national interest; nor indeed does it mean that Congress cannot influence the legislative agenda or take important legislative initiatives. Yet, in the end, members of Congress owe their election – and re-election – to their ability to represent their local constituents' interests, rather than those of the nation, and local and state interests are not only different from the national interest, they may actually conflict with it. In short, Congress stands accused of *parochialism*, a narrowness of vision and a self-interest which gives priority to local concerns over those of the nation. This parochialism contrasts with the national outlook, standing and responsibility of the president. He is chosen by a national constituency, all voting on the same day and on the same set of contemporary issues. Even a president who does not gain a majority of the votes cast in his election, such as Bill Clinton in 1992 and George W. Bush in 2000, can claim a mandate because he is the nation's choice to provide national leadership.

Institutional factors in congressional decline

In relation to the presidency, Congress has serious institutional weaknesses which inhibit its ability to provide legislative leadership. These weaknesses stem from disadvantages in both organisation and capacity.

Bicameralism

The internal organisation of Congress leads to a fragmentation of power that makes legislative coherence extremely difficult. In one basic respect, this fragmentation has its roots in the Constitution. The framers decided that Congress should be a bicameral body, composed of two chambers with more or less equal legislative power. By stipulating that all bills must be approved by both chambers in identical form, they established the possibility that one house could negate the legislative initiatives of the other. This potential for inter-chamber conflict was made all the greater by designing different electoral bases for the House of Representatives and the Senate. This constitutionally ordered fragmentation of the Congress contrasts with the unitary design of the presidency. Furthermore, Congress established internal structures which only exacerbate the problem.

Committee power

One of the conditions for providing leadership *outside* of Congress is effective leadership *within*, yet the committee structure of Congress makes coherent, unified policy leadership difficult to achieve. Congress carries out its legislative tasks by delegating substantial authority to specialist committees. Although each chamber as a whole must approve any bill, that approval is often a formality, a largely unproblematic ratification of the decisions taken by the committee. Moreover, power is fragmented still further by the fact that committees in turn delegate considerable power to their sub-committees. The practical result is that, on most occasions, the subcommittee recommendation is accepted by the full committee and the full committee recommendation is accepted by the chamber as a whole.

Unsurprisingly, then, congressional committees and subcommittees are frequently spoken of as 'little legislatures'. As long ago as the late nineteenth century, Woodrow Wilson observed that 'Congress in session is Congress on public exhibition, whilst Congress in its committee rooms is Congress at work' (Bailey, 1989, p. 103).

Leadership and party weakness

At one time, this fragmentation of power towards committees was compensated by strong party leadership, particularly in the House of Representatives. The key figure here was the speaker. At first little more than a formal presiding officer, the speaker, chosen by the majority party, gradually accumulated important powers. The most significant of these was control over appointments to committees, including the committee chairs. Eventually, however, members rebelled against this control of their interests and careers. A series of decisions in 1910–11 stripped the speaker of some of his most important powers, including his right to make committee assignments and his position on the Rules Committee. This inevitably resulted in a fragmentation of authority, which persists to this day.

As for the Senate, it has never experienced the kind of centralised power that the House once knew. It has been noted that 'senators tend to regard themselves as unregimented ambassadors from their states' (Bailey, 1989, p. 154). They are, therefore, most reluctant to subordinate themselves to others and expect to be treated as a co-equal by those at the head of the party.

Without an effective and coherent internal leadership, Congress is simply incapable of either putting together a legislative agenda or ensuring that an agenda is acted upon. Such leadership as Congress recognises, therefore, must come from outside, and that means, first and foremost, the presidency.

A further disadvantage of the Congress is its relative lack of specialised knowledge compared with the presidency. The president is the head of a vast federal bureaucracy, employing thousands of specialists on every aspect of likely legislation. Whenever a problem arises, then, the president is well placed to ascertain its origins and scope and to draw up legislative proposals accordingly.

Members of Congress are in essence amateurs in policy matters, although they may have a measure of expertise in one or two areas thanks to previous careers or service on specialist committees. Nevertheless, they can rarely match the bureaucratic experts.

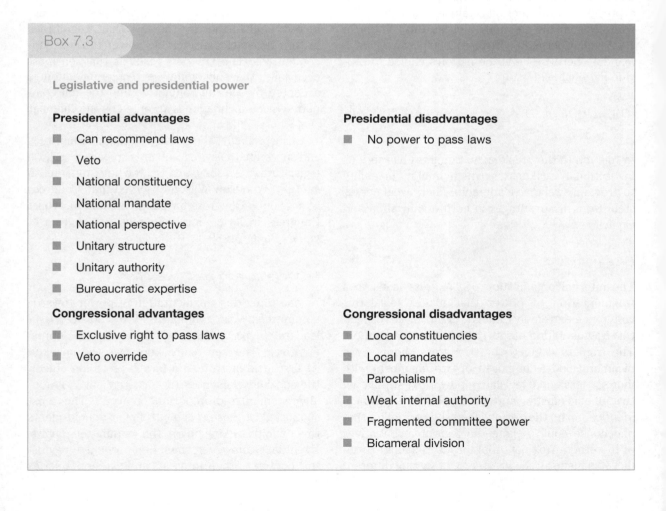

Box 7.3

Legislative and presidential power

Presidential advantages
- Can recommend laws
- Veto
- National constituency
- National mandate
- National perspective
- Unitary structure
- Unitary authority
- Bureaucratic expertise

Presidential disadvantages
- No power to pass laws

Congressional advantages
- Exclusive right to pass laws
- Veto override

Congressional disadvantages
- Local constituencies
- Local mandates
- Parochialism
- Weak internal authority
- Fragmented committee power
- Bicameral division

Since the 1970s, Congress has taken steps to establish its own bank of policy specialists in an attempt to reduce its dependence upon executive branch expertise. It established new specialist support agencies, such as the Congressional Budget Office (1974). Furthermore, between 1970 and 1986, the number of committee staff increased by 250 per cent and the personal staff of members by 60 per cent (Mezey, 1989, p. 133).

While these changes have undoubtedly provided Congress with an independent source of expertise and information, it is by no means clear that they have enabled Congress to perform its legislative tasks any better.

The rise of the legislative presidency means that Congress is left only with what Arthur Maas has called leadership reserve. Congress may still exercise leadership, but only when the president chooses not to lead. 'As a general rule, whenever the president is disposed toward leadership, it is his to be had' (Maas, 1983, p. 14).

However, the fact that the president may choose to lead at any time does not mean that the Congress is bound to follow.

Congressional cooperation and resistance

It is worth emphasising that this fundamental shift in legislative power from the Congress to the presidency was accomplished without any significant formal change in the constitutional structure. The president is now expected to do far more than in 1787, but there has been no constitutional recognition of the fact. Congress, then, retains 'all legislative power'.

Many have recognised what Godfrey Hodgson called this 'paradox of presidential power' (Hodgson, 1980, p. 13). In terms of practical politics, it means that the president is powerless to command Congress to act. All he can do is urge, bully, cajole, woo and induce legislators to pass his proposals. In the famous phrase of Richard Neustadt, presidential power is 'the power to persuade' (Neustadt, 1960). If so, then the legislative power of Congress can

be described as 'the power to refuse'. For in the final analysis, Congress, or even just one of its chambers, retains the autonomy to refuse the president outright or to amend his proposals out of all recognition.

For any legislation to pass, therefore, Congress and the president must cooperate. Yet cooperation is not easily achieved. As we have already noted, the president and members of Congress operate on different electoral cycles and are answerable to different constituencies. In other words, over and above any policy differences, they do not necessarily share the same legislative interests in terms of political survival.

Congressional–presidential liaison

Congressional liaison is one of the most important aspects of the modern presidency. To a significant extent, a president's legislative success or failure turns upon the skill of his liaison staff in operating the politics of persuasion. Nevertheless, both liaison staff and members of Congress have no illusions about the extent to which their real differences of interest can be ignored. Larry O'Brien, chief of congressional liaison under Presidents Kennedy and Johnson, and one of the most skilful practitioners of his art, put it this way: 'I never expected any member to commit political suicide in order to help the President, no matter how noble our cause. I expected politicians to be concerned with their own interests; I only hoped to convince them our interests were often the same' (Wayne, 1978, p. 155).

Party ties

In many political systems, party is the mechanism which links the executive to the legislature, but, as we saw in Chapter 4, parties in the United States are relatively weak. Nevertheless, party *is* one of the levers a president has in trying to persuade Congress to act, and so he will, if wise, make a considerable effort to liaise with his party's congressional leadership. For their part, party leaders in Congress do generally see one of their most important duties as maximising support for (or opposition to) the president's legislation. The speaker of the House of Representatives and the majority and minority leaders and whips in both chambers are right in the middle of executive–legislative relations. If of the same party as the president, they will represent his wishes to fellow party members. In turn, however, the members also expect their leaders to represent their views to the president. Party leaders are thus engaged in a fine balancing act. They must avoid being seen as those who fail to defend the interests of the institution and membership to which they themselves belong (Keefe and Ogul, 1993, pp. 270–1).

Even if they wished to do so, party leaders have little power to compel members to follow the party line. An interesting example of this occurred in 2005, when President Bush and the Republican party leadership in the Senate were heading for a showdown with the Democrats over judicial appointments. The Democrats had employed the device of the filibuster to delay indefinitely a confirmation vote on those judicial nominees they

considered to be too extreme. Supported by President Bush, Senate leader Bill Frist threatened to remove the right of filibuster. Senate Democrat leader Harry Reid was equally determined to stand his ground and refused to allow a vote on certain nominees. The Senate was heading for a crisis. At the last minute, seven Republican senators and seven Democrat senators simply abandoned their party's position and forged a compromise that Bush, Frist and Reid had no choice but to accept.

On some occasions, even the party leaders do not follow the party line. President Clinton experienced this in 1993, when he was trying to secure passage of the North American Free Trade Agreement (NAFTA). Among those leading the fight against NAFTA were House Majority Leader Richard Gephardt (Missouri) and House Majority Whip David Bonior (Michigan).

It is not altogether surprising, then, that presidents are by no means guaranteed passage of their legislative proposals, even when they have given a clear lead and their party controls both houses of

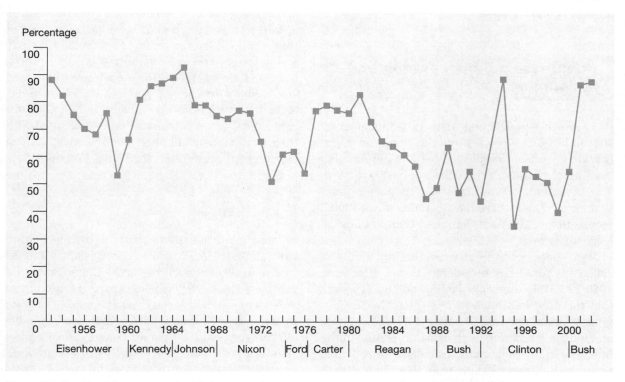

Figure 7.1 Presidential success on legislative votes, 1953–2002.

Source: Keefe and Hetherington, 2003, p. 157

Congress. However, presidents whose party does not control Congress are at a disadvantage, as are those in their second term of office and therefore in the process of becoming 'lame ducks'.

Congressional support for presidents

Many factors help to explain why Congress supports some presidents more than others. Most obviously, a majority of members will support a president when they believe that his proposals are likely to solve a particular problem in an appropriate and successful manner. In these instances, Congress and president are of the same mind and there is relatively little need for either to draw upon its 'heavy guns'.

What about those instances where there is no easy agreement to be reached? This is often the case when controversial or difficult legislation has been proposed. What are the factors that come into play when members of Congress are reluctant to support the president, but he is determined to secure passage of his legislation? What induces members to vote for legislation when appeals to ideology, party and the public interest have failed?

As with most aspects of the congressional process, the electoral connection is vital here. The president has a number of carrots and sticks with which he can win over recalcitrant members by supporting or threatening their chances of re-election.

Where a bill involves the expenditure of money, the most powerful inducement a president can offer is to ensure that some of it will be spent in the member's district or state. This will benefit the member's constituents by providing them with jobs or services and make them more disposed to re-elect the member who secured these benefits.

Presidents can also grant access to the White House to a member and, perhaps, some of her constituents. The visit can be publicised back home, as can a photograph of the event signed by the president. All of this can be used to convey the impression that the member is an important and influential player in national politics.

More aggressively, a president can bring pressure to bear by appealing over the heads of members to their constituents. President Reagan used this tactic, sometimes called 'going public', to considerable effect. The basic method was to appear on television, present his proposals and then ask all the viewers who wanted to see them passed to call or write to their members of Congress to urge them to support the president. Members who were subsequently inundated with tens of thousands of letters and calls would thus feel the electoral heat and perhaps think twice about defying a popular president. In other words, a president on occasion will challenge members for the loyalty and support of their constituents.

The legislative power of Congress, then, is severely constrained by institutional weaknesses and outside political pressures. Initiative and leadership have passed to the executive branch. There was, however, an attempt to break this presidential grip on legislative leadership in the form of the so-called Republican Revolution of 1994.

The Republican 'Revolution' of 1994

In 1994, the Republican party captured the House of Representatives for the first time since 1952. It also captured a majority in the Senate. Even more impressively, the Republicans held on to the House (and the Senate) in 1996, thus winning consecutive House majorities for the first time since 1928.

Under the aggressive leadership of Newt Gingrich (R – Georgia), the House Republicans fought the 1994 elections in a manner that sought to remedy some of the long-standing weaknesses in congressional power described above. Thus they attempted to overcome the parochialism of both congressional elections and congressional legislative activity by 'nationalising' their approach.

The Contract with America

Gingrich was determined that the House Republicans should fight the 1994 elections on the basis of a common manifesto which, if successful, would provide a mandate for party unity and legislation in the 104th Congress (1995/96). The so-called Contract with America was something of a gimmick and, right from the start, its impact was in doubt. A survey undertaken at the time of the 1994 election revealed that 71 per cent of voters had never heard of it. Moreover, while 7 per cent said the Contract was more likely to make them vote Republican, 5 per cent said it was less likely to do so (Jacobson, 1996, p. 209). Furthermore, there was absolutely no guarantee that any of the measures proposed in the Contract would ever become law: even Republicans in the Senate did not pledge their support for it.

However, Gingrich's main aim was to challenge the leadership of the Democrat in the White House, President Bill Clinton. The climactic battle came with the struggle over the 1995 budget. The House rejected Clinton's budget, pushing instead for cuts in expenditure that would produce a balanced budget. In turn, the president refused to sign the congressional budget bill because it threatened important programmes such as Medicare and education. The new fiscal year came into force on 1 October 1995, with the impasse still in place. In the past, Congress had dealt with this by authorising temporary funds to keep the wheels of government in motion. With Gingrich to the fore, however, the Republicans refused to do this, which in turn led to the shutdown of many government offices and government-run tourist attractions.

This tactic rebounded badly on Gingrich and the Republicans. Cleverly exploiting his role as the nation's leader, President Clinton was able to portray his opponents as irresponsible extremists. When public opinion polls decisively pinned the blame for the crisis on the Republicans, they were forced to back down. Indeed, only when, in the summer of 1996, House Republicans decided to revert to the time-honoured strategy of compromise with the president and Senate on a number of important issues did they succeed in putting onto the statute books any elements of the Contract with America (Hershey, 1997, p. 216).

The Republican Revolution of 1994 was a failure. A bold attempt at party government foundered on the rocks of the Constitution's structures and the political and legislative constraints they impose. It is also significant that once the House Republicans had one of their own in the White House, in the form of George W. Bush, they were happy to cede leadership to him and to play a supportive role. In that sense, the Republican Revolution was perhaps never much more than a 'second-best' option, born, in part, of the failure to capture the natural home of political leadership in the United States – the presidency.

Congressional oversight

You will search the Constitution in vain for an explicit reference to the oversight function of Congress, yet the very notion of 'checks and balances' invites Congress to ensure that the executive branch does not abuse its power.

Moreover, there are clauses of the Constitution which do explicitly give Congress the right to constrain executive power. For example, the president is required to obtain the support of two-thirds of the Senate before any treaty he has negotiated can become law (Article II, Section 2(ii)). The same clause requires a simple majority of the Senate to approve presidential nominations for the Supreme Court, ambassadorships, cabinet secretaries and, indeed, all federal officials save those exempted by Congress itself. Congress may also exploit the 'power of the purse' given to it by the Constitution: for the exercise of executive power depends to a considerable extent on the willingness of the legislature to vote the necessary funds.

To these constitutional controls, Congress itself added the right to hold public investigations into the activities of the executive branch. This has been described as an 'inherited power' of Congress, because it follows from the British Parliament's practice of conducting investigations for the purpose of gathering information with a view to legislation (Peltason, 1988, p. 74). It has not been restricted to the generation of new legislation, but also includes the right to investigate whether the executive branch is properly administering existing legislation.

Instruments of congressional oversight

- Hearings/investigations
- Legislative veto
- Appointments
- 'Power of the purse'
- Required reports
- Sunset legislation*
- Informal contact

* Acts which cease to exist after a specified date

Congressional oversight is best seen as a series of practices by which Congress can project its power into the executive branch. The purpose of oversight *may* be to ensure bureaucratic efficiency and responsibility, but it may also be exercised in pursuit of institutional and individual aggrandisement.

Effectiveness of oversight

There is a broad consensus among scholars that Congress does not perform its oversight functions very well. Most recently, the 9/11 Commission criticised the ineffective process and structures of congressional oversight of intelligence and homeland security policy. Despite such criticism, the initial response of Congress was not impressive, as members seemed reluctant to give up their vested interest in the existing system.

Oversight of anti-terrorism policy v. interests of members of Congress

The independent 9/11 Commission report of 2004 concluded that 'congressional oversight for intelligence – and counterterrorism – is dysfunctional'. What explains the failure of Congress to put its house in order some three years after the traumatic attacks of September 11th, 2001? The answer lies in a familiar tale of 'turf wars' and 'pork barrel' politics. And the problem pre-dates 9/11. According to one account, responsibility for intelligence oversight rests with 'at least 17 committees' (*New York Times*, 23 August 2004) and according to another '88 separate committees and sub-committees' (Newsday.com, 23 August 2004). Despite numerous attempts since the 1970s to consolidate intelligence oversight and make the process more coherent, there has been no effective action. Part of the reason is that members of the various committees are reluctant to give up their power, or 'turf'. More important still, members are reluctant to lose their ability to channel homeland security funds into their districts – 'pork barrel'. In the three years following 9/11, Congress had some $23 billion to distribute for enhanced homeland security. Rather than giving this money to the areas most at risk of terrorist attack, however, it was divided up to give each state a share. This may help members of Congress to get re-elected, but it is not an effective way to improve homeland security. As a result, the 9/11 Commission recommended either the creation of a joint Senate–House committee with sole responsibility for intelligence and security, or perhaps one permanent committee with sole responsibility in each chamber. The 9/11 Commission also recommended major changes in the intelligence and security structures of the executive branch. However, as Senator Susan Collins (R – Maine) commented: 'It's extraordinarily difficult to reorganize the executive branch, but that is going to be a piece of cake compared to reorganizing Congress' (*Washington Post*, 23 August 2004).

The Senate exercises oversight in the form of its power to confirm or reject presidential nominees to federal posts. However, with one important exception, the Senate confirmation of these nominees is usually routine. This is not to say that some nominations don't run into trouble, as did that of John Bolton to become US Ambassador to the United Nations in 2005. President Bush's nominee to become attorney-general in his second term, Alberto Gonzalez, was also fiercely resisted by Senate Democrats, but was still confirmed by a comfortable margin.

The exception mentioned above concerns nominees to federal judgeships. As we will see in Chapter 8, until quite recently nominations to the federal district and appeals courts were routinely confirmed. However, during President Clinton's second term, the Republican majority in the Senate began delaying consideration of nominated judges whom they considered to be too liberal. The Senate Democrats responded in kind under President George W. Bush. Nevertheless, although the judicial confirmation process is less automatic than before, this does not necessarily constitute good use of the oversight power. Judges should be confirmed mainly on their fitness for office, in terms of skills, experience and temperament, rather than upon their political ideology. When a tit-for-tat, partisan war breaks out, as it did under Presidents Clinton and George W. Bush, it results in many judgeships being left vacant and thus a more inefficient federal judiciary.

Nevertheless, while public, formal oversight by Congress may produce little tangible evidence of effectiveness, it may be that informal oversight is more productive. By definition, the effect of informal oversight is impossible to measure. Yet, it seems logical, at least, to assume that the daily, routine contacts which members of Congress have with federal bureaucrats attune the executive branch to the preferences, interests and objections of the legislative branch. Bureaucrats, therefore, will try to anticipate the views of legislators and, if possible, accommodate those views when devising and implementing policy (Keefe and Ogul, 1993, pp. 411–12).

Political education for the public

The legislative and investigative functions of Congress involve informed, public debate on the major political issues confronting the nation. As a result, Congress may be said to have an important role to play in educating the public. It may further be argued that an increasing tendency in recent years to allow hearings, floor debates and even committee sessions to be televised has enhanced the importance of this function of Congress.

Congress has lost some of the will and capacity to perform the legislative role envisaged in the Constitution. Yet this is a common development in many democratic systems where there has been a drift of power from the legislative to the executive in the twentieth century. This is true even where, as in the UK, party ties are stronger and internal structures less fragmented. Nevertheless, it cannot be denied that internal congressional structures and processes do make the task of legislative leadership even more difficult for Capitol Hill.

Congressional structures and processes

A bill becomes law

There are many bills introduced into Congress every session, but very few become law. Many bills are introduced without any serious expectation that they will be passed. However, even the most earnestly and widely supported bills have to struggle to overcome the many obstacles and opportunities for sabotage and derailment that await them. As we have seen, the parochialism and fragmentation of power within Congress, combined with the absence of strong party loyalties and disciplines, makes the path of legislation unusually incoherent and uncertain.

In formal terms, all bills follow more or less the same route. The complexity of the legislative process stems from the fact that problems may arise at

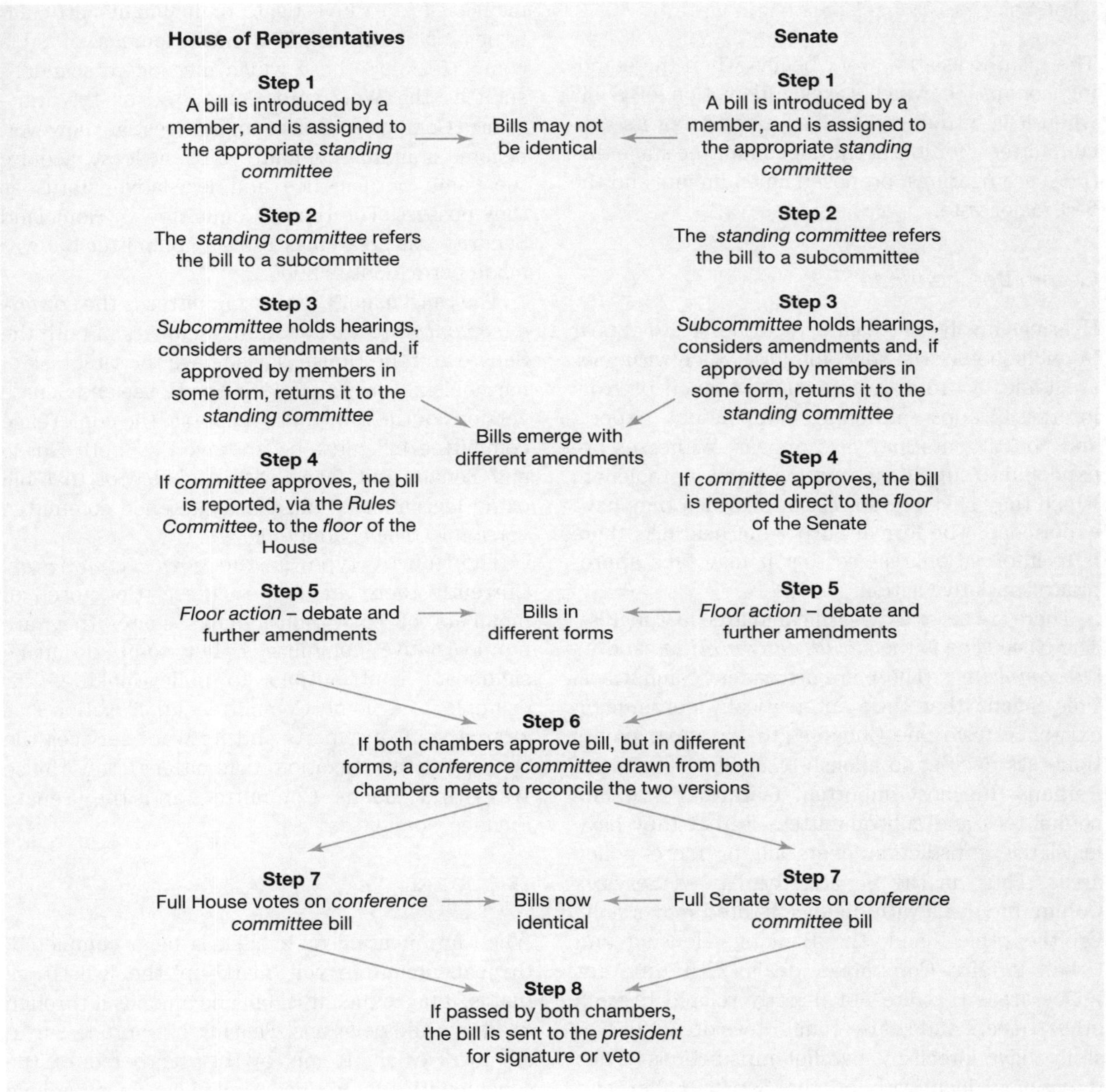

House of Representatives

Step 1
A bill is introduced by a member, and is assigned to the appropriate *standing committee*

Senate

Step 1
A bill is introduced by a member, and is assigned to the appropriate *standing committee*

Bills may not be identical

Step 2
The *standing committee* refers the bill to a subcommittee

Step 2
The *standing committee* refers the bill to a subcommittee

Step 3
Subcommittee holds hearings, considers amendments and, if approved by members in some form, returns it to the *standing committee*

Step 3
Subcommittee holds hearings, considers amendments and, if approved by members in some form, returns it to the *standing committee*

Bills emerge with different amendments

Step 4
If *committee* approves, the bill is reported, via the *Rules Committee*, to the *floor* of the House

Step 4
If *committee* approves, the bill is reported direct to the *floor* of the Senate

Step 5
Floor action – debate and further amendments

Bills in different forms

Step 5
Floor action – debate and further amendments

Step 6
If both chambers approve bill, but in different forms, a *conference committee* drawn from both chambers meets to reconcile the two versions

Step 7
Full House votes on *conference committee* bill

Bills now identical

Step 7
Full Senate votes on *conference committee* bill

Step 8
If passed by both chambers, the bill is sent to the *president* for signature or veto

Figure 7.2 The path of legislation.

any step along the path. For example, the requirements of bicameralism mean that separate bills must be introduced into both House and Senate. However, not only may the two chambers pass different amendments, but the two bills may be different from the outset, depending on the distinctive goals and strategies of the bills' sponsors. The wording of a bill is vital if its sponsor has a strong preference for a particular committee to take jurisdiction of it. Thus seeking a 'friendly' home in each of the two chambers may require differences in the initial House and Senate bills.

Committees and legislation

The main legislative work begins when the standing committee which takes jurisdiction of a bill when it is introduced assigns it to one of its subcommittees, for it is at the subcommittee stage that there are hearings, proposed amendments and the first major vote.

Committee hearings

Hearings involve the calling of witnesses to appear in public before the subcommittee. Such witnesses are typically from the executive branch or from interest groups, although independent experts and constituents may also appear. Witnesses are expected to supply information about a problem in which they have an interest or of which they have experience. The formal purpose of hearings, then, is to inform Congress so that it may take appropriate legislative action.

There are several types of committee in Congress. The basic type is the *standing committee* and its *subcommittees*. These are permanent committees. This means that they automatically continue in existence from one Congress to the next, unless Congress decides to abolish or amalgamate them. Perhaps the most important feature of standing committees and subcommittees is that they have legislative jurisdiction over one or more policy areas. Thus, in the Senate, the Armed Services Committee deals with defence-related issues only. On the other hand, the Banking, Housing and Urban Affairs Committee deals with different policy areas that are not directly related to each other. Senate and House committees do not necessarily have precisely parallel jurisdictions. Thus the issues dealt with by the Senate Labor and Human Services Committee are handled in the House by the Appropriations Committee. The fact that the House has 435 members, compared with just 100 senators means that the House has greater scope for both more and larger committees and subcommittees.

The second type of committee is the *select* or *special committee*. These are not formally permanent, nor do they have legislative authority. Their main task is to investigate or highlight particular issues or problems. The most famous of such committees are those which investigate scandals, such as the Watergate Committee or the Iran–Contra Committee. Select committees can, however, become standing committees or, at least, acquire the same permanence and legislative status as they possess. The House Committee on Homeland Security was created as a select committee but was made permanent in 2005.

The third major type of committee is the *conference committee*, made up of members of both the Senate and the House. These have the vital task of harmonising, or *reconciling*, the House and Senate versions of the same bill. Of course, the conference committee bill must be approved by both House and Senate, but faced with a choice of that bill or no legislation at all, the conference committee version is usually adopted.

The fourth type is the *joint committee*. Currently there are four of these. Composed of members of both House and Senate, they are non-legislative committees, but some do make significant contributions to policy-making. For example, the Joint Committee on Taxation has a large staff of experts and its work services the two legislative taxation committees, the House Ways and Means Committee and the Senate Finance Committee.

Mark-up sessions

When any hearing on a bill has been completed, the subcommittee will 'mark up' the legislation: that is, it takes the initial bill and amends it through additions and deletions. This mark-up process usually involves an attempt by the chairperson of the subcommittee to produce a broad consensus among the members. Thus mark-up sessions may involve intense political bargaining between individual members of the committee and between members of the majority and minority parties. Bargaining and compromise are desirable because a bill with broad support stands a much better chance of surviving the later stages of the legislative process than one which is divisive and likely to attract hostile actions (Woll, 1985, p. 117).

Box 7.6

Committees in the 109th Congress (2005/6)

Senate

Standing committees
- Agriculture, Nutrition and Forestry
- Appropriations
- Armed Services
- Banking, Housing and Urban Affairs
- Budget
- Commerce, Science and Transportation
- Energy and Natural Resources
- Environment and Public Works
- Finance
- Foreign Relations
- Governmental Affairs
- Health, Education, Labor and Pensions
- Judiciary
- Rules and Administration
- Small Business and Entrepreneurship
- Veterans Affairs

Select and special committees
- Intelligence (Permanent Select)
- Ethics (Select)
- Indian Affairs
- Aging (Special)

House

Standing committees
- Agriculture
- Appropriations
- Armed Services
- Budget
- Education and the Workforce
- Energy and Commerce
- Financial Services
- Government Reform
- Homeland Security
- House Administration
- International Relations
- Judiciary
- Resources
- Rules
- Science
- Small Business
- Standards of Official Conduct
- Transportation and Infrastructure
- Veterans Affairs
- Ways and Means

Select and special committees
- Intelligence (Permanent Select)

Joint committees
- Joint Economic Committee
- Joint Committee on the Library
- Joint Committee on Printing
- Joint Committee on Taxation

The subcommittee stage of a bill's progress is usually the most important. Although not the final stage, it is at this point that the real specialist members of Congress, together with their even more specialised staff, have the opportunity to define the basic shape of the bill. Other members not on the subcommittee tend to defer to the expertise of those who are, unless they have a particular reason for opposing them.

'Subcommittee Bill of Rights'

In the 1970s, several important reforms enhanced the power and prestige of subcommittees. The reforms had two main goals: first, to free subcommittees from the control of full committee chairpersons, and, secondly, to disperse power more widely among members. In 1973 came the 'Subcommittee Bill of Rights'. This transferred significant power over subcommittees from full committee chairpersons to the Democratic group, or *caucus*, on each committee. Henceforth, the caucus would decide who would chair the subcommittees and also ensure that all members be given a major subcommittee assignment.

More changes followed, all with the same aim of increasing the power and autonomy of subcommittees. As David Vogler wrote: 'The greatest effect of these reforms was to shift the site of most congressional lawmaking from the full committee to the subcommittee level. . . . It is clear that subcommittees in the House have come into their own as new centres of power' (Vogler, 1983, p. 154).

Power in the Senate had always been more decentralised than in the House, but in 1977 it too reorganised its committee and subcommittee structures. The number of committees was reduced by one-fifth and subcommittees by one-third. Each senator would also now be limited to service on no more than three committees and eight subcommittees. Furthermore, no senator could chair more than three committees and subcommittees.

Whatever benefits the subcommittee reforms produced, they also exacerbated the problem of fragmentation within Congress. Congress has itself recognised this and there were attempts to modify some of the measures of the 1970s. These attempts failed, however, largely because, for most members, the admitted loss in institutional coherence was outweighed by the gain in the power and autonomy of subcommittee members. Subcommittees give members their best chance to make their mark in the legislature and, consequently, with the voters back home. Too many of them are therefore simply unwilling to forgo the opportunities the strengthened subcommittees offer them.

The Republican Revolution of 1994 involved a further attempt to reduce the autonomy of committees, by giving more power to the speaker. Yet by the beginning of the 105th Congress (1997/98), the committees had regained their former position. As with other aspects of the 'revolution', the roots of this return to traditional arrangements lie in the failure of the House Republicans to secure passage of their key legislative priorities by pure partisanship. Forced in 1996 to compromise in order to get action on welfare reform and other items, the House Republicans found that committees were the best forum for bargaining and making deals across party lines (*Congressional Quarterly*, 22 March 1997, p. 9).

For similar reasons, committee chairs have regained much of their power to initiate and control legislative initiatives; where bipartisanship is essential to enacting legislation, committee leaders are better placed than party leaders to assess and manage the potential for acceptable compromise.

Reporting bills

Many bills fail to progress beyond the subcommittee stage. If, however, the subcommittee can agree and approve a version of the bill, then it is sent back to the full committee for consideration. The full committee may choose to hold further hearings and mark-up sessions, though on the whole it will accept the recommendations of the subcommittee. At this point, if the committee approves the bill, it is reported to the floor for consideration by the full chamber. The vast majority of bills are never reported: one count in the mid-1980s revealed that only 12 per cent of House bills and 24 per cent of Senate bills survived the committee stages of the legislative process (Bailey, 1989, p. 98).

House rules

At this point, the House and Senate processes diverge. In the House, the reported bill must go to the *Rules Committee* where it will be given a 'rule' determining the conditions of debate and the extent to which amendments may be offered. If the majority party is united on the bill and wishes to protect it, the committee can give it a rule which forbids amendments altogether. In the Senate, however, this is possible only where there is a unanimous vote to limit debate or amendment. Given that just one senator alone can prevent such limitation, Senate bills are more vulnerable to hostile amendment on the floor than House bills.

Floor action

Floor action refers to the activities of the whole chamber when a bill is reported to it. In essence this means debate, amendments (unless a 'rule' determines otherwise) and the final vote.

The extent of such activities may be restricted in the House, but the Senate has a rule of unlimited debate. Because senators may talk for as long as they like, they can exploit it to try to exact further concessions from the bill's supporters or even to kill the legislation altogether. When organised with real determination, this is known as a filibuster.

During the presidency of George W. Bush, the minority Democrats in the Senate employed the filibuster to block some of the president's more conservative judicial nominees. This led Senate Republican leaders to threaten to restrict the uses of the filibuster, something which made even some other Republicans very anxious. As noted above, a compromise was finally reached, although this may have merely delayed the problem, rather than resolve it. The fact is that the filibuster is not merely a traditional power of senators, but one valued by members of both parties. Although it cannot be used as a matter of routine, it does serve a useful purpose by forcing a choice between consensus or inaction on issues where passions run high.

Conference

If both the Senate and the House pass a bill, it goes to a *conference committee*. A conference committee is composed of a delegation of members from both the House and the Senate. Their task is to take the two versions of the bill passed by the Senate and the House and reconcile them: that is, produce a common version of the bill. An agreed version, known as the Committee Report, is accepted once it has been signed by a majority of each chamber's delegation. It is then sent back to the House and Senate for a final vote. It is rare for a Committee Report to be defeated in the Senate or House. Equally important, no amendments to a Committee Report are permitted. Senators and representatives are therefore confronted with what is called a straight 'up or down' vote – a simple choice between approving or disapproving the report as it stands. Whatever is agreed in the conference committee, therefore, will almost certainly be what becomes law.

Bargaining and compromise in the legislative process

The legislative process as outlined above offers a series of points at which a bill may be fundamentally altered or defeated altogether. Each stage provides individual members of Congress, interest groups and representatives of the executive branch with a point of access to the legislative process. Combined with a set of detailed and complex rules governing legislative procedure, this makes negative legislative action far easier than positive legislative action. In simple terms, it is easier to prevent than to secure the passage of a bill.

Given the difficulty of operating on partisan lines, the best method for securing the passage of a bill is to ensure that it serves the interests and needs of as many individual members as possible. This means that for each new bill, its sponsors must try to build a coalition which will support it through the difficult process which lies ahead. However, since the specific interests and needs of individual members may vary considerably, this inevitably entails bargaining and compromise on the details of the legislation. If a bill involves a distributive policy, that is, one which involves the allocation of funds or other benefits, then the simplest method of building a successful coalition is to make sure that enough members' constituencies benefit from the expenditure. If little or no money is involved, as with a civil rights bill, then bargaining and compromising will revolve around the terms and language of the legislation: some members may seek to strengthen the bill whereas others try to dilute it.

In either case, the effect on the original bill can be very significant. Ensuring the passage of a distributive bill may simply necessitate spending more money than the nation's financial position makes desirable. This could contribute to a budget deficit or to other programmes being starved of vital finance. Diluting the terms and language of legislation may render it less effective or even completely worthless.

In short, the need to bargain, compromise and make deals may well undermine the achievement of good public policy. Nevertheless, it continues to be a central feature of the congressional process because there is no other, more effective method of aggregating the interests of individual members in a fragmented legislative body.

Members of Congress

Although Congress is a representative institution, its members are not at all typical of the population at large. They are disproportionately old, male, white and wealthy compared with those who elect them.

Table 7.1 Portrait of the 109th Congress (2005/6)

	Senate	House
Average age	60.35	55.07
Women in Congress	14	68
Minorities		
Black	1	42
Hispanic	2	24
Asian	2	5
American-Indian	0	1
Career background		
Law	58	160
Public Service	32	164
Business	30	163

Source: *CQ Guide to the New Congress*

Some of these imbalances are less worrying than others. For example, the predominance of lawyers is hardly surprising given that politics is all about the making of laws. The gender and ethnic imbalances, on the other hand, indicate that there remain considerable barriers preventing members of historically disadvantaged groups from entering the corridors of power. Nevertheless, there are more women members of Congress today than there have ever been. There has also been progress in the number of members who come from ethnic minorities.

For minority candidates, it is clearly easier to get elected to the House than to the Senate. This reflects two main factors. First, because House districts are smaller than those for the Senate, they may contain concentrations of minority voters who constitute a relatively high percentage of the district's electorate. This factor was given added impetus in the early 1990s, when the Justice Department put pressure upon states to create 'majority-minority districts'. However, a series of Supreme Court decisions, beginning with *Shaw* v. *Reno* (1993) has ruled many of these districts unconstitutional as racial gerrymanders.

The second, and closely related, factor which makes it difficult for minority candidates to get elected to the Senate is that many white voters seem very reluctant to support them. Since whites constitute a large majority in all states, the state-wide electoral constituency of senators militates against the success of minority candidates. As a result, unless there is a marked change of attitude on the part of white voters, minority membership of the House may already be close to its maximum possible level. It is likewise difficult to imagine much further progress being made in the Senate. Nonetheless, the 2004 Senate race in Illinois produced the unprecedented phenomenon of both major party candidates being black.

Congressional careers

Once elected to Congress, however, members from all backgrounds face a similar career structure. Apart from their own talents and ambitions, the main determinant of their success is committee work. As we have seen, it is in committee that the main legislative work of Congress is done, and so it is also here that members have a chance to make their name. The first aim of a new member of Congress is to secure a seat on the most electorally advantageous committee.

Committee assignment

All committees and subcommittees are organised along party lines. That is to say that the party which has an overall majority in the chamber as a whole is entitled to have a majority of the seats on every committee and subcommittee. Logically enough, then, it is the two parties who allocate their members to committees. In order to share membership of committees on a reasonably fair basis, Senate committees are divided into A, B and C classes, and no senator may be a member of more than two A class and one B class committee.

Members' committee preferences differ according to their personal interests and how they choose to attempt to advance their careers. A member bent on building up his power within the House might well aim for the House Rules Committee since this has considerable sway over the progress of most legislation. On the other hand, a member from a mainly rural area might request a place on the Agriculture Committee in order to ensure that she can protect the interests of the farming communities in her constituency. Then again, a senator with presidential aspirations might seek a place on the Foreign Affairs Committee in order to acquire and demonstrate expertise in matters that preoccupy most residents of the White House.

The seniority principle

Once on a committee and subcommittees, members will almost invariably rise through the ranks largely on the basis of seniority. Seniority is acquired by years of continuous service on a committee. Thus a member who has served twelve years continuously on the same committee outranks one who has served only ten years.

The seniority system has certain advantages for members of Congress. First, those with most

legislative experience of the issues dealt with by a committee will also be its highest ranking and most influential members. Secondly, it guarantees all members 'promotion' on a neutral basis: a member knows she need only wait her turn to rise to the top, probably to become chairperson of a subcommittee or even full committee. This also helps to avoid recriminations and feuds between members over promotions.

There are disadvantages to the seniority system, however. For example, it promotes the longest-serving committee members regardless of their talent, diligence or loyalty to party and colleagues. Seniority thus also frustrates more able but junior members of Congress. It was for reasons such as these that Congress gradually abandoned the absolute application of the seniority rule in the 1970s. A series of changes gave the party caucuses the ultimate power to overturn the assignment of committee chairs based on seniority. In 1995, House Speaker Newt Gingrich, backed by the Republican caucus, ignored seniority in regard to the chairs of three committees.

Despite these exceptions, however, seniority remains the dominant principle in determining who shall rise to become chairpersons of congressional committees. To a considerable extent, this is because it avoids the problem of finding a better method of appointment: 'Reliance on seniority, unless there is an overwhelming reason to oppose the most senior member, resolves the question of choosing between the alternatives and minimises internal party strife' (Smith and Deering, 1990, p. 134).

Party leadership

Apart from the power that comes through committee service, members of Congress may also seek to become party leaders. As we saw above, party leaders do not have the disciplinary powers that would enable them to control party members. This is particularly true when party policy conflicts with members' constituency interests. Nevertheless, party leaders in Congress are in position to command the respect, if not the absolute loyalty, of fellow party members. Tact, persuasion and

Box 7.7

Party leadership in Congress
Main office-holders in the 109th Congress
(2005/6)

Republicans	Democrats
House	**House**
Speaker	–
Dennis Hastert (Illinois)	–
Majority leader	*Minority leader*
Tom DeLay (Texas)	Nancy Pelosi (California)
Majority whip	*Minority whip*
Roy Blunt (Missouri)	Steny Hoyer (Maryland)
Senate	**Senate**
Majority leader	*Minority leader*
Bill Frist (Tennessee)	Harry Reid (Nevada)
Majority whip	*Minority whip*
Mitch McConnell (Kentucky)	Dick Durbin (Illinois)

goodwill towards colleagues are usually among the required qualities of party leaders.

Speaker of the House

Speaker of the House is the most important party position in either chamber of Congress. This is in part due to the fact that it is the only leadership position created by the Constitution. Originally intended as a non-partisan presiding officer, the speaker is today the leader of the majority party in the House. All members take part in the election of the speaker at the beginning of each new Congress. However, the vote is normally strictly partisan.

The speaker possesses important powers which help him lead his party and the House. He is influential in determining the committee assignments of members of his party, who are therefore mindful of his opinion of them. He can influence the outcome of legislation through his power to choose the committee to which a bill is assigned, and he largely controls appointments to the Rules Committee, which determines how a bill will be handled on the floor of the House.

When the president is of a different party, the speaker can also take on the role of unofficial 'leader of the opposition'. Speaker Tip O'Neill tried to do just this during the first six years of the Reagan administration. Even so, O'Neill was not able to hold his party together in opposition to President Reagan's tax and budget proposals, thus underlining once again the limits of party authority in Congress. As we saw above, Speaker Newt Gingrich sought to go beyond oppositional status in the 1990s and tried to wrest national political leadership from President Bill Clinton. However, this failed and Gingrich succeeded only in lowering his standing in public opinion polls, as respondents saw him as aggressive and extreme.

In 1997, Gingrich's bid for power was further reined in when there were two attempts by some House Republicans to unseat him as speaker. Finally, as a result of the poor showing by Republican House candidates in the 1998 mid-term elections, Gingrich was obliged to step down as speaker. Gingrich was succeeded by Dennis Hastert, who has shown himself to be more conciliatory and collegial than his predecessor – and is all the more popular for it. Ultimately, therefore, the speaker's power is dependent upon the will of the party caucus in the House. If it wants a strong leader, it will have one; but if it prefers to devolve power to committee chairs, there is little the speaker can do about it.

House majority and minority leaders and whips

House majority and minority leaders and whips are chosen in intra-party elections. The majority leader's principal task is to support the work of the speaker. The minority leader, by definition, has no supportive relationship with the speaker. He does, however, carry out similar functions to those of the majority leader – liaising between party members, gathering intelligence and trying to persuade them to follow party policy. If the president is of the same party, then the minority leader will have an additional important task of liaising with the White House.

House caucus and conference chairpersons

The Democratic caucus and the Republican conference consist of all the members of the respective parties. If members wished it, the chairpersons of these two groups could wield considerable power, even more than that of the speaker and majority and minority leaders. Since the caucus or conference chooses all other party leaders, it has the potential to define the hierarchy of party leadership.

In practice, members who do not accept binding party discipline see little need for powerful caucus or conference leaders. Nevertheless, chairing the caucus can be a useful step on the political ladder for an ambitious member of Congress.

Senate party leaders

There is no equivalent position to that of the speaker in the Senate. The presiding officer stipulated in the Constitution is an outsider, namely the vice-president of the United States.

This means that the majority and minority leaders take on the mantle of party leaders. The majority leader, for example, has some of the same responsibilities as the speaker, including scheduling legislation, organising the chamber and acting as a focal point for party unity. The minority leader, when the president is of the other party, may also try to emulate the speaker by assuming the role of 'leader of the opposition'.

However, owing to the differences in culture between the two chambers, these positions are of less importance in the Senate than they are in the House. Senators are more individualistic and less deferential than members of the House. This means that leadership in the Senate must be even more collegial in nature.

Congressional staffs

Senators and representatives are clearly the most prominent members of the Congress, but they are not the only important group in the legislature. Increasingly, the staff who support congressional committees and the individual members themselves are being seen as vital participants in the legislative process. Indeed, these congressional staff have been characterised as 'the invisible force in American lawmaking' (Fox and Hammond, 1977).

There has been a rapid increase in the number of these personal and committee aides in the past fifty years, as well as in the number of those working for congressional support agencies. Between 1967 and 1977, the number of staff working in the offices of members of Congress in Washington almost doubled, from 5,804 to 10,486. In the case of senators, in 1967 they had an average of 17.5 staff per member, including those working back at the offices in the state; by 1991, the average was 57 per member. Committee staff also grew rapidly in number, from a total of 1,337 in 1970 to 3,231 in 1991. When those working for support agencies, such as the Congressional Research Service were included, it made for a total of some 24,000 staff working for Congress in the early 2000s (Davidson and Oleszek, 2004, p. 28). Although the levels stabilised at the end of the 1970s, owing mainly to financial constraints, and were then cut by the Republicans when they captured Congress in 1994, the thousands of congressional staff who remain must clearly fulfil important functions.

Committee staff

The number of committee staff has grown rapidly in recent decades. This is due principally to the increase in government activities in the modern period. Altogether, there are some 2,000 staff attached to congressional committees and subcommittees (Schneider, 2003, p. 3).

Committee staff are closely involved in all the main functions of Congress. They organise hearings, draft legislation, meet interest groups and negotiate between members on details of policy and votes.

Critics argue that they have become more influential than the elected legislators themselves, or that rather than help deal with the congressional workload, they actually increase it unnecessarily in order to justify their existence. While the ultimate approval of legislation remains with members themselves, there can be little doubt that the duties of congressional staff afford them considerable opportunities for influencing the content of national legislation.

Personal staff

Some of the staff attached personally to members of Congress carry out legislative and oversight functions. There is evidence to suggest, however, that most of the work done by personal staff is connected to the representative roles of members (Vogler, 1983, p. 130). Employed either in Washington, DC, or in offices back in the state or district, they deal with constituents' complaints and problems, schedule meetings and personal appearances for the member and try to ensure a flow of good publicity. They also conduct frequent polls in order to try to keep their member in tune with political developments and moods among their constituents.

As usual with members of Congress, the electoral connection here is all too apparent. The ultimate task of personal staff engaged in representative work is to provide the high level of constituency service and political intelligence that will ensure their member's re-election. Given today's incumbency re-election success rates of better than 90 per cent, the creation of large personal staffs seems to have paid off.

Chapter summary

Although Congress retains its exclusive power to enact laws, much of the initiative in legislation has passed to the presidency. This is due largely to the institutional advantages enjoyed by a unitary executive compared with a fragmented legislative branch. Another major cause, however, is the tendency of members of Congress towards parochialism and the desire to serve their constituents in order to enhance their prospects of re-election. The central feature of legislative and most other activity in Congress is the committee. Although the precise amount of power wielded by committees and their chairpersons varies over time, committees remain central because it is in committee that the details of legislation are hammered out. Legislating in Congress is a complex and difficult process. It requires considerable bargaining and compromise in order to accommodate the diverse interests of members – for without such accommodation, it is relatively easy for a minority of members to block the legislative process.

Discussion points

1. What explains the shift in legislative initiative from the Congress to the presidency since 1789?

2. How accurate is the view that Congress is a fundamentally parochial institution?

3. What are the most important differences between the Senate and the House of Representatives?

4. What are the advantages and disadvantages of the committee system in the legislative process?

5. How important are party ties in Congress?

Further reading

A useful introductory text is R. English, *The United States Congress* (Manchester: Manchester University Press, 2003). Two comprehensive and authoritative works on Congress are R. Davidson and W. Oleszek, *Congress and Its Members* (9th edn, Washington, DC: CQ Press, 2004) and L. Dodd and B. Oppenheimer (eds), *Congress Reconsidered* (8th edn, Washington, DC: CQ Press, 2005). An interesting sociological approach to changes in Congress is taken in N. Polsby, *How Congress Evolves: Social Bases of Institutional Change* (Oxford: Oxford University Press, 2004). For an analysis of congressional elections see M. Nelson (ed.), *The Elections of 2004* (Washington, DC: CQ Press, 2005). If you are fortunate to have access to it, *Congressional Quarterly* is a marvellous source of up-to-date information and analysis.

Websites

http://thomas.loc.gov/
http://www.house.gov/
http://www.senate.gov/

References

Bailey, C. (1989) *The US Congress* (Oxford: Basil Blackwell).

Davidson, R. and Oleszek, W. (2004) *Congress and Its Members* (9th edn, Washington, DC: CQ Press).

Fisher, L. (1985) *Constitutional Conflicts between Congress and the President* (Princeton: Princeton University Press).

Foley, M. and Owens, J. (1996) *Congress and the Presidency: Institutional Politics in a Separated System* (Manchester: Manchester University Press).

Fox, H. and Hammond, S. (1977) *Congressional Staffs: The Invisible Force in American Lawmaking* (New York: Free Press).

Hershey, M. (1997) 'The congressional elections', in Pomper, G. *et al.* (eds) *The Elections of 1996: Reports and Interpretations* (Chatham, NJ: Chatham House).

Hodgson, G. (1980) *All Things to All Men* (New York: Simon & Schuster).

Jacobson, G. (1996) 'The 1994 House elections in perspective', *Political Science Quarterly*, vol. 111, no. 2, pp. 203–23.

Keefe, W. and Hetherington, J. (2003) *Parties, Politics and Public Policies in America* (9th edn, Washington, DC: CQ Press).

Keefe, W. and Ogul, M. (1993) *The American Legislative Process: Congress and the States* (8th edn, Englewood Cliffs, NJ: Prentice Hall).

Maas, A. (1983) *Congress and the Common Good* (New York: Basic Books).

Mayhew, D. (1974) *Congress: The Electoral Connection* (New Haven, Conn.: Yale University Press).

Mezey, M. (1989) *Congress, the President and Public Policy* (Boulder, Col.: Westview).

Neustadt, R. (1960) *Presidential Power* (New York: Wiley).

Peltason, J. (1988) *Corwin and Peltason's Understanding the Constitution* (11th edn, New York: Holt, Rinehart & Winston).

Schneider, J. (2003) *The Committee System in the US Congress* (Washington, DC: Congressional Research Service).

Smith, S. and Deering, C. (1990) *Committees in Congress* (2nd edn, Washington, DC: CQ Press).

Vogler, D. (1983) *The Politics of Congress* (4th edn, Boston: Allyn & Bacon).

Wayne, S. (1978) *The Legislative Presidency* (New York: Harper & Row).

Woll, P. (1985) *Congress* (Boston: Little, Brown).

Chapter 8

The Supreme Court and judicial politics

'We are under a Constitution, but the Constitution is what the judges say it is.' So said Charles Evan Hughes, politician and jurist, and later to become chief justice of the United States Supreme Court. His perceptive remark succinctly identifies the vital connection between the American political system and the American judiciary. The Supreme Court is the ultimate interpreter of the Constitution and that means it has a profound impact upon politics as well as upon law. In this chapter we will examine how a court of law became a powerful political body and why judicial power is important but controversial in contemporary American politics.

Judicial review

The foundation of the Supreme Court's legal and political power is the American version of the doctrine of *judicial review*. This empowers the Court to declare any law or action of a governmental institution – whether federal state or local – to be unconstitutional. This entails a majority of the nine justices deciding that a challenged law or administrative action violates one or more clauses of the Constitution.

A second form of judicial review involves *statutory interpretation*. This is where the Court decides whether a state or local government measure violates a federal law. In both constitutional interpretation and statutory interpretation, the outcome is the same: if the Supreme Court believes a violation exists, then the inferior law is declared null and void.

There is, however, a crucial difference between constitutional interpretation and statutory interpretation. If the Supreme Court interprets a federal statute in a way that offends Congress, then the legislators can simply amend the law to nullify the Court's decision. If, on the other hand, a Court decision is based upon constitutional interpretation, then Congress has no power to overturn it. True, it can initiate the process of constitutional amendment, but this is extremely difficult to bring to a successful conclusion. In virtually all cases, then, a decision of the Supreme Court based upon constitutional interpretation is final, unless the Court can be persuaded to change its mind.

The power of judicial review, therefore, has serious implications for the operation of American democracy. Since, in principle, all government policies can be challenged in the federal courts as unconstitutional, it can be argued that the Supreme Court, as the final court of appeal, is superior to both the Congress and the president in matters of legislation and public policy. Indeed, critics of the Court have sometimes alleged that the United States has 'government by judiciary'.

In fact, such charges are a gross exaggeration. As we shall see, there are many practical restrictions on the power of judicial review. Nevertheless, because the Supreme Court is recognised as the authoritative interpreter of the Constitution, it has a stature and role in American government that makes it a political force to be reckoned with. Remarkably, however, it is not at all clear that the framers of the Constitution intended the Court to play such an important role.

Inventing the Supreme Court

Article III of the Constitution clearly created a *court* when it opened with the words 'The judicial power of the United States shall be vested in one Supreme Court, and in such inferior courts as the Congress may from time to time ordain and establish.'

As many scholars have pointed out, however, Article III makes no mention of judicial review or of the power of the Supreme Court to declare legislation unconstitutional. Nor does the Judiciary Act of 1789, by which Congress created the first federal court system. In other words, both the Constitution and the first Congressional legislation on the matter are silent on the very power that today makes the Supreme Court a major actor in American politics.

The explanation for this silence is not entirely clear, but there was certainly a disagreement about the legitimacy of allowing an unelected judiciary to overturn the acts of an elected representative body such as Congress. Nevertheless, the proponents of judicial review continued their campaign. Most famously, in the course of the public debates over ratification of the new Constitution, Alexander Hamilton established their basic case in a three-step argument in *The Federalist* (no. 78). First, he pointed out that since the Constitution was the supreme law of the United States, legislative Acts which conflicted with it must be illegitimate. Secondly, in the event that such a conflict was alleged to exist, some body or another must be empowered to interpret the Constitution in order to arbitrate the dispute. Thirdly, Hamilton argued that the Supreme Court was the logical institution to play this role: after all, courts had traditionally performed the task of interpreting other forms of law. Moreover, to allow legislative bodies to exercise review, as some suggested, would create the unsatisfactory situation in which legislators would sit in judgement on the constitutionality of their own actions. To say the least, this would raise doubts about their impartiality in the matter.

Hamilton made one further argument of great importance: he denied that giving the Court the power to strike down Acts of Congress and state legislatures would make the federal judiciary the most powerful branch of government. On the contrary, he famously predicted that a Supreme Court endowed with judicial review would prove 'the least dangerous branch' of the government, because it possessed 'neither Force nor Will, but only judgment'.

By this, he meant that the Court was inherently weaker than either the Congress or the presidency. Those two branches controlled both expenditure and law enforcement and the Court would have to rely on the cooperation of Congress and the president. Furthermore, Congress and the president were driven by the will and desires of the population, something which could lead to rash actions. The justices of the Supreme Court, on the other hand, would not be ideological partisans: they would be impartial legal technicians – judges – who merely established the facts of whether a given law conflicted with a given clause of the Constitution.

Plausible as it was, Hamilton's argument did not yet convince the country. As a result, the early years of the Supreme Court were exceedingly dull and uneventful. Without the power of judicial review, the Court lacked stature compared with the Congress, the presidency or even the higher offices of state government. As a consequence, it proved difficult to persuade people of high standing to serve on the Court and it appeared destined to play only a minor part in the nation's government.

Marbury v. *Madison*: a political coup

The transformation in the role and power of the Supreme Court came in 1803, as a direct result of the bitterly fought presidential election of 1800. The more conservative Federalist party, having lost that election to the Jeffersonians, sought to use their remaining months in office to make the unelected judiciary a bastion of Federalist power.

Most significantly, the outgoing Federalist secretary of state, John Marshall, was appointed chief justice of the Supreme Court.

In the case of *Marbury* v. *Madison* (1803), Marshall and his colleagues staged a political coup by claiming the power to declare an Act of Congress unconstitutional. With consummate skill, Marshall avoided a political war with the Jeffersonians – a war the Court was bound to lose – yet simultaneously won implicit acceptance of the power of judicial review. To Chief Justice John Marshall, then, goes the ultimate credit for making judicial review of legislation a significant reality of American political life.

We will examine later how the Marshall Court and its successors used the power it had awarded itself. First, though, it is important to understand how the process of judicial review works. For this reminds us that, no matter how embroiled it becomes in politics, the Supreme Court operates in a manner quite different from other political institutions. Quite simply, it is a *court*, and therefore its procedures are those of a court.

Box 8.1

Marbury v. Madison (1803) and the creation of judicial review

Towards the end of the outgoing Federalist administration of President John Adams (1797–1801), several new justices of the peace were appointed, all staunch Federalists, but their commissions were not delivered before the new administration of President Thomas Jefferson (1801–9) took over. The new secretary of state, James Madison, refused to complete delivery of the commissions, one of which was destined for William Marbury. Marbury went to court, claiming that Section 13 of the Judiciary Act of 1789 empowered the Supreme Court to order Madison to complete delivery of his commission.

The Court sympathised with Marbury, but knew that a decision in his favour would invoke the wrath – and disobedience – of the Jefferson administration. Marshall craftily argued that he could not order Madison to complete Marbury's commission because Section 13 of the Judiciary Act had enlarged the Court's power of *Original Jurisdiction*; but since such an enlargement could only be achieved by constitutional amendment, and not by federal statute, Section 13 was unconstitutional. Many scholars doubt the validity of Marshall's argument. However, it was politically adroit. Mollified by their immediate victory, the Jeffersonians denounced the chief justice and his concept of judicial review, but did nothing substantial to negate the Court's claim to possess the power to declare an act of Congress unconstitutional.

Stages of judicial review

Initiating a case

There are several formal steps through which any Supreme Court case proceeds. The first is that an individual, organisation or government body must decide to *litigate*, that is, to bring a lawsuit in a lower federal court or a state court. These litigants must do more than merely allege that someone has violated the Constitution: they must show that they have personally suffered some concrete harm as a result of the violation.

In theory, this first stage means that litigation cannot be used simply as a forum for political debate or controversy. For example, the requirement that the litigants must have a real stake in the case aims to prevent people from challenging laws simply because they oppose them on political grounds.

It is also important to note that the judiciary cannot take the initiative on an issue, unlike the president or the Congress. Rather, it must wait until the issue is placed before the courts in the form of a lawsuit. Moreover, it is not usually possible to take a case straight to the Supreme Court: litigants must work their way up through the hierarchy of lower courts and so a case may take several years before the justices settle the question definitively.

These constraints on the Court's freedom of manoeuvre are in line with the language of Article III of the Constitution, which says that the Court's power extends to all 'cases and controversies' arising under the Constitution. Cases must be real legal disputes, not merely hypothetical or political arguments.

Interest group intervention

In practice, litigation today is frequently initiated by specialist interest groups whose strategies are legal but whose mission is entirely political. These groups seek out individuals who have real cases and effectively take them over. They provide individual litigants with the legal and financial

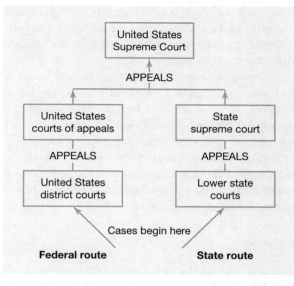

Figure 8.1 Basic court structure.

resources to take their case through the expensive minefield of preparing and arguing cases in the judicial system, if necessary going through one or more appeals to get to the Supreme Court. These organisations hope that by winning a concrete case for the individual, they will simultaneously win a constitutional ruling that will benefit others. In short, these interest groups sponsor or manufacture test cases which they hope will have wide social and political significance.

Perhaps the most famous example of the successful use of the courts to bring about political reforms is that by the National Association for the Advancement of Colored People (NAACP). This group sponsored some of the main cases in the racial segregation controversies of the 1950s and 1960s and became a role model for other litigation groups. The American Civil Liberties Union (ACLU) is another group which frequently sponsors litigation on behalf of liberal political causes.

Class-action suits

An important legal device which greatly aids the political use of the courts by interest groups is the so-called class-action suit. This means that an individual who brings a case may do so not merely on her own behalf, but also for all those similarly situated. An example would be that of an African-American parent whose children are denied entry to a school because of their race. As well as suing to have her own children admitted, a class action enables her to sue on behalf of all African-American parents throughout the entire country whose children are similar victims of racial discrimination. Class actions, then, combined with the activities of litigation interest groups, ensure that major political issues are frequently brought to the courts, albeit in the guise of lawsuits.

Appeals

As noted above, the first round of a constitutional case takes place in a federal district court or a state court. (The only exceptions are the one or two cases each year which come direct to the Court under its *Original Jurisdiction*). When the decision is announced in the lower court, the loser may appeal to either a federal appeals court or a state's highest court. These courts may affirm or reverse the lower court's decision but, either way, the loser may then try an appeal to the Supreme Court.

At this point, however, we come to a most important feature of the Supreme Court. It is not obliged to hear any appeal. Originally, there were a considerable number of appeals that the Court was obliged to hear. Owing to the Court's increasingly heavy workload, however, Congress has removed virtually all mandatory appeals and has left the Court with full discretion over its docket. Thus, the justices receive thousands of petitions for appeal each year, mostly in the form of petitions for review called *writs of certiorari*. From these, however, the Court frequently accepts less than one hundred for full consideration: that is, cases accepted and decided with written opinions.

The Supreme Court's agenda

The Supreme Court, then, has a large measure of control over its own agenda and this flexibility can at times be most useful. On the other hand, the Court does have an obligation to settle constitutional

Table 8.1 The Supreme Court's discretionary control

Term	Cases decided with full opinions	Review denied
1998/99	81	6,866
1999/2000	77	7,197
2000/1	86	7,500
2001/2	81	7,865
2002/3	78	8,186

Source: Adapted from the annual statistical review of the Supreme Court, *Harvard Law Review*, various years

conflicts and it would be of little value as an institution if it avoided every controversial issue. As Justice William O. Douglas (1939–75) once observed, 'Courts sit to determine questions on stormy as well as calm days.' Moreover, as we shall see below, the cases that are brought before the Court are often precisely those which are politically controversial. As the nineteenth-century commentator Alexis de Tocqueville famously said (admittedly with a measure of exaggeration), 'Scarcely any political question arises in the United States that is not resolved, sooner or later, into a judicial question.'

Judicial decision-making: the formal procedures

The basic procedures that the justices of the Supreme Court follow in deciding a case are relatively straightforward. First comes the decision whether or not to take an appeal at all: five votes are formally needed to grant judicial review of a case, but the custom is that the 'rule of four' applies. Thus if four justices favour review, a fifth justice will supply the additional vote.

Next, the Court schedules a date for *oral argument*. This is when lawyers for each party to the case will appear before the justices and in public to present the arguments for their clients. Normally, each side is allowed thirty minutes to speak, but the lawyers may be frequently interrupted by questions from the justices. The record suggests that the justices are rarely swayed by the oral arguments, and the questions they put to the lawyers are intended mainly to draw attention to

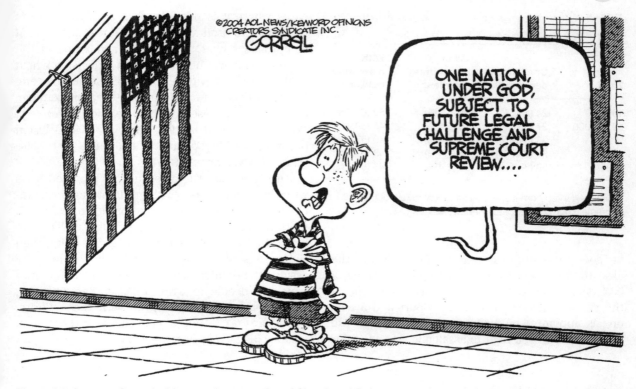

Figure 8.2 Supreme Court decisions on the separation of Church and State suggest that even the Pledge of Allegiance may be declared unconstitutional due to its mention of God.
Source: © Bob Gorrell

a point which they have already decided is dispositive, one way or the other.

This is in part because before oral argument, the lawyers will have submitted detailed, written *briefs* stating their arguments in full. Furthermore, interest groups also frequently submit briefs at this stage. Although not always a party to the case, an interest group is allowed to participate as an amicus curiae (literally, friend of the court). Some briefs rely on the special expertise of the group concerned. For example, in cases concerning abortion rights the American Medical Association submitted briefs which addressed the specifically medical aspects of the abortion issue. Other groups may offer innovative legal arguments or, like the National Organization for Women, hope to impress the justices with the fact that their large membership deems abortion rights to be fundamental to their lives.

Another significant participant at this point may be the federal government, in the form of the solicitor-general. Coming below the attorney-general, the solicitor-general is the second-ranking member of the Department of Justice. The solicitor-general frequently appears before the Court, either because the United States is itself a party to the case, or because it has a particular view to articulate as an amicus curiae.

Case conference

After reading the briefs and hearing the oral arguments, the justices meet in a *case conference* to discuss and to take preliminary votes. Many cases are decided unanimously. However, of those cases deemed sufficiently important to warrant written opinions, over half involve at least one dissenting justice.

In theory, a 5–4 decision is as authoritative as a unanimous decision. In practice, however, the former is far more vulnerable to attack than the latter. First, a 5–4 split indicates that there may

Table 8.2 Unanimity rates on the Court: decisions with full opinions

Term	Unanimous decisions	With concurring opinions	With dissenting opinions
1998/99	24 (29.6%)	5 (6.2%)	52 (64.2%)
1999/2000	27 (35.1%)	5 (6.5%)	45 (58.4%)
2000/1	30 (34.9%)	7 (8.1%)	49 (57.0%)
2001/2	27 (33.3%)	6 (7.4%)	48 (59.5%)
2002/3	30 (38.5%)	5 (6.4%)	43 (55.1%)

Source: Adapted from the annual statistical review of the Supreme Court, *Harvard Law Review*, various years

be good constitutional reasons for believing the case to have been decided wrongly. Secondly, a 5–4 decision can easily be reversed when one of the majority justices leaves the Court and a new one is appointed. A unanimous decision, on the other hand, is well-nigh unassailable. In the major

cases where it is possible, therefore, the justices work hard to produce unanimity, including making compromises over the wording and scope of the opinion. This will help to sustain a decision which is likely to meet with resistance in some quarters. Unanimity was an important feature, for example, of the Court's desegregation decision, *Brown* v. *Board of Education* (1954), and also of its decision ordering President Nixon to release the 'Watergate tapes' (*US* v. *Nixon*, 1974).

After the vote, the chief justice, provided he is with the majority, assigns himself or another member of the majority the task of producing a formal, written *opinion* explaining the Court's decision. If, however, the chief justice is in the minority, then the most senior associate justice in the majority assigns the opinion. Those justices in the minority may well decide to write a *dissenting opinion*, explaining why they disagree with the majority. Yet a third type of opinion is the *concurrence*, in which a justice usually explains that he agrees with

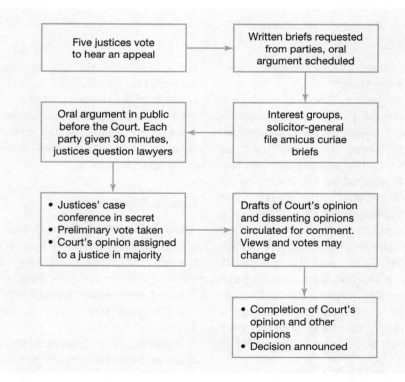

Figure 8.3 Typical stages of a Supreme Court case.

the majority's decision but for different reasons than those given in the Court's opinion.

Before the Court's decision is formally announced, draft versions of these opinions are circulated among the justices for their comment and may well be amended as a result. Votes may even be switched at this stage. Eventually, the Court announces its decision and the opinion(s) are published.

Although few people outside of politics, the law schools and the media actually read Supreme Court opinions, they are nevertheless very important. The opinion of the Court is both an explanation and a justification of the Court's decision. An opinion which fails to convince those who read it will give ammunition to those who disapprove of the result. For example, the opinion of the Court in *Roe* v. *Wade* (1973), which announced a new right to abortion, was deemed seriously flawed even by some who support abortion rights. This has strengthened the hand of pro-life activists who wish to see *Roe* overturned.

Judicial reasoning and politics

The procedures outlined above are those of a court, not those of what we traditionally think of as a political institution. Moreover, as we saw from Alexander Hamilton's defence of judicial review, Supreme Court justices were expected to eschew politics and to carry out their duties in a politically neutral manner. Yet today there are many judicial scholars who argue that it is neither possible nor even desirable for the justices to escape from their own political, philosophical or moral values. Others, however, believe that the Court can usually make decisions that are politically neutral and that it should at least always attempt to do so. Let us examine each of these arguments in turn.

Judicial traditionalism

Until the twentieth century, the notion of politically neutral, or value-free, Supreme Court justices was largely accepted. At the heart of this concept

was the belief that when a justice struck down a law as unconstitutional, he was not enforcing his own values but rather the values enshrined in the Constitution by the framers. The justice merely used his legal knowledge and skills to discover what the will, or intention, of the framers actually was and how it should be applied in the particular case before the Court.

Justice Owen Roberts expressed this view of judicial neutrality in 1936 in the case of *US* v. *Butler*. The decision in *Butler* was one of a series in which the Court struck down some key elements of President Franklin D. Roosevelt's New Deal. Many people thought the justices were simply motivated by their ideological conservatism. Roberts, however, rejected this accusation:

It is sometimes said that the Court assumes the power to overrule or control the action of the people's representatives. This is a misconception. The Constitution is the supreme law of the land ordained and established by the people. All legislation must conform to the principles it lays down. When an Act of Congress is appropriately challenged in the courts as not conforming to the constitutional mandate, the judicial branch of government has only one duty – to lay the article of the Constitution which is invoked beside the statute which is challenged and to decide whether the latter squares with the former. All the Court does or can do is to announce its considered judgment upon the question. The only power it has, if such it may be called, is the power of judgment. This Court neither approves nor condemns any legislative policy.

Roberts sought to make a vital distinction between the *political result* of a Supreme Court decision and the *process* by which that decision was made. Thus, although the decision in *Butler* had great political significance because it scuppered President Roosevelt's policy for agricultural recovery, this did not mean that the Court's decision was motivated by a desire to defeat that policy. All Roberts and his colleagues had done, he maintained, was judge that the policy was at odds with the design of the Constitution. That was a quite separate question from whether the policy was good for the country.

Today, judicial traditionalists emphasise that the justices of the Supreme Court must follow the original intentions of those who framed the Constitution. They argue that the doctrine of *original intent* prevents justices from inflicting their personal policy preferences on the country. In turn, this secures the legitimacy of judicial review in a democracy. For if, on the contrary, the justices abandon original intent and substitute their own or some other set of values for those intended by the framers, then unelected judges are in effect selecting the values and policies that govern the country. Such a situation, they claim, is more akin to judicial autocracy than representative democracy.

There is certainly some evidence that justices see an important distinction between their personal views on an issue and what the Constitution commands. For example, in 1989, in the highly emotive decision in *Texas* v. *Johnson*, Justice Anthony Kennedy voted to uphold the right to burn the American flag as a political protest, even though he expressed his distaste for that activity. He ruefully noted that, 'The hard fact is that sometimes we must make decisions we do not like. We make them because they are right, right in the sense that the law and the Constitution, as we see them, compel the result.'

Judicial modernists

Other justices and scholars see many problems in the doctrine of original intent. In the first place, it is by no means always easy to establish exactly what the framers did intend. However, modernists believe that even if the original meaning of a clause is clear, it does not follow that the justices should be bound by it. After all, they argue, much of the Constitution was written in 1787 and those who drafted it could not possibly foresee the needs and values of American society in future centuries. Chief Justice Marshall, the architect of judicial review, identified this dilemma early on. In 1819, in *McCulloch* v. *Maryland*, he wrote that the Constitution was 'intended to endure for ages to come, and, consequently, to be adapted to the various crises of human affairs.' Marshall thus created the concept of the *living Constitution*. In this view, the Constitution is an organism which must grow and adapt as society develops. It is the duty of the Court to interpret it flexibly, so that the country is not oppressed by the dead hand of the past.

In effect, this power to reinterpret the Constitution in the light of changing societal needs can amount to the power to amend the Constitution. For this reason, Woodrow Wilson once famously wrote that 'the Supreme Court is a constitutional convention in continuous session'. Of course, the original Constitution did provide for a process of amendment in Article V, but this is too cumbersome to be invoked on every occasion when a significant innovation is required. Many scholars and, indeed, judges believe that while the Supreme Court must be faithful to the spirit of the original Constitution, it must define that spirit by reference to contemporary values. As Justice William Brennan said in 1985 in response to traditionalist criticisms: 'We current justices read the Constitution in the only way that we can: as twentieth-century Americans.'

Virtually all justices today accept that their task of interpreting the Constitution involves some measure of 'updating'. A clear example is the current interpretation of the Eighth Amendment's ban on 'cruel and unusual punishments': even those who most admire intentionalism agree that ear-clipping, branding and other punishments familiar to the framers in 1787 are no longer permissible.

What divides the justices, then, is the degree of creativity they allow themselves in applying the Constitution. At one end of the spectrum is the 'intentionalist' or 'strict interpretivist' whose ideal it is to follow closely the will of the framers. At the opposite end are the 'non-interpretivists' who not only pay little or no heed to the original meaning of the Constitution, but are also willing to create new rights on subjects that the framers had never even contemplated. Between these two extremes are those justices, probably a majority, who take a pragmatic approach, trying to harmonise

Box 8.2

Approaches to constitutional interpretation

Traditionalist	Pragmatist	Modernist
Strict interpretivism or 'Strict Construction'	Balances traditionalist concerns against those of modernists	Non-interpretivism or 'Broad Construction'
Follows the original intent of the framers		Disregards original intent; creative in applying contemporary values to interpret the Constitution

fidelity to original meaning with the demands of contemporary realities.

Judicial role

We can see from the foregoing discussion that the concept of 'judicial role' is an important one in understanding how the Court works. Unlike others involved in making decisions that determine public policy, most Supreme Court justices do not believe that they can simply vote for their own political preferences. Even the most non-interpretivist of justices will at least argue in her written opinion that her vote is explained by her understanding of what the Constitution requires, rather than her personal notions of good public policy.

The Supreme Court therefore has a delicate role to perform in American politics. On the one hand, it is expected to be a judicial body which is politically impartial, and which must attempt to transcend passing political passions and uphold the eternal values of the Constitution. On the other hand, it is expected to resolve the sometimes highly charged political controversies which come before it in the form of lawsuits, with the inevitable result that its decisions will have a profound political impact and be attacked vehemently by whichever party has lost the case. Moreover, these judicial decisions are often made under considerable political pressure, since the presidency, the Congress, interest groups, legal scholars, the media and the public may all seek to influence the Court in its decision.

Politics and the Court

The Supreme Court's role as the authoritative interpreter of the Constitution has been applied to two broad areas of government and politics. First, the Supreme Court defines the powers of other government offices established by the Constitution. Thus it settles disputes over the relative powers of Congress and the presidency, and over the relative powers of the federal government and the governments of the fifty states. In other words, the Court interprets the Constitution to determine exactly what is required by the separation of powers and by the principle of federalism. Thus, in *Clinton* v. *New York* (1998), the Court declared unconstitutional the congressional grant of a line-item veto to the president. The Court reasoned that the Constitution empowered the president to veto only an entire bill, rather than a part of one, and therefore that the only way he could acquire a line-item veto was through the process of constitutional amendment.

Secondly, the Supreme Court settles disputes over the constitutional legitimacy of particular legislative acts or other policy decisions. Of course, sometimes both these kinds of dispute are involved in the same case. However, it is useful to bear this distinction in mind when considering the controversies that have arisen over the Court's decisions, for, generally speaking, decisions on the precise parameters of the powers of the president or Congress do not generate much public excitement.

Box 8.3

Politics, statesmanship and the Court: *Bush* v. *Gore* (2000)

No other modern Supreme Court case has provoked accusations of political decision-making by the justices as much as *Bush* v. *Gore*. The case arose out of the close and confused presidential election in Florida. Victory in Florida was originally awarded to George W. Bush, but the margin was extremely narrow – the first official figure was 1,784 (out of almost 6 million votes cast), but this was to fluctuate over the following weeks. The Democratic candidate, Al Gore, challenged the result, arguing that some ballot papers had not been counted even though it was possible to see in them a clear intention to vote for a candidate. This was the issue of the 'hanging chads' – ballot papers which the voting machines had failed to punch a clear hole through. The Gore campaign asked several counties to undertake a manual re-count, with a view to including those previously rejected ballots. The Constitution assigns the supervision of presidential elections to each of the states and their judicial systems. The pro-Bush Florida secretary of state, Katherine Harris, insisted that any re-counts had to be finished within one week of the election. There then began a series of cases in the Florida courts over what deadlines should be imposed on the re-counts. As the weeks passed, and re-counts were started and stopped and then re-started, the situation became even more confused. Eventually, the Bush campaign asked the Supreme Court to intervene, arguing that the re-counts in the various counties were using different criteria to assess the intention of the voter and that this violated the Equal Protection clause of the Fourteenth Amendment.

In a 5–4 vote, the most conservative justices stopped the re-counts and effectively handed victory to George W. Bush, while the four more liberal members would have left the issue with the Florida courts, with the possibility that Al Gore might eventually take the state and the presidency.

Most observers believed the justices had all decided the case on the basis of who they wanted to see elected president. The accusation was all the more serious because whoever won the election would nominate the replacement justice for any who retired in the next four years. To many, this was an inexcusable and unacceptable violation of the separation of powers. However, there is another possible explanation. The Court may, with some justification, have decided that the wrangle over Florida needed to be brought to an end. The election had taken place on 7 November and over a month had passed by the time the Court issued its decision on 12 December. There was also the distinct possibility that the wrangle would continue well into the future. If Gore was declared the winner, the Bush camp would certainly have challenged *that* result in the courts. Moreover, there was the suspicion that Florida judges, as well as its politicians, were engaged in a partisan struggle to ensure their preferred candidate became president. It is plausible, therefore, to think that the nation needed an end to the Florida wrangling and needed to know who would be president in January. In short, while the Court may have intervened when it was not constitutionally required to, it acted in a diplomatic fashion by bringing a political crisis to an end. A majority of the public approved of the Court's decision even though, of course, a majority had not voted for George W. Bush. The episode shows that the Court is held in high esteem by the public and is trusted to settle disputes in a manner that the other branches of government are not.

When a case involves the legitimacy of particular policies, however, that is when the Court is likely to occupy the public limelight simply because such policies tend directly to affect the daily lives of individuals, interest groups and various sections of the community. This does not mean that decisions regarding federalism and separation of powers are not important: they unquestionably are since they can have significant implications for the operation of government throughout the United States. However, as we now go on to examine the uses of judicial review in American history, we will find that, on the whole, the power of the Court becomes controversial when it decides cases that involve controversial policy decisions.

Judicial activism and judicial self-restraint, 1789–1954

The prominence and power of the Court has varied over the years. In some eras, the Court has practised *judicial activism*: this means that the Court has asserted its power even when faced with hostile challenges from the Congress, the president or the public. Such periods of activism are indicated by the unusually large number of federal or state laws which the Court has struck down as unconstitutional. They may also be characterised by innovations in constitutional interpretation and the suspicion that the justices are motivated by their own political viewpoints. As a result, judicial activism has usually been controversial.

In contrast to judicial activism stands *judicial self-restraint*. When the Court practises restraint, it is cautious, passive and, above all, shows great deference to the elected branches of government. The Court seeks to avoid making controversial decisions and rarely declares an Act unconstitutional. It also tends to avoid innovations in constitutional interpretation and instead follows precedent, that is, the principles announced in past decisions.

We have already noted that, after a quiet start, the Supreme Court became a dynamic institution under the leadership of Chief Justice John Marshall. After the Marshall Court (1801–35) had established

the legitimacy of judicial review in *Marbury* v. *Madison*, it proceeded to make bold decisions which had a major impact upon the political and economic future of the United States. In particular, the Marshall Court strengthened the federal government at the expense of the power of the individual states and also ensured that national commerce and capitalism were given free rein.

Under the leadership of Chief Justice Roger B. Taney (1836–64), the Court generally practised self-restraint. Unfortunately for the Taney Court, however, it is remembered less for its characteristic restraint than it is for its lone, disastrous foray into judicial activism. In *Dred Scott* v. *Sanford* (1857) the Court helped to precipitate the Civil War (1861–65). Giving a much broader ruling than was required by the facts of the case, the southern-dominated Court declared that the Missouri Compromise on slavery, worked out by Congress, was unconstitutional. This meant not only that the westward expansion of slavery could continue, but also that Congress could not fashion a compromise between pro-slavery and anti-slavery forces.

It should be noted, however, that under both Marshall and Taney it was rare for a law to be declared unconstitutional. Between 1800 and 1860, just two federal laws and thirty-five state laws suffered this fate. To a great extent, these figures reflect the fact that levels of legislative activity were still low at this stage in the nation's history.

This situation began to change drastically with the onset of industrialisation in the last quarter of the nineteenth century. As government tried to regulate the explosion in economic activity and cure the social ills which accompanied it, the Supreme Court established itself as the last bastion of laissez-faire economics. While it did permit some economic regulation and some social reform, the Court increasingly interpreted the Constitution's guarantees of liberty to protect the economic rights of individuals and corporations against interference from both federal and state government. For example, in *Adair* v. *United States* (1905) the Court struck down a congressional Act outlawing 'yellow-dog contracts'. These obliged workers to agree not to join a union as a condition of employment. The justices reasoned that the Act violated

Table 8.3 Federal and state laws declared unconstitutional by the Supreme Court, 1790–2002

Decade	Federal laws	State laws
1790–1799	0	0
1800–1809	1	1
1810–1819	0	7
1820–1829	0	8
1830–1839	0	3
1840–1849	0	9
1850–1859	1	7
1860–1869	4	24
1870–1879	7	36
1880–1889	5	46
1890–1899	5	36
1900–1909	9	41
1910–1919	6	112
1920–1929	18	131
1930–1939	14	84
1940–1949	2	58
1950–1959	5	59
1960–1969	19	123
1970–1979	20	181
1980–1989	16	161
1990–2002	30	57

Source: adapted from Epstein *et al*., 2003, pp. 163–93

the constitutionally guaranteed freedom of contract of both employer and employee to make any agreement they wished.

In the same year, the Court decided in *Lochner* v. *New York* (1905) that freedom of contract also prevented the state from restricting the maximum hours of work of bakery workers to sixty a week; and in yet another infamous case, *Hammer* v. *Dagenhart* (1918), the Court ruled that Congress had no power to prohibit factories from using child labour.

Although these decisions were by no means without constitutional basis, they were activist and controversial. The Constitution makes no mention of freedom of contract, for example. Rather, the justices interpreted the general guarantee of liberty in the Fifth and Fourteenth Amendments to include freedom of contract, and then exalted that right above the general power of government to provide for the public welfare. In simple political terms, however, the Court was imposing a set of values and policies upon the country which

the electorate and their chosen representatives no longer supported.

The Court in political crisis

This ongoing crisis came to a head during the Great Depression of the 1930s. In the presidential elections of 1932 and 1936, the nation gave impressive victories to the Democratic party candidate, Franklin D. Roosevelt. He had promised the voters a 'new deal'. Together with a large Democratic majority in Congress, Roosevelt experimented with various forms of government intervention in an attempt to alleviate the economic and social catastrophe that had befallen the country. The Supreme Court, however, declared some of his most important policies unconstitutional. The National Industrial Recovery Act of 1933 was struck down in *Schechter* v. *United States* (1935) and the Agriculture Adjustment Act of 1933 in *US* v. *Butler* (1936).

Roosevelt's response was to do battle with the Court. In 1937, he proposed a bill that purported to aim at helping the ageing justices to cope with their workload. For each justice over the age of 70, the president would be empowered to appoint an additional member of the Court. As it so happened, six of the nine current justices were over 70, so at one fell swoop Roosevelt would be able to make six new appointments to the Court. Assuming he would appoint only those known to support the New Deal, this would bring an end to the Court's resistance. It was clear to all that this was a crude attempt to bring the Court to heel and the proposal became known as the Court-packing plan.

There was considerable opposition to the Court-packing plan, even among Roosevelt's regular supporters in Congress. They feared that, if passed, it would violate the principle of the separation of powers and create a dangerously dominant presidency. Before Congress had to vote, however, the Court itself rendered the bill politically unnecessary. In *West Coast Hotel* v. *Parrish* (1937), the Court surprised everyone by upholding the constitutionality of a minimum-wage law of a type that it had previously struck down. Moreover, language in the Court's opinion suggested that, henceforth, economic liberties would take second place to government's view of what was required by the public welfare. And so it proved. Since 1937, the Supreme Court has virtually abandoned the field of economic regulation to the Congress, the president and the states.

Political lessons of the Court-packing plan: the Supreme Court and the political majority

The Court's strategic error in the 1930s was in overestimating the degree to which the Supreme Court can resist an insistent political tide. Ultimately, the power of the Court rests upon the respect it can command. For this reason it has been argued that the Court never remains out of step with the national political majority for very long (Dahl, 1957).

This in turn highlights a very important aspect of the Court's role in American government: it acts as a legitimator of political change. The New Deal involved a marked break with American traditions of politics and governmental responsibility, yet by eventually conferring its constitutional blessing upon this shift, the Court signalled that it was an acceptable addition to the fundamental political values and practices of the nation.

The Supreme Court since 1954

With hindsight, the year 1954 can be recognised as a watershed in the history of the Supreme Court. For it was then that the Court took on not just a new agenda of issues, but a significantly different method of constitutional interpretation.

Brown v. Board of Education (1954)

The catalyst for these changes was a decision ordering an end to racial segregation in the nation's school systems. It had long been the practice, particularly but not exclusively in the southern and border states, to require black and white children to attend separate schools. The Supreme Court had validated this and other forms of racial segregation

in *Plessy* v. *Ferguson* (1896). There the Court ruled that, provided facilities were 'separate but equal', racial segregation did not violate the Fourteenth Amendment's guarantee of equal protection of the laws.

In *Brown* v. *Board of Education* (1954), the Court unanimously voted to reverse its *Plessy* decision. Under the leadership of its new chief justice, Earl Warren (1953–69), it argued that separate facilities were inherently unequal: the mere desire to segregate by race implied the inferiority of one of the races compared with the other. Therefore, racial segregation did indeed violate the Fourteenth Amendment's command that the states must give all persons the 'equal protection of the laws'.

Although unarguably the right moral decision, *Brown* was rather unconvincing in terms of constitutional interpretation, as even sympathetic scholars acknowledged. The decision could not be justified by original intent, as the historical record made clear. In fact, the members of Congress who approved the Fourteenth Amendment in 1866 lived and worked in a Washington, DC, which itself operated a racially segregated school system. There was not the slightest indication that they intended to put an end to that system.

In *Brown*, therefore, the Court ignored history and judicial precedent, and relied instead upon some rather flimsy social science evidence purporting to show that black children suffered psychological damage as a result of segregated schooling. The Court's reasoning, however, was regarded as secondary to the overwhelming moral rightness of the decision. Legal scholars, in spite of their misgivings, applauded the decision. This encouraged the Warren Court along a new path of using constitutional interpretation as a means of promoting what many Americans considered to be benign social reforms. The *Brown* decision thus illustrates the fact that the Court can sometimes get away with decisions the constitutional underpinnings of which are shaky, provided they are viewed as just and desirable by other politicians and the public.

The Warren Court became increasingly bold, activist and, eventually, bitterly controversial. After *Brown*, a series of decisions swept away every law which required racial segregation. The Court also turned its activist guns onto other targets, most controversially in 1963 banning compulsory prayer in public schools (*Abington School District* v. *Schempp*). This rising tide of judicial activism brought much criticism and, eventually, a political backlash.

When the Republican Richard M. Nixon became president in 1969, he was determined to curb liberal judicial activism by appointing tradition-alist justices. By 1975, Nixon and his Republican successor, Gerald Ford, had appointed five new justices, including Warren Burger as Chief Justice. However, with a few exceptions, the counter-revolution failed to materialise. Indeed, in many respects, the Burger Court was even more activist than the Warren Court. Many scholars took this as a sign that the Court's role in the political system had undergone a fundamental change. No longer would there be cycles of activism and restraint:

the Court would now be more or less permanently activist. Judicial review, it seemed, had become the means through which policy on socio-moral issues would be made in the United States.

The Burger Court's decisions certainly gave ammunition to this theory. It announced innova-tions in constitutional interpretation by holding that the Fourteenth Amendment banned traditional gender classifications (*Reed* v. *Reed*, 1971); that the Eighth Amendment banned all existing state death penalty laws (*Furman* v. *Georgia*, 1972); that women had a constitutional right to terminate pregnancies by abortion (*Roe* v. *Wade*, 1973); and that the Constitution's requirement of race equality in the law did not disbar affirmative action policies that avoided 'quotas' but which were intended to give racial minorities certain advantages in col-lege applications (*Regents of the University of California* v. *Bakke*, 1978).

Box 8.4

The Supreme Court, gay rights and same-sex marriage: *Lawrence* v. *Texas* (2003)

The capacity of the Supreme Court to set off a political firestorm was illustrated by this case dealing with privacy rights under the Constitution. Texas law criminalised certain sexual acts when practised by homosexuals. Two men convicted under the statute appealed to the Supreme Court, arguing that the 'liberty' to which they were entitled under the Constitution was violated by the Texas legislation. The Supreme Court had dealt with this issue before, in *Bowers* v. *Hardwick* (1986). The Court had ruled in a 5–4 vote that the US Constitution did not protect the right claimed by homosexuals and that it was up to each state legislature to decide for itself whether these homosexual acts should be legal or not. The *Bowers* decision had been roundly condemned in many quarters for its insensitivity to personal privacy rights and it came as no surprise when, in *Lawrence*, the Court overruled *Bowers* by a 6–3 vote. Since the earlier decision, changes in Court personnel and the progress made by gay and lesbian groups in fighting discrimination had significantly altered attitudes to homosexuality. However, *Lawrence* proved controversial because one of the dissenting justices, Antonin Scalia, suggested the decision could lead a later Court to rule that gay marriage was also protected by the Constitution. Certain religious and conservative groups went into immediate action and tried to pass an amendment to the US Constitution declaring that marriage could only be between a man and a woman. Although it failed, over forty states have banned same-sex marriage under their own statutes or constitutions and the issue was much debated in the presidential election of 2004. In the face of such political pressure, the Supreme Court will surely tread cautiously if the issue of gay marriage comes before it. On the other hand, its decision in *Lawrence* shows once again that the Court plays a vital role in defending the rights of minorities.

Decisions such as these provoked considerable anger among conservatives and, at both the state and federal levels of government, there were determined and partially successful attempts both to reverse them and to force the Court to abandon its activism. This backlash revealed once again that, when it provokes significant and sustained opposition, the Court's decisions can suddenly take on the appearance of great vulnerability.

Supreme Court decisions: implementation and resistance

There are several formal means at the disposal of other branches of government if they wish to reverse a constitutional decision by the Court. Most obviously, they can attempt to pass a constitutional amendment. However, this is a difficult, time-consuming and uncertain device. As a result, it has been employed successfully on only four occasions in American history. The Eleventh Amendment overturned *Chisholm* v. *Georgia* (1793); the first part of the Fourteenth Amendment overturned *Dred Scott* v. *Sanford* (1857); the Sixteenth Amendment reversed *Pollock* v. *Farmers' Loan and Trust Co.* (1895); and the Twenty-sixth Amendment reversed *Oregon* v. *Mitchell* (1970).

Nevertheless, despite the slim prospects of success, members of Congress often introduce constitutional amendments as a symbolic gesture to express their hostility to the Court. Thus, for example, within eighteen months of the Court's decision banning any kind of school prayer (*Engel* v. *Vitale*, 1962), no less than 146 constitutional amendments to reverse it were introduced into Congress.

An even worse success rate characterises a second device to overturn a Court decision: *withdrawal of appellate jurisdiction*. The Constitution allows Congress to vary the kinds of case which may be taken on appeal to the Supreme Court. If Congress dislikes the Court's decisions on, say, abortion, it can simply remove the Court's right to hear appeals in cases involving abortion. In fact, such withdrawal of appellate jurisdiction has happened on only one occasion: just after the

Civil War, Congress removed the Court's right to hear appeals involving convictions for sedition by a military commission.

In 2005, the arch-conservative Republican leader in the House of Representatives, Tom Delay, attacked federal judges for their handling of the Terri Schiavo case. Schiavo had been kept alive for years only by life-support mechanisms and her family was divided over whether these mechanisms should be switched off. The case went through the hands of several courts, including the Supreme Court, with the end result that Schiavo was allowed to die. Delay launched a broadside against the federal judiciary, threatening to impeach certain justices and remove federal court jurisdiction over these kinds of issues. The reaction even within his own party was to criticise Delay for seeking to undermine the independence of the judiciary and he was forced to apologise.

The failure of so many proposals to reverse the Court by withdrawing appellate jurisdiction or amending the Constitution reveals something important about the Court's power. No matter how much the justices may anger Congress by particular decisions, a majority of its members are deeply reluctant to inflict permanent, structural damage upon the Court. Frequent surgery upon the Court with such blunt instruments would soon leave it incapable of truly independent decision-making – and it is that independence which makes the Court so valuable in settling constitutional conflicts.

We noted above Alexander Hamilton's observation that the Court was inherently weak because it had to rely on others to implement its decisions. The history of the Court bears this out. An early illustration came in *Worcester* v. *Georgia* (1832), when the Marshall Court offended anti-Indian sentiment by telling the state it could not make laws for the local Cherokee nation. Not only did Georgia refuse to obey the order, but President Andrew Jackson is reputed to have said: 'John Marshall has made his decision. Now let *him* enforce it.' Three years after the Court's decision, most of the Cherokees were forcibly removed from the state.

In modern times, non-compliance with Court decisions is fairly common. The most famous example concerns the 'massive resistance' to the

Brown school desegregation decision, organised by southerners. Ten years after the Court made its order, hardly any black children in the Deep South were attending integrated schools. It is obvious that the mere fact that the Court ordered states to desegregate their schools was wholly insufficient to bring about any significant change. Compliance with *Brown* only came in the late 1960s, after Congress and President Johnson combined to produce legislation which allowed stricter enforcement and which provided financial 'carrots and sticks' for state school systems.

The Court's 1973 abortion decision produced several forms of resistance. States which opposed liberal abortion statutes placed many obstacles in the path of women seeking terminations. Many refused to allow abortions to be performed in public hospitals, leaving women reliant upon private clinics which might be located hundreds of miles away. Others introduced cumbersome administrative procedures which required women to attend the abortion facility more than once. A favourite strategy, emulated by Congress in 1976 with the passage of the Hyde Amendment, was to withdraw public funds for poor women seeking abortions, even though funds were available for childbirth expenses and, indeed, all other types of medical treatment. In the first full year of the operation of the Hyde Amendment, the number of Medicaid (publicly funded) abortions fell from 200,000 to less than 2,000. The Reagan administration also joined the attack by banning any federally funded pregnancy counselling service from providing advice or information on abortion. On several occasions, President Reagan's solicitor-general also intervened as amicus curiae, urging the Court to reverse its decision in *Roe*.

The Court had thus ruled that states could not ban abortions; but the response of many states and the other branches of the federal government was to do their utmost to undermine that policy. The result was that although women retained a theoretical right to abortion, many experienced some difficulty in turning that right into a practical reality. The constraints upon the Court, then, are less the formal ones of reversal by constitutional amendment or withdrawal of appellate jurisdiction; rather, they are the pressures and indirect restrictions which arise from the unwillingness of the elected branches to implement the Court's decisions. In short, the main constraint upon the Court is the political hostility that its decisions engender.

There is, however, yet one other major way in which Supreme Court decisions may be changed by the actions of elected politicians. That is through the appointment process.

Supreme Court appointments

The power to appoint Supreme Court justices is shared by the president and the Senate. Article II, Section 2(ii) of the Constitution stipulates that the president shall nominate new justices 'with the advice and consent of the Senate'. In other words, the Senate has the power to confirm or reject the president's nominees. Here again the constitutional system of checks and balances provides the executive and legislative branches with an 'invitation to struggle'. Yet the president usually has the upper hand in such struggles, simply because the Constitution gives him the initiative in the appointment process. The Senate can reject the president's nominee, but it knows it cannot replace that nominee with its own preferred candidate. It must always calculate, therefore, whether the rejection of one nominee will lead to the appointment of a better one. Nevertheless, in recent decades, the Senate has become a lot more assertive in the appointment process than in the first two-thirds of the twentieth century.

Presidential nominations to the Court

Presidents have no power over how many nominations they can make to the Court. With justices being appointed for life, presidents must wait until a member of the Court either resigns or dies. Some presidents are luckier in this respect than others. Most obviously, President Carter had no opportunity at all to nominate a justice during his single term, while President George H. Bush made two

Table 8.4 Number of Supreme Court vacancies per president since 1945

President	Years in office	Number of vacancies
Truman	1945–53	4
Eisenhower	1953–61	5
Kennedy	1961–63	2
Johnson	1963–69	2
Nixon	1969–74	4
Ford	1974–77	1
Carter	1977–81	0
Reagan	1981–89	3
Bush	1989–93	2
Clinton	1993–2001	2
Bush	2001–5	2

nominations during his single term; and while Presidents Johnson and Nixon served for similar lengths of time, the latter filled twice as many vacancies as the former. President George W. Bush had to wait until his second term before he had a vacancy to fill.

Presidents rightly cherish their opportunities to make nominations to the Court. In the short term, it allows them to place political allies and sympathisers in another branch of the federal government. In the long term, those justices and their political viewpoints will still be influencing government long after the presidents themselves have left office.

Take the case of Justice William O. Douglas, nominated by Franklin D. Roosevelt in 1939. Roosevelt died in office in 1945, but Douglas did not retire from the Court until 1975, some thirty years after Roosevelt died. In fact, while no president may serve more than eight years (up to ten years exceptionally), the average length of service of justices appointed since 1937 is fifteen years (excluding those still serving). Moreover, of those twenty-two justices, three served more than thirty years, a further three more than twenty years, and a further eight more than fifteen years.

Criteria for nomination

There are no formal requirements for those who serve on the Court. While it is convention that nominees should possess a law degree, they are not required to have practised law, never mind have experience as a judge. Many of the justices considered to be outstanding had no judicial experience prior to their nomination: thus, Chief Justice Warren had been governor of California and an unsuccessful Republican vice-presidential candidate.

There would appear to be no connection between prior judicial experience and greatness on the Court, perhaps because the functions of the Court require political and philosophical skills as much as they require purely legal skills. However, recent Republican presidents, all striving to appoint strict constructionists, have nominated only those with at least some judicial experience. The thinking is that those with personal experience of judging, as opposed to politics, will behave more 'judicially' and less 'politically' once they are on the Court.

The overwhelming criterion for nomination is political compatibility with the president. This can be identified in a number of ways. Most obviously, presidents usually nominate those affiliated with their own party. Of the 109 justices who served on the Court up to 2004, only 13 had not been members of the nominating president's party. Even then, such cross-party nominees have usually been known to share the president's ideology.

It was President Reagan, however, who established the most elaborate method of screening nominees for political compatibility. During his administration, all potential candidates for nomination to the Supreme Court, or lower federal courts, were vetted by a President's Committee on Federal Judicial Selection. This committee analysed all the published writings and statements of those being considered for nomination. Candidates would be interviewed and asked their views on issues about which the administration felt strongly. Indeed, under Presidents Reagan and Bush, it was widely perceived that the 'litmus test' for any nominee to the Court was opposition to the *Roe* v. *Wade* (1973) abortion decision, although both administrations denied this.

Beyond political compatibility, the president may have a variety of secondary, and in essence symbolic, criteria for nomination. Until the early twentieth century, presidents considered the nominee's home state to be important, because it was thought desirable that the Court should reflect the country's regional diversity. In the twentieth century, a desire for ethnic diversity has been a factor. In 1916, Louis Brandeis became the first Jew to be appointed to the Court and the tradition of a 'Jewish seat' continued until the retirement of Abe Fortas in 1969. In 1967, Thurgood Marshall became the first black Supreme Court justice. When he retired, President Bush nominated another black, Clarence Thomas, to fill his seat.

Such nominations are not free of political calculation. The president will hope to reap electoral rewards for his actions by showing his symbolic support for the group concerned. President George W. Bush is thought likely to give serious consideration to nominating the first ever Hispanic-American to the Court when a vacancy occurs. His political strategy since his days as governor of Texas has involved cultivating the Hispanic vote and a historic appointment to the Court would set the seal on his political relationship with the Hispanic community.

Senate confirmation and rejection

The president has sole prerogative over who is *nominated* to the Court, but the Senate has equally sole prerogative over who is *confirmed*. Historically, about one in five presidential nominees to the Court fails to be confirmed by the Senate. Sometimes they are rejected outright by Senate vote; sometimes their nominations are withdrawn before a vote because of the certainty of defeat.

The historical frequency of Senate rejections of presidential nominees to the Court is not, however, even, and a marked change in that respect took place at the end of the 1960s.

Two facts stand out in the confirmation statistics. First, in the earlier period, all twenty-two nominees

Table 8.5 Senate confirmation/rejection of Supreme Court nominees, 1937–2004

1937–67			1967–2004		
Nominee (year of Senate action)	Result	Vote	Nominee	Result	Vote
Hugo Black (1937)	Con.	63–16	Abe Fortas[a] (1968)	With.	–
Stanley Reed (1938)	Con.	–	Warren Burger (1969)	Con.	74–3
Felix Frankfurter (1939)	Con.	–	Clement Haynsworth (1969)	Rej.	45–55
William Douglas (1939)	Con.	62–4	G. Harrold Carswell (1970)	Rej.	45–51
Frank Murphy (1940)	Con.	–	Harry Blackmun (1970)	Con.	94–0
Harlan Stone[a] (1941)	Con.	–	Lewis Powell (1971)	Con.	89–1
James Byrnes (1941)	Con.	–	William Rehnquist (1971)	Con.	68–26
Robert Jackson (1941)	Con.	–	John Paul Stevens (1975)	Con.	98–0
Wiley Rutledge (1943)	Con.	–	Sandra Day O'Connor (1981)	Con.	99–0
Harold Burton (1945)	Con.	–	William Rehnquist[a] (1986)	Con.	65–33
Fred Vinson (1946)	Con.	–	Antonin Scalia (1986)	Con.	98–0
Tom Clark (1949)	Con.	73–8	Robert Bork (1987)	Rej.	42–58
Sherman Minton (1949)	Con.	48–16	Douglas Ginsberg (1987)	With.	–
Earl Warren (1954)	Con.	–	Anthony Kennedy (1988)	Con.	97–0
John Harlan (1955)	Con.	71–11	David Souter (1990)	Con.	90–9
William Brennan (1957)	Con.	–	Clarence Thomas (1991)	Con.	52–48
Charles Whittaker (1957)	Con.	–	Ruth Bader Ginsberg (1993)	Con.	96–3
Potter Stewart (1959)	Con.	70–17	Stephen G. Breyer (1994)	Con.	87–9
Byron White (1962)	Con.	–	John G. Roberts (2005)	Con.	78–22
Arthur Goldberg (1962)	Con.	–	Harriet E. Miers[b] (2005)		
Abe Fortas (1965)	Con.	–			
Thurgood Marshall (1967)	Con.	69–11			

Con. = Confirmed   Rej. = Rejected   With. = Withdrawn
[a] Sitting associate justice nominated to the chief justiceship
[b] Senate vote pending

were confirmed, while in the later period five out of eighteen failed to make the Court.

Secondly, in only seven of the twenty-two earlier nominations did the Senate bother to record a vote: even then, not one of the recorded votes indicated substantial opposition to the nominee. In the second period, however, all nominations were subject to a recorded vote, save those which were withdrawn. Moreover, those votes show that, as well as the three rejections, there was a serious attempt to deny confirmation on three further occasions, most notably in the case of Clarence Thomas.

The Supreme Court appointment process has become controversial for one reason above all: the increasing tendency of the Supreme Court to behave in ways that have a major impact upon politics and public policy. Quite simply, both presidents and senators have come to realise that justices of the Supreme Court are major players in American politics.

Senate confirmation battles

When the president and the Senate do battle over a Supreme Court nominee, they are fighting for a major political prize: influence over the future direction of a co-equal branch of the federal government. The more political the Court's decisions, the more both president and Senate want that influence.

Take, for example, the historically unprecedented rejection of two successive nominees under President Nixon. During the 1968 presidential election campaign, Nixon had attacked the Warren Court for a number of its liberal-activist decisions. He promised to appoint new justices who would practise strict construction. The president also had a second political goal: to appoint a southerner to the Court. Nixon believed, rightly, that the traditionally Democratic, but conservative South was potentially a Republican stronghold. The appointment of a southerner, Clement Haynsworth of South Carolina, was therefore part of Nixon's plan to woo the region away from the Democrats.

Haynsworth was undoubtedly qualified for the office, but Democrats seized upon an alleged minor breach of judicial ethics as an excuse for rejecting him. Nixon's response was to nominate G. Harrold Carswell of Florida, a federal judge with a background of racial bigotry and incompetence. Nixon wanted to punish the Senate for the rejection of Haynsworth by obliging them to accept someone far worse. Nixon falsely assumed that the Senate would not dare reject two successive nominees. However, he made it easy on the Democrats by nominating a man who was clearly unsuitable. Senator Roman Hruska unintentionally damned Carswell with faint praise when he famously remarked of the nominee: 'Even if he is mediocre, there are a lot of mediocre judges and people and lawyers. They are entitled to a little representation, aren't they?'

The politics of appointment reached new heights of intensity with the nominations of Robert Bork and Clarence Thomas. On each occasion, the nomination was believed to be more than usually important because the other justices were more or less evenly divided on many of the big issues. The appointment of one new justice could swing the Court one way or the other on abortion rights, for example. As a result, both president and Senate went all-out for victory against the backdrop of a massive lobbying campaign by interest groups on both sides. Senate hearings were televised live and the whole nation became absorbed in the fate of a Supreme Court nominee.

Also, on both occasions, both proponents and opponents of the nominee tried to play down their ideological motives and find other reasons to justify their position. Presidents Reagan and Bush repeatedly stated that they had chosen nominees whose views on controversial issues they did not even know. Opponents sought to show that the nominees were not temperamentally fit for office or were 'outside the judicial mainstream'. The Thomas nomination became especially rough after one of his former colleagues, Professor Anita Hill, alleged that Thomas had sexually harassed her some ten years before. Thomas denied the allegations and there was an absence of corroborative evidence to determine which of the two was the more credible. Despite this, liberals now had a 'legitimate' and 'non-political' reason for doubting Thomas's fitness for a seat on the Court. As a result, the anti-Thomas campaign gathered sudden momentum and only fell short of securing his rejection by three votes.

Thomas survived because although there was again a strong partisan aspect to the Senate vote, this was qualified by other political considerations for some senators. Only two Republicans voted against Thomas, but eleven Democrats voted for him. Of these, eight were from the South and were particularly dependent for election upon the support of black voters. When polls told them that, in spite of Professor Hill's allegations, these voters believed Thomas should be confirmed, they cast their votes in line with constituency opinion. Thus, even though the Thomas vote was not simply partisan, it was wholly political.

Post-appointment performance: do presidents get what they wanted?

Nothing guarantees that a president's successful nominee will vote as anticipated once on the Court. Justices of the Supreme Court are answerable to no one for their decisions, and it may be that their behaviour on the Court departs significantly from what their pre-Court record suggested. President Eisenhower expected Chief Justice Warren to be a moderate conservative, just like himself. Instead, Warren led the Court in a liberal-activist direction, causing Eisenhower to comment later that nominating Warren was 'the biggest damned-fool mistake I ever made'. President Nixon nominated Justice Blackmun as a strict constructionist, but on abortion and many other issues Blackmun voted with the liberal non-interpretivists. Likewise, current Justice David Souter, nominated by President George H. Bush, has turned out to be much more liberal than many Republicans expected.

These, however, are the exceptions that prove the rule. By and large, justices *do* turn out the way their nominating president had hoped. If the president gets the chance to fill sufficient vacancies, he can change the Court's direction altogether. Although President Franklin D. Roosevelt's Court-packing plan was never passed by Congress, his eventual nominees to the Court ensured that New Deal-type legislation was deemed acceptable under the Constitution. The more recent Reagan–Bush campaign to shift the Court in a more conservative direction also paid off in many ways, though not as decisively as conservative Republicans had hoped: abortion rights have been significantly undermined, affirmative action policies much more difficult to pursue and convicted murderers more likely to be executed.

At the same time, on particular issues or in particular cases, justices do not necessarily do what their nominating presidents desire. Thus, although Justices O'Connor, Kennedy and Souter have narrowed the Court's 1973 abortion decision, they have not squarely reversed it, as both Presidents Reagan and Bush urged. In part, at least, this is owing to the fact that most justices of the Supreme Court are not simply politicians in disguise. They cannot escape their political environment entirely, but there are also judicial imperatives that may constrain them. Law, even constitutional law, requires a good measure of stability and consistency of principle. If the Court simply tacks with every change in the prevailing political winds, it risks losing the very character that makes it distinctive and authoritative in American politics. As the three justices wrote when refusing to reverse *Roe* v. *Wade*:

> The Court must take care to speak and act in ways that allow people to accept its decisions on the terms the Court claims for them, as grounded truly in principle, not as compromises with social and political pressures having no bearing on the principled choices that the Court is obliged to make. Thus, the Court's legitimacy depends on making legally principled decisions under circumstances in which their principled character is sufficiently plausible to be accepted by the Nation.
>
> Joint opinion of Justices O'Connor, Kennedy and Souter, *Planned Parenthood of Southeastern Pennsylvania* v. *Casey* (1992)

Chapter summary

The Supreme Court was established as a judicial body and thus its formal structures and processes are those of a court of law. However, the acquisition of the power of judicial review transformed the Court.

Authorised now to declare legislation and executive decisions unconstitutional, the Court necessarily became involved in the policy-making process. The Supreme Court therefore has a dual nature, part judicial and part political. Its decisions can have a major impact on public policy and its judicial decision-making processes require an infusion of political, moral and philosophical reasoning.

Throughout American history, the Supreme Court has oscillated between judicial activism and judicial self-restraint. When the Court has been activist, opponents have charged that the supremacy of the Constitution has been perverted to create the supremacy of the Supreme Court in the American political system. In fact, there are enough formal and informal constraints upon the Supreme Court's power to ensure that this does not happen, and in the long term, the Court usually does comply with the wishes of the majority. Nevertheless, precisely because the Supreme Court is a judicial body endowed with significant political power, presidents go to considerable lengths in the appointment process to shape the direction and decisions that the Court will take.

Supreme Court of the United States, ed. Kermit L. Hall (2nd edn, Oxford: Oxford University Press, 1999) and *The Supreme Court Compendium: Data, Decisions and Developments*, eds Lee Epstein *et al.* (3rd edn, Washington, DC: CQ Press, 2003). A basic introductory level book on the Supreme Court is Kenneth Jost (ed.), *The Supreme Court A–Z* (Washington, DC: CQ Press, 2003). More sophisticated discussions of the interaction between politics and law and the policy-making role of the Court include: David M. O'Brien's *Storm Centre: The Supreme Court in American Politics* (6th edn, New York: Norton, 2002) and Robert J. McKeever's *Raw Judicial Power: The Supreme Court and American Society* (2nd edn, Manchester: Manchester University Press, 1995). On the appointment process, the most comprehensive work is Henry Abraham's *Justices and Presidents* (Lanham, Md.: Rowman & Littlefield, 1999). See also Robert J. McKeever, 'Presidential Strategies in the New Politics of Supreme Court Appointments', in George Edwards and Philip Davies, *New Challenges for the American Presidency* (London: Pearson, 2004).

Discussion points

1. What are the distinguishing features of the concepts of *judicial activism* and *judicial restraint*?

2. How powerful is the Supreme Court?

3. To what extent is constitutional interpretation an inherently political exercise?

4. Is it acceptable from the point of view of democratic principles that the Supreme Court can 'update' the Constitution?

5. What does a president look for in a Supreme Court nominee?

Further reading

Two very useful reference works on the Supreme Court are: *The Oxford Companion to the*

Websites

http://www.findlaw.com
http://www.supct.law.cornell.edu
http://court.it-services.nwu.edu/oyez

The first two contain the opinions of the Supreme Court and other useful data. The latter contains audio materials, such as tapes of the oral arguments before the Court in major cases.

References

Dahl, R. (1957) 'Decision-making in a democracy: the Supreme Court as a national policy-maker', *Journal of Public Law*, vol. VI, pp. 279–95.

Epstein, L. *et al.* (2003) *The Supreme Court Compendium: Data Decisions and Developments* (3rd edn, Washington, DC: CQ Press).

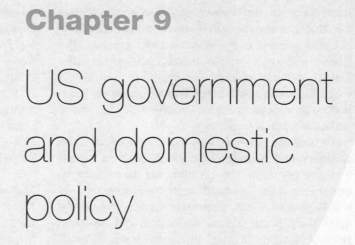

Chapter 9

US government and domestic policy

One explanation given by non-voters for their lack of engagement is the complaint that it makes no difference who is elected, that politics goes on in much the same way. Adding to this impression, observers have sometimes pointed to the United States as a nation where the two major political parties have much in common. For example, Democrats and Republicans do not differ in their fundamental commitment to the capitalist, private-enterprise market system. Nevertheless, many areas of domestic policy are the subject of fierce argument and negotiation between America's politicians. The presidency of George W. Bush was built on two of the closest elections in American history, and the president's pursuit of a forceful policy agenda launched the new century in America with a vigorous debate in several key areas of domestic policy.

The twenty-first century policy debate

When President George W. Bush took office for his second term, in January 2005, it was the first occasion that the Republicans had held the presidency and simultaneously had a Republican-majority Senate and a Republican-majority House of Representatives since the 1920s.

The second half of the twentieth century had been characterised by a period of 'divided government', during which, more often than not, control of the elected branches and chambers of government was divided between the two major political parties. By the end of the 1900s national authority in terms of control of elective office was very finely balanced between Democrats and Republicans. When opinion is so evenly matched, it takes but a small shift in the public's voting patterns to tip the scales. The election result of 2004 suggested a small, but telling change, moving the Republican policy agenda firmly to centre stage for the opening years of the twenty-first century.

Election results as close as those for the presidency in 2000 and 2004 are especially open to competing interpretations. In both years the shift of one closely-fought state would have put a different person into the White House. It is perhaps inevitable, when a result prompts such nail-biting among the politically involved, that many elements within the winners' electoral coalition should claim it was their group's support that was the key to victory.

As analysts and advocates alike pored over the entrails of the 2004 election result, different supporters of George W. Bush were not hesitant in laying their claims to have energised the support that the Bush camp had needed for re-election. Richard Viguerie, a campaigner for conservative positions with a record of campaign innovation, wrote that 'conservative Christians and "values voters" won this election for George W. Bush and Republicans in Congress', and said, 'If you don't implement a conservative agenda now, when do you?' In similar vein, James C. Dobson, of the group Focus on the Family, pressed the point that 'the involvement of millions of evangelicals, and mainline Protestants and Catholics' had helped President Bush to re-election, and that they would expect to see the administration's policies reflecting the positions taken by these groups.

Around 60 million Americans voted for George W. Bush, and even a supportive electorate that large is going to be driven by a variety of issues. Republicans with a conservative view on economic affairs, but more libertarian views on social and lifestyle policies point out that they too form an important part of any successful Republican coalition. Republican Hispanic leaders point to 2004's sharp rise in the Hispanic Republican vote as indicating their significance to the victory, and other groups contribute to a white noise of demands that the interests of their constituents be taken into account by the administration.

Special interests in the USA are highly skilled in putting their cases. In spite of this pressure, the Republican domestic policy agenda that had been followed in the 43rd president's first term, and that looked likely to set the tone for the rest of the Bush administration, concerned matters that have been central to American political debate for many years: the role of government in supporting individual Americans; the extent of government involvement in guiding social policy; and the cost to Americans of implementing these policies.

The first Bush administration saw the passage in 2001, 2002 and 2003, of legislation selectively reducing taxes. Some of these cuts were time-limited. A debate over national welfare provision continued in the context of discussions over the long-term shape that the existing Temporary Assistance for Needy Families (TANF) programme should take. The health care system was modified, with altered prescription benefits for Medicare recipients. The federal role in education provision increased, with the passage of the No Child Left Behind Act.

This Republican agenda, together with the increased foreign policy spending prompted by the administration's increased defence and security activities in the wake of September 11th, 2001, contributed to a considerable increase in the national debt, and an apparent change of attitude to deficit spending since the 1990s. With a clear margin of public as well as electoral college support, the Bush second term opened with commitments to continue on the same path, with proposals for income tax and Social Security reform, permanent tax cuts, and more education initiatives. All of these fit into the historic debates of American domestic policies over the years.

America's public support policies

Competing philosophies of the American welfare state

There has been historically a strong tendency to avoid US federal intervention in areas of social policy. The proponents of this position consider that American beliefs in federalism, and in individual self-reliance, both underpin their case.

The Tenth Amendment of the US Constitution reserves to the states and the people those powers not particularly delegated in the body of that document. The eighteenth- and nineteenth-century development of US politics saw federalism observed as a division in which the vast majority of domestic policy was decided and implemented at the state level, and often delegated by states to local governments. While the division of authority between governments at national and state level was never entirely clear-cut, the tradition that decisions on the level of provision, and allocation of costs for social policies such as education and welfare should be taken at the state level – close to constituencies that are affected – is well established and respected in the United States.

The provision of any social goods, whether it be roads, health facilities, educational opportunities or public welfare, inevitably throws up the question of cost. Questions of how much provision should be provided on the public purse have a context both of what is an adequate level of service, and of how much can be afforded. A community facing the question of what services to provide is inevitably faced with the parallel question of what taxes will be needed to pay for them. In spite of having used income tax to collect revenue in the Civil War era, an attempt in 1894 to introduce a more permanent income tax was declared unconstitutional by the Supreme Court (*Pollock* v. *Farmers Loan and Trust Co.*), and it took the passage of the Sixteenth Amendment to the Constitution in 1913 before the federal government had the opportunity to use this flexible tax resource – probably an essential tool of modern social welfare.

The debate over social policy adapts according to changing definitions of need and adequate provision, but the competing schools of thought have developed relatively consistent approaches.

On the one hand there is the position that the freedom and liberty of the American polity and economy also imply an obligation and responsibility to make the best use of opportunity. In this scenario, citizens and their families should make adequate provision for their own long-term needs. In case of difficulties, people should be relied on to remedy social problems, acting individually or through charitable or other community organisa-tions. Government intervention, according to this school of thought, will lead to higher taxes, which undermines individual opportunities to act in a civically responsible manner. Furthermore, government will expand if it is required to make increased provision for social policy, and large agencies become wasteful, inefficient and distanced from the ordinary citizen.

This position on policy is often reinforced by a commitment to the devolution of policy decision-making and delivery to states and localities. The advocates of this approach argue that locally taken decisions are most likely to reflect local opinion and to be most appropriate to local policy needs. Furthermore, devolved decision-making keeps spending choices closer to those capable of assessing, and committed to working with, appropriate levels of local resources.

In contrast to this is the position that while the freedom and liberty of American society may create much opportunity, equality of opportunity cannot be assumed to arise for absolutely everyone in contemporary American society. Not all citizens will have the same chance to succeed. Opportunity has to be underpinned by service provision, and government has an obligation to ensure that appropriate provision exists to support adequately its citizens in their pursuit of their target lifestyles and standards of living. Furthermore, some individuals and families will still fail to provide for themselves, and society has the obligation to ensure guaranteed standards of support for all of its citizens.

This more interventionist position is often accompanied by a more centralist approach to government activity. The proponents of this argument are unconvinced that social policy-making benefits from a piecemeal regional approach. They support the establishment of national standards to underpin these areas of policy. They suggest that states and localities are not always willing to address problems, but that the social welfare of the population is too important to leave without the imposition of national minimum standards.

There are many subtle variations on these positions. There are, for example, spectrums of opinion regarding which public services should be considered a broad public right, and which should not. And there are divisions of opinion regarding whether some parts of the population are more or less deserving of public service support. The roots of these debates sometimes lie in the early history of particular social service provision.

Early social welfare policy

Debates over the nature and extent of provision have been nowhere more vigorous than in the area of welfare. Many community practices in the early United States were continuations of colonial practices that in their turn had been imported from England. Welfare provision was no exception.

These imported traditions underpinned a restricted idea of general welfare. The stress was on the rights and responsibilities of the individual in a land of opportunity and resources. However, some researchers into modern US welfare consider it to be a twentieth-century innovation, sharing many conceptual foundations with poor relief, but emerging more directly from a concern to support poor mothers and their children, especially those in single-parent households.

After the stock market crash of 1929 the US economy slumped into a period that is now recalled as the Great Depression. Employment opportunities collapsed, throwing millions out of work, and putting unprecedented demands on the jigsaw of welfare provision made by the states at that time. In a nation hit so hard by economic conditions beyond any individual's control it was hard to distinguish between those poor who were deserving, and those who could be thought of as not. That body of opinion that supported universal standards for all gained strength in the face of the Depression's reality. Models provided by various state initiatives to give limited support through 'mother's pensions' were drawn on in the creation of a national system of aid within the Social Security Act of 1935.

From New Deal to War on Poverty

Democratic President Franklin D. Roosevelt took office in 1933 with a mandate to tackle the problems of what appeared to a national economic and social crisis. The Republican party's faith in the economic system to correct itself with very limited intervention had apparently failed. Michael Heale (2004) estimates that up to 50 million Americans were in desperate poverty when Roosevelt became president. There followed a period of energetic expansion of the federal government's role in domestic policy as the administration used legislation proactively in a range of initiatives design to combat the crisis.

The Civilian Conservation Corps (CCC) and the Civil Works Administration (CWA) were used to provide work relief, while the Federal Emergency Relief Act (FERA) made direct grants to the poor as well as providing funding through grants to state and local governments. The government sought directly to create jobs through such initiatives as the Works Progress Administration (WPA) and the Public Works Administration (PWA), which funded a huge range of building projects from modest local post office buildings to vast hydro-engineering projects. The government sought to lift and protect rural incomes through the price supports and production controls in laws such as the Agricultural Adjustment Act (AAA). This New Deal alphabet of legislation signalled an extension of federal government activity into domestic social policy, and the Social Security Act was a very significant element.

Over time the term Social Security has increasingly been applied solely to the system of benefits and pensions to which retired or disabled persons and their families are entitled, which were established by the Act. The original Social Security Act also contained other critically important sections setting up a system of unemployment benefits, and creating the programme that was to become the bedrock of federally funded poverty relief, Aid to Families with Dependent Children (AFDC).

All of these programmes had a long-term effect on the social and economic security of American workers. In particular many of the elderly have been protected by their Social Security pension, a federal entitlement that does not depend on state-level intervention, from descending into poverty once their working lives are completed. Others have found periods of temporary unemployment easier, receiving support as of right, though these benefits do vary between states. By the end of the twentieth century Social Security entitlements accounted for 22 per cent of federal budgetary expenditure.

From an early stage there was a clear distinction between the entitlement programmes within the Social Security Act, and AFDC. The latter, a means-tested welfare programme, was a regular source of controversy. Voices within the administration of the new welfare system certainly existed to support the idea that the needy should have simple and universal access to support, but there also existed resistance to this. By definition AFDC appeared to deem mothers and their children as more clearly deserving support than other poverty-hit groups in society, and the administration of the welfare system seemed to its critics to emphasise the grudging and selective nature of welfare support.

States used residency laws to cut the costs of help for poor people. People who had migrated across state borders were in some states refused support until they had been resident in the state for long periods. Some states required up to five years' residence. States on occasion attempted to restrict the freedom of women on welfare to form sexual relationships, or imposed other regulations on recipients' behaviour. In some states, welfare applicants were threatened with home inspections that could result in children being taken into care. In few states did welfare payments come close even to the US government's own definition of the poverty income level. There was also a steady shift from a position that saw welfare support, however limited, as a right to enable poor women to stay at home with their children, towards one that perceived the working mother as a virtuous model, towards which welfare recipients should be guided.

These complex and adapting regulations, predominantly imposed by the states who were obliged to administer this federal programme, helped maintain a debate about the fairness of America's web of welfare provision. Arguments over the success of welfare support were themselves complicated by differing definitions of how success should be measured. Nevertheless the US Congress, where the US House of Representatives especially was dominated by the Democratic party with only very brief interruption for more than half a century beginning in the 1930s, acted to make AFDC available to more categories of Americans, for example in 1954 expanding it to include agricultural workers who had previously been excluded.

During this period two very different visions of AFDC emerged. On the one hand the poor and their advocates were conscious of a welfare system that varied considerably, almost capriciously, between states, and within which some states supported the nation's poor at an unbearably low standard of living. While addressing health, education, training or child care needs might help some recipients change their circumstances, programmes were limited and underfunded. These critics felt, furthermore, that regulation of the system was at times conducted in a punitive fashion, and regulatory impositions such as those on sexual partners could be positively destructive to the family.

A very different perspective was held by those who criticised the system as becoming too unwieldy, too expensive, and accused it of 'featherbedding' unworthy recipients. Certainly the expense of the system was growing apace. There was a twofold increase in those eligible for AFDC in the fifteen years from 1950 as Congress expanded coverage, and as demographic and social changes in the USA led to a growth of households headed by females. Regardless of state-level restrictions, the overall cost to the taxpayer of welfare was growing steadily. Perceptions grew of a welfare population that chose dependency, of a system that was inefficient and corrupt in its operation, and of a programme that shifted resources from middle-class white taxpayers to unemployed black welfare recipients. However mistaken, these images of the welfare system in operation took firm root.

Research consistently found little fraud in American welfare provision; identified the vast majority of welfare recipients as genuinely needy; pointed out that the number of white poor and welfare beneficiaries exceeded the number of blacks on the rolls; and found that almost all recipients had ambitions to improve their lot and were willing to make the most of the limited opportunities available. In spite of the understandable anxiety expressed by American taxpayers that welfare was helping to drive an expansion of provision and feeding a tendency towards 'big government', the 1960s was also a period which saw an expanded belief in the effectiveness of government as a positive force for change, which could reach out through its agencies to identify and solve social problems with interventionist legislation.

There was a brief period of enhanced government activism in social policy. Some older politicians may have felt that extended and supportive social policies were a natural heritage of the New Deal. A younger generation of politicians looked to research and experimental work on poverty and urban sociology, which appeared to indicate new approaches to long-lasting problems.

The proposals of the War on Poverty, and of Lyndon Johnson's Great Society programme emerged out of this political and conceptual coalition. The mid-1960s produced a range of legislation that affected social welfare support in various areas of policy, including the US Civil Rights Act, the introduction of food stamps, and the critically important Economic Opportunity Act, all in 1964, and the legislation introducing Medicare and Medicaid, the Elementary and Secondary Education Act and the Higher Education Act in 1965. Johnson asserted that his target was an end to poverty in America. In order to achieve this his administration adopted the approach that poverty is the sum of many parts. While income support is a major element of an anti-poverty strategy, such matters as health care, jobs training, education and skills development, and motivation cannot be ignored.

Food stamps aimed to help the poor purchase food, the Education Acts included elements intended to provide targeted support to improve schools in poor areas. Related legislation provided breakfast programmes in schools, and the Headstart programme funded extra tuition for children from deprived areas. The federal support for benefits available under AFDC was expanded, and the numbers on the public welfare rolls grew by about 4 million between the mid-1960s and 1970. This period also saw a reduction in poverty among the sharpest ever measured, from 22 per cent to 13 per cent in the decade to 1970.

A small but widely noted element of the anti-poverty strategy was to encourage client participation in local decision-making. This was prompted by research indicating that people who engaged

with local issues with some chance of solving problems not only benefited their community, but also gained skills and self-confidence that could help their personal development. To the embarrassment of the federal government, some community action was so energetic that city, state and local governments felt threatened by the emergence of communities ready to make challenges against existing centres of power.

In health care, Medicare provided some health insurance benefits for the elderly, while Medicaid was a parallel programme designed to help the poor. These programmes of health care support repeated the distinction made between Social Security and AFDC, a generation earlier. Medicare, like Social Security, was introduced as a federal government funded programme paid to recipients as a matter of right. Eligibility for Medicaid, however, as for AFDC, has to be established through fulfilling various criteria, and both eligibility requirements, and degree of coverage are set variously and locally by the states, through which the federal government channels the funds for these programmes. These programmes helped increase government spending considerably and, especially given very substantial rises in the fiscal demands made in other areas of policy, maintained the heated debate over government policies on taxing and spending.

From Nixon's plan to Newt's contract

Levels of direct economic aid to the poor remained low even in the most generous states, and ancillary programmes were often under-funded and bureaucratically complex, given their broad social aims. Nonetheless, the broader range of programmes and of eligibility increased total cost to the taxpayer. President Richard Nixon's administration saw a shift away from the vision of government as a problem-solving and interventionist force, and towards an interpretation of social welfare policy as a major cost to American taxpayers.

Setting themes that have resonated in American government ever since, the Nixon White House launched a vigorous attack on high-tax, high-spending, big government policies that were portrayed as the heritage of a generation of Democratic party political dominance. At the core of Nixon's response was a proposal for welfare reform, a theme taken up by successive presidents for the rest of the twentieth century. Nixon's proposal, the Family Assistance Programme, including a minimum wage that would be guaranteed to employed persons through both regulation and payments made through the taxation system, was not wholly antagonistic to centralised social welfare policies, but was defeated by an unusual coalition of the right, who felt the programme too expensive for the taxpayer, and the left, who felt it too inadequate for the recipients' needs.

The big cost increases for social welfare were in Social Security and Medicare, those policies that could be expected automatically to deliver benefits to most of the population. Nevertheless, it was means-tested benefits that generally came under attack. President Ronald Reagan employed anti-welfare rhetoric in his campaigns, and his administration tightened eligibility requirements, increased state-level flexibility on regulation, and increased work requirements.

The growing influence of conservative interest groups gave new validation to the old distinctions between those more or less deserving of public support through social policies. A debate on 'family values' that was to continue to influence American politics into the twenty-first century emerged strongly under Reagan. Conservative critics of welfare and other forms of public support argued that these policies generated a condition of social dependency that undermined both the American individual and the traditional structure of the family. In spite of actual support levels being very low, this school of thought argues that the nation's network of support offers the choice to be unemployed, and to indulge in creation of families of illegitimate children.

The shift in the late twentieth century was such that its last president, Bill Clinton, a Democrat, pledged an end both to big government, and to 'welfare as we know it'. Any doubt that substantial change would be achieved was eradicated when the Republicans took control of the US Congress after the 1994 elections. The new Speaker of the House,

Newt Gingrich, had placed his Contract with America at the centre of the election campaign that had brought the Republicans victory, and he took this list of proposals as his agenda for the foundation of a new political approach for the new century.

The Contract with America continued the attack on big government, and the political engagement with concepts of family values. Among the Contract's proposals were that funding would shift from social programmes to prison-building; welfare spending would be cut; under-age welfare mothers would lose benefits; welfare mothers with new illegitimate children would receive no benefits for the new children; welfare periods would be limited; work requirements would be increased; and job creation would be encouraged through benefits to business. The Contract was not passed in full, but formed part of a contest between the Republican Congress, and President Clinton's Democratic White House that produced the 1996 Personal Responsibility and Work Opportunity Reconciliation Act.

The debates and legislation of the turn of the century continue to underpin the social support system on which President George W. Bush's administrations have since made their mark. Welfare, education, health care and pensions are so important that a presidential administration will inevitably address at least some of these areas of social policy. President Bush made education reform a core issue in his first presidential campaign, his administration initiated some health care reforms, and it has proposed adaptations to the new welfare system. The Bush second term began with targets to reform Social Security. All of this social policy activity takes place within a context of an overall commitment to cutting taxes.

Items from a twenty-first century agenda

Health care

Current health care provision in the USA reflects the complexity found in all areas of the nation's social support policies. In the main, US health care is funded from private rather than public or government sources. In 2002, total health expenditure in the USA exceeded $1.5 trillion, and was rising by about 8 per cent annually. Less than half of this total, or about $736 billion, was public expenditure, primarily paid through Medicare and Medicaid. Most of the rest of America's health expenditure came from its citizens through their health insurance premiums ($550 billion) and their direct out-of-pocket cash expenditure on health services and supplies ($213 billion).

Most Americans are covered by health insurance either through private purchase, as an employee benefit, or through coverage by one of the government programmes for the elderly, disabled or poor. Not all health insurance policies cover all eventualities, leaving part of the population underinsured, and in 2002 over 15 per cent of the US population had no health insurance at all.

The Medicare programme provides benefits to the elderly and to certain categories of disabled persons specified in the legislation. The core provision, an entitlement to certain hospital care, is funded from federal taxes on workers, with extra Medicare benefits covering physicians' fees available through a federally sponsored contributory insurance programme. The number enrolled on Medicare exceeded 40 million persons in 2002. At the same time there were also around 40 million on the Medicaid programme. Targeting the poor, this programme is supported by federal grants to state health authorities, and varies in its coverage according to the level of added state support and state regulation. As with all welfare-oriented programmes, Medicare can be controversial, but government spending on its Medicare recipients was lower than on the similar number entitled to Medicaid. While the 2002 cost of the entitlement programme, Medicare, was $267 billion, all public assistance medical payments, primarily accounted for by Medicaid, amounted to $256 billion.

Inflation in medical costs has affected the whole range of health provision. Health care costs reached 16 per cent of US gross domestic product in 2000, a figure well ahead of other developed countries. At state level, Medicaid programmes have faced repeated examination for savings opportunities,

continuing a long tradition of rationing social support provision for the poor.

Dealing with a broader and more affluent population, private insurers in America have attempted to protect themselves by regulating closely the procedures for which they provide coverage. The threat that cost limitations imposed by insurers may extend some elements of health care rationing beyond the poor to the majority of Americans, has prompted calls for a 'Patients' Bill of Rights' placing obligations on the insurers.

Costs did not prevent President Bush in late 2003 succeeding in getting a Medicare prescription drug benefit passed through Congress which is the largest single expansion in Medicare expenditure in the forty years since it was founded. The benefit, met critically by some who felt it did not go far enough and was too complex in its operation, was nonetheless a burden on government finances at a time when other pressures, most notably the combination of expensive foreign and defence policies and a commitment to tax cutting, were producing a substantial national deficit. Not all conservative Republicans were happy with their president's enthusiasm for further Medicare provision and expenditure. That having been said, the retired population which benefits most from Medicare has a high election turnout rate, and is a prime target for the Republican party.

Temporary Aid for Needy Families (TANF)

The Bush White House website points out that the welfare reform law of 1996 marked a turning point in national welfare policy. When President Clinton signed the bill at a high profile ceremony held on the White House lawn in the run-up to that year's Democratic National Convention it signalled the end, after sixty years, of AFDC at the centre of welfare policy, and its replacement by TANF.

The US government's stated core objectives for TANF are that the programme provides assistance to families with children or where there is a pregnant woman. The legislation establishing this programme sets itself firmly against what conservative critics perceived as the dependency culture

Box 9.1

Goals and methods of TANF

The four purposes of TANF are:

- assisting needy families so that children can be cared for in their own homes;
- reducing dependency of needy parents by promoting job preparation, work and marriage;
- preventing out-of-wedlock pregnancies;
- encouraging the formation and maintenance of two-parent families.

Selected highlights of TANF:

- Recipients (with few exceptions) must work as soon as they are job-ready or no later than two years after coming on assistance.
- Failure to participate in work requirements can result in a reduction or termination of benefits.
- Families with an adult who has received federally funded assistance for a total of five years (or less at state option) are not eligible for cash aid under the TANF programme.
- States (may) create jobs by taking money that is now used for welfare payments and using it to create community service jobs, provide income subsidies or provide hiring incentives for potential employers.

Source: US Department of Health and Human Services, Administration for Children and Families Office of Public Affairs Fact Sheet: http://www.acf.hhs.gov/opa/fact_sheets/tanf_factsheet.html

infecting the welfare system. The current legislation concentrates on job preparation and employment. Furthermore, the TANF vision puts a high value on the importance of the family unit. Promoting marriage, reducing illegitimacy and encouraging two-parent families are seen as proper elements of this twenty-first century policy.

Federal funds distributed to the states underpin the finances of the new welfare system. Within parameters set by the federal legislation the individual states have some discretion regarding the regulation of eligibility and participation. The states also contribute some matching funds from their own resources, and may fund additional public welfare initiatives of their own. The shift from welfare based on the principle that recipients should have

some basic level of income, however minimal, to a programme stressing the centrality of work, is especially evident in the funding limitations and reporting requirements that are contained within the legislation.

States receive federal block grants under TANF, which means that they are required to design their own individual plans to achieve the targets set by the federal government. Funding penalties are threatened if states fail to meet targets without acceptable explanation. Among the targets set are minimum employment participation rates by the recipients.

Sensitive to the criticism that welfare might be an incentive for single parents to stay home and bring up children, TANF may allow a period of home-based child care, but requires that after a maximum of twenty-four months parents in families receiving TANF must be engaged in work activities. States have the discretion to tighten this requirement, and about a quarter of the states demand immediate work activity from their TANF recipients. States are also free within limits to define what they mean by work activity, which may be staged from active and evident job-seeking, through participation in education and job training programmes, to community service and various categories of part-time and full-time employment.

Employment requirements on the individual vary from 20 hours per week for the single parent of a child under the age of 6 years, to a work requirement of 55 hours shared between the two parents if both are present, neither is disabled, and federal child care is available. The requirements on the states, as they stood in financial year 2004, were that 50 per cent of all families and 90 per cent of two-parent families on TANF must be participating in work activities. Discretion exists to vary these benchmarks in special conditions, for example in case of a severe economic recession in a region, or if a state has been able significantly to reduce its aggregate welfare caseload.

The Bush administration claims that nearly 3 million families had left welfare by 2002, with over 2 million families remaining on the rolls. The administration's aim continues to be the redeployment of welfare recipients out of welfare provision and into work. Academic research on poverty confirms that the number of people on welfare in the USA fell by about 60 per cent in the first few years that the new system was in operation. It is not entirely clear what all of these people found on leaving welfare, but certainly the employment rates among single mothers and other affected groups rose significantly.

Other forms of aid, such as Medicaid and food stamps, continued to form part of the welfare support system, and another Clinton initiative, the Earned Income Tax Credit, helped reduce the tax burden on low-income groups. While engagement with the workforce and the employment pool are generally seen as positive, there is concern among some observers that the current welfare system is promoting these features at the expense of providing a guaranteed and humane standard of living. Poverty and the associated need for welfare support are not always associated with unemployment. The poor in America are more typified by those who work in minimum wage, or low-paying, and often very hard jobs, and who nevertheless do not earn enough to break out of poverty. A system that increasingly forces welfare recipients into the low-wage job market may in some states benefit some former welfare cases, persuading them of their skills, helping them with job training, and even adding child care to ease their entry to the job market. In other states the support systems may be meagre, and the results may look more like pushing an unskilled and unwaged group of people off welfare to create a labour pool that will help maintain low wages in parts of the employment sector.

Poverty rates fell dramatically in the second half of the twentieth century, but, while people have been leaving the welfare system, there has been no significant fall in poverty rates since the 1990s, and some signs of an increase in measured poverty. The Bush administration nevertheless remains committed to the TANF approach. TANF should have been re-authorised in 2002, but as of early 2005 the Bush administration and Congress had not been able to agree the required new legislation. TANF has been continued by a series of six-month extensions of the initial legislation. There is no indication that the TANF approach to welfare will be abandoned, and the administration has affirmed its belief in the programme, listing as key aims promoting work, strengthening families, devolving authority to the states and localities, and denying access to most welfare benefits to immigrants until they have been in the USA for five years. These aims, and debates on adjusted work requirements and child care funding, will underpin the continuing debate on re-authorisation of TANF.

No Child Left Behind

As a first-time candidate for the presidency in 2000, then Texas governor George W. Bush needed to draw at least to some extent on his experience in office to provide him with executive credibility.

One policy that he brought from Texas to the campaign was his active promotion of standards in education in his own state. Texas, with over 7,500 schools, nearly 300,000 schoolteachers, and well over 4 million school students, has the second largest state education system (after California), and is responsible for almost 9 per cent of all America's school students. In the late twentieth century there were concerns, nevertheless, that educational standards were failing the clients of Texan schools.

Moves to improve matters in Texas pre-dated the Bush governorship. Future independent presidential candidate H. Ross Perot cut his political teeth leading a commission calling for improvements in the state's delivery of education. The call for educational improvements supported by some system of public accountability appealed to a wide cross-section of the public, gained bipartisan support, and was taken up at the national campaigning level. The Texan reforms pre-dated Bush's governorship, but his administration could claim to have tightened the regime of school-based tests in reading and mathematics. And that state operated vigorously the Texas Assessment of Academic Skills (TAAS) tests which students had to pass in order to fulfil their high school completion requirements. The aggregate student performance on these standardised tests also fed into the assessment of schoolteacher and school management performance, providing a loop that connected student success or failure with the fate of educational personnel and institutions.

The American public often lean marginally towards the Democratic party on issues of domestic and social policy, but opinion polls suggest that on education at least the Bush proposals convinced potential voters enough that any advantage for the Democrats was eliminated. The importance that the Bush presidential administration attached to this domestic policy, and perhaps their eagerness to prove that faith in Republican domestic policy was not misplaced, was indicated when the new administration issued a full legislative proposal only three days after taking office in January 2000, although the new Act was not passed until December 2001.

Some Republicans were worried that the Bush proposals indicated a level of federal intervention into state affairs that went beyond the normally conservative approach espoused by that party. In 1999/2000 the federal government provided only 6.4 per cent of the funding for public schools. All of the rest of the funding came from state and local governments, divided approximately evenly between the states and the localities. Primary and secondary education, almost above all other policy areas, was one where the traditional federal approach of devolving important local decisions to state and local governments had been well entrenched throughout American history. The establishment of a federal Department of Education had been achieved over the opposition of many Republicans. A far-reaching education policy seemed to some Bush supporters to be precisely the kind of big government to which they are opposed, interfering in its regulation, expensive in its provision, and with the potential to expand.

It is nonetheless difficult for any government to remain entirely distant from a social policy area that delivers services to a shifting population of about 50 million school students, and which impacts not just on those clients, but on their parents, their family, and their future employees and colleagues. The Bush administration could also project the policy as part of its support both for work-oriented policies and of the poor through improving their opportunities to create their own wealth, and ultimately reducing the numbers who would be claiming welfare through lack of preparation for the jobs market. These targets are encapsulated well in the political rhetoric of the legislation's name: the No Child Left Behind Act.

As passed, the legislation requires annual state-imposed tests on all children in grades 3 (about age 9) to 8 (about age 14) with another test for school students during their final couple of years at school. The test results are made public, and, as well as being subject to scrutiny through the publication of these results, schools are required to meet target overall standards, as well as to achieve standards within substantial ethnic minority groups represented in the school. Schools can be identified as failing, parents have the right to move children between school on the basis of results, and failing schools and school districts may be restructured by state authorities. The legislation also allows considerable state-level discretion over high school graduation requirements, variation in methods of tallying, tracking and reporting results, and envisions a twelve-year period for full implementation. The debate and adjustment in federal education policy that is likely to go on through that period could be a significant bell-wether for general debates over social and domestic policies in the first part of the twenty-first century.

The context and the future

The 2000 Bush campaign had placed tax cuts at its centre, in a way reminiscent of Ronald Reagan's focus on tax reductions just twenty years before. The argument had similarities, too. If big government is starved of funds, then it must necessarily shrink, and if people have more money left in their pockets, they will be more economically active, and generate more wealth. As more wealth circulates, continues this logic, jobs are created, and some of the costs of big government, such as welfare and social support policies, decrease, completing the circle. Among its first acts, the administration demanded tax cuts in excess of $1.6 trillion, and, on the basis of strong partisan support in Congress, managed to come close to this target in its first tax reduction efforts.

The context of American domestic spending became radically different after the attacks of September 11th, 2001 prompted a vigorous response in terms of security-related legislation. As well as Homeland Security measures, active military engagements were undertaken in Afghanistan and Iraq. The various elements of what the US administration styled a 'war on terror' combined to place a huge financial cost on the nation. The labour needs of the new policies were large, adding to the government's wage bill both through its own employment, and through the awarding of contracts for the new and expanded services. The hardware costs are also high, in terms both of the equipment needed to maintain a domestic security operation, for example in airport security, and of the military equipment committed to the engagements overseas.

In spite of these budgetary pressures, the Bush administration did not deviate from its aim to reduce taxes. Tax cut proposals that came after September 2001 faced a tougher passage through Congress, but in 2003 the administration managed to enact a further cut of $350 billion over ten years. By the beginning of the second Bush term the fiscal context had changed from a projected budget surplus of $5.6 trillion in 2000, to a projected budget deficit of at least $2.3 trillion, but the prospect of increased deficit spending did not appear to check the administration's enthusiasm for tax cuts. Bush re-entered office suggesting more tax reductions should be made, for example by making permanent those among the previous tax cuts that had been time-limited, by increasing the availability of tax-free savings opportunities, by abolishing tax on dividends, and possibly as part of a major overhaul of income tax and other tax sources.

Together these proposals would increase the government's requirement to borrow to support its foreseeable expenditures. Given that a reduced pattern of social spending has already been set, and that security and foreign policy costs have been pushed higher, there appear few areas for savings, but one of these could be Social Security. George W. Bush entered his second term expressing a wish to part-privatise the US Social Security system, persuading employees to invest more funds in private insurance and investment policies, and to reduce national dependence on taxpayer-funded Social Security pensions. Any such proposal is likely to face considerable scepticism. Unlike social programmes like TANF and Medicare, Social Security pays out on a non-means tested basis, as of right. A threat to Social Security is not just a threat to poor people, but a threat to all potential American pensioners. The promise not to mess with Social Security has been a touchstone of American politics for more than a generation, and launching into a public debate around the topic is a bold move.

Tax cuts and Social Security reform are all part of an approach that places the opportunity for entrepreneurship and wealth creation at the centre of domestic policy. Critics argue that further tax cuts increase inequality in the population, by benefiting the high tax payers much more than those paying few or no taxes. Others, with a concern that owes less to a liberal position regarding the welfare state, are not sure that tax cuts, Social Security privatisation, and the general levels of policy provision seen at the beginning of the twenty-first century can be maintained in the face of increasing government deficits.

Chapter summary

Debate on American social and domestic policy provision has always contained the strands of two arguments in addition to the content of the policy. One of these strands has been the ever-present tension over state versus federal authority in the provision of domestic policies. The other is the continuing debate over the proper reliance that should be made on public versus private spending in these policy areas.

While never embracing European models of state provision, for much of the twentieth century successive American administrations created a complex welfare state providing health, education, welfare and other supports.

The Bush administrations of the early twenty-first century continued with Clinton's aim to 'end welfare as we know it', and pursued domestic strategies through tax cuts. It also showed willing to challenge its own ideological right wing at times, to be interventionist, for example in education and Medicare, in order to achieve its policy aims. Nevertheless, the policy debate has steadily shifted from one based on a conception of a right to particular standards of social and welfare support, to one based on taxpayers' rights and the obligation of the state-supported population to undertake work activities, and to take responsibility for themselves.

Discussion points

1. Can the USA be said to have a 'welfare state'?

2. Why do domestic policy aims vary between the states of the USA?

3. Are US administrations more likely to be associated with leaving a lasting imprint on domestic policy or on foreign policy?

Further reading

Gwendolyn Mink and Rickie Solinger (eds), in *Welfare: A Documentary History of US Policy and Politics* (New York: New York University Press, 2003), provide nearly 1,000 pages of documentation and commentary. In *No Child Left Behind? The Politics and Practice of School Accountability* (Washington, DC: Brookings Institute, 2003), editors Paul E. Peterson and Martin R. West provide valuable insights into both the politics and the educational theory behind the federal government's expanded education role. A useful contemporary overview is provided by John Iceland, *Poverty in America* (Berkeley: University of California Press, 2003).

References

Heale, M.J. (2004) *Twentieth Century America: Politics and Power in the United States, 1900–2000* (London: Arnold).

Chapter 10

Foreign policy

The role of the United States in world politics has changed beyond recognition since 1776. The new, vulnerable country of thirteen states strung out along the eastern Atlantic coast of the New World has become the world's sole superpower. This transformation happened gradually but saw a rapid acceleration with the onset of the Cold War in the period following the end of the Second World War. Yet there are features of American foreign policy today which have strong roots in the early history of the Republic. The most important of these are, first, the structures and process of foreign policy-making, the basis of which was laid down in the Constitution of 1787. Secondly, it is important to understand the ideology which underpins American foreign policy: a unique blend of national self-interest and mission – a mission not merely to defend but also to spread American values around the world. In this chapter we examine how these deep-rooted factors interact with contemporary circumstances in order to explain how and why the United States plays the role it does in international politics.

Ideology and self-interest, 1776–1945

The study of international relations and foreign policy has been dominated by variations of the *realist school*. Realism holds that any nation's behaviour is determined mainly, if not exclusively, by its self-interest. This includes core concerns such as national security and economic self-interest. Realism has been opposed by variations of *idealism*. This argues that nations also act on the basis of its values, whether or not these values coincide with national self-interest defined in economic or security terms. In the case of the United States, both realism and idealism play an important role in foreign policy.

Like any other nation, the newly minted United States of America had interests to protect. In the first place, it had to deal with the fact that three major European states still occupied a substantial portion of the North American continent – Great Britain, France and Spain. These constituted a potential threat to both American national security and economic interests. Being far weaker than these powers militarily, the foreign policy of the United States had as one key goal the avoidance of war with these nations. An essential element of this policy was to avoid being caught up in Great Power conflicts that might, in the end, force the United States to become an ally of one Great Power in its struggle against the others.

While this policy is clearly understandable in realist terms, it also has an ideological basis. And here we must go back to the way Americans saw themselves as a nation: new, different from and superior to the societies and governments of the Old World. This self-image further entailed the belief that the United States was a role model for the future development of other nations.

This sense of *mission* inevitably found its way into American foreign policy. After all, a belief in one's distinctiveness and superiority as a nation is bound to colour one's relations with other nations not so blessed. Yet this 'myth of superiority', as Henry Steele Commager called it, did not demand an inflexible policy in dealing with the outside world. On the contrary, it justified both remaining aloof from international politics and leading crusades for a better world (Commager, 1974). Thus, whether discussing nineteenth-century isolationism or twenty-first century globalism, we quickly encounter the moralistic underpinnings of American foreign policy.

Some believe that such American idealism is little more than rhetoric, designed to cloak the presence of the baser motivations of national self-interest. Indeed, it would be foolish to argue that politicians do not attempt to dignify their policies, foreign or domestic, with the language of higher moral purpose. On the other hand, as Michael Hunt has pointed out, such rhetoric only works and continues to be employed because it taps deep-seated beliefs in American culture:

In the United States, foreign-policy rhetoric has been peppered with widely understood codewords. References in speeches, school texts, newspaper editorials, and songs to liberty, providential blessings, destiny, and service to mankind have been fraught with meaning shared by author and audience. Precisely because of their explanatory power and popular appeal, such simple but resonant notions become essential to the formulation and practical conduct of international policy.

Hunt, 1987, p. 16

This does not mean that we must accept that American foreign policy actually is more moral than that of other nations. Rather, it means that we must seriously consider the possibility that American foreign policy-makers – and the American public at large – do conceive of their foreign policy as something more than the mere pursuit of national self-interest. When we examine American foreign policy therefore, we must always calibrate the effects of *realism* and those of *idealism* on that policy at any given time.

Two episodes from American history provide an insight into how the combination of realism and idealism was to support quite different foreign policies. If we read the words of Presidents George Washington (1789–97) and Thomas Jefferson (1801–9), we can see that American superiority was used to support the doctrine of neutrality and the avoidance of entangling alliances with other nations. It is evident that Washington, for example, sees no contradiction between realism and idealism: American self-interest is intimately bound up with the enlightened and just nature of American society.

A few decades later, the United States was a more confident and assertive nation, a development greatly aided by the victory over the British in the War of 1812. The greater confidence was encapsulated in the famous address by President James Monroe in 1823, which became known as the Monroe Doctrine. This in effect told the European powers that the western hemisphere should no longer be considered land for their colonisation. By the 1840s a new term had been coined to describe the role of the United States in North – and quite possibly, South and Central – America: *Manifest Destiny*.

Box 10.1

American neutrality in foreign affairs

Presidents George Washington and Thomas Jefferson made a strong stand in favour of neutrality in international politics, fearing in particular that joining permanent alliances with other nations would inevitably drag the United States into wars that were not in its interests. Furthermore, they believed that adherence to such neutrality placed the United States upon superior moral ground.

Extract from George Washington's farewell address, 1796

'Observe good faith and justice toward all nations. Cultivate peace and harmony with all. . . . It will be worthy of a free, enlightened and at no distant period a great nation to give to mankind the magnanimous and too novel example of a people always guided by an exalted justice and benevolence. . . .

  The great rule of conduct for us in regard to foreign nations is, in extending our commercial interests, to have with them as little political connection as possible. . . .

  Europe has a set of primary interests which to us have none or a very remote relation. Hence she must be engaged in frequent controversies, the causes of which are essentially foreign to our concerns. Hence, therefore, it must be unwise in us to implicate ourselves by artificial ties in the ordinary vicissitudes of her politics or the ordinary combinations and collisions of her friendships or enmities.'

Extract from Thomas Jefferson's first inaugural address, 1801

'About to enter, fellow citizens, on the exercise of duties which comprehend everything dear and valuable to you, it is proper you should understand what I deem to be the essential principles of our Government. . . . Equal and exact justice to all men, of whatever state or persuasion, religious or political; peace, commerce, and honest friendship with all nations, entangling alliances with none.'

This justified the expansion, by conquest and diplomacy, of the United States across the continent to the Pacific coast. The superiority of American values explained and justified war against Mexico and Native Americans that yielded vast new lands including Texas, California and the Plains states.

By the end of the century, the United States had consolidated its continental land mass and began to turn its attention outwards to fulfil its mission and manifest destiny.

The Spanish–American War of 1898

Our second example of the blend of realism and idealism in American foreign policy arose from the Spanish–American War of 1898. As the remnants of the Spanish empire in the Caribbean and the Pacific fought for independence, the United States declared war on Spain, supposedly in the spirit of the Monroe Doctrine. However, the outcome was that the United States gained new territory in one guise or another. Hawaii eventually joined the United States, while Cuba became a protectorate. Interestingly, Cuba was persuaded to grant the United States a 99-year lease on a naval base at Guantanamo Bay. This was later granted in perpetuity.

The war also saw the United States annex the Philippines, something the Filipinos resisted through a bloody guerrilla war that lasted three years. It eventually required some 120,000 US troops to subdue the Filipinos, whose deaths from the fighting, starvation and the American concentration camps may have reached 200,000 (LaFeber, 1989, p. 202). In the wake of the war, it was clear that the United States was now behaving as an imperial power, much like the nations of Europe. This was difficult to justify in terms of American exceptionalism – the notion that the United States was a different and morally superior nation to those of Europe.

An oft-repeated, though apocryphal story reveals how Americans rationalised their imperialism at the end of the nineteenth century. The story has President McKinley telling an audience of churchmen how he had prayed late into the night for divine guidance on what to do with the Philippines after the Spanish had been defeated:

And one night it came to me in this way – We could not give the Philippines back to Spain: that would be cowardly and dishonourable. We could not turn them over to France and Germany, our commercial rivals in the Orient: that would be bad business. There was nothing left to do but take them all, and educate the Filipinos, and uplift and civilise them, and by God's grace do the very best by them as our fellow men for whom Christ also died. And then I went to bed, and went to sleep and slept soundly.

LaFeber, 1989, p. 200

Once again, realism and idealism combined to explain US foreign policy.

The First World War and the inter-war years

On the outbreak of the First World War in Europe in 1914, the familiar combination of economic self-interest and American values persuaded President Woodrow Wilson to remain neutral. Gradually, however, the war encroached unbearably on American freedom to trade, particularly German U-boat attacks upon American merchant ships. By 1917, Wilson realised that the United States must become a belligerent if it wished to protect its economic interests. Moreover, Wilson understood that if the United States was to influence the post-war

settlement and international order, it would have to negotiate as a victor.

In April 1917, Wilson sought and obtained a declaration of war from Congress. Declaring that neutrality was no longer feasible or desirable, Wilson proclaimed a crusade to make the 'world safe for democracy'. The president continued in idealistic vein in his 'Fourteen Points' speech to Congress, in January 1918. Although it played to the economic interests of the United States, with its advocacy of absolute freedom of navigation and the open door in trade, the speech also envisaged self-determination for all nations and international peace based upon collective security. This latter idea would lead to the creation of the League of Nations. While President Wilson wanted the US to join the League, isolationist feeling was strong in the Senate and it refused to ratify American membership.

The Second World War

Wilsonian internationalism still had its supporters in the United States in the inter-war years, particularly among the makers of foreign policy. However, many Progressive politicians from the Midwest and western states were principled opponents of what they saw as the threat to American virtue stemming from involvements in Europe. Congress took this view and passed three separate Neutrality Acts in the period from 1935 to 1937.

America was forced into the war by the decision of Hitler's ally, Japan, to attack the American Pacific Fleet at Pearl Harbour, Hawaii, on 7 December 1941. In the light of such aggression, President Franklin D. Roosevelt had no difficulty persuading Congress to declare war on Japan. Germany responded by declaring war on the United States. Thus the Americans, who had spent the past twenty years desperately trying to avoid military entanglements, now found themselves at war across both the Atlantic and the Pacific.

The United States emerged from those conflicts as the world's dominant economic and military power. During the war years, the American economy had recovered fully from the Great Depression. While the American economy boomed, the major

European powers, whether in victory or defeat, had suffered economic devastation. Consequently, the end of the Second World War saw the United States uniquely positioned to lead the world out of the economic chaos of the previous two decades.

Moreover, economic dominance translated ineluctably now into political and military dominance. The United States needed a thriving capitalist world economy if its own businesses were to prosper. However, the world capitalist economy could only recover if stable and supportive political conditions existed: and the sole country with the power to assure such conditions was the United States. American policy-makers recognised this and moved their country towards a position in international politics that in some respects reversed 150 years of foreign policy tradition. It also required an overhaul of the apparatus of American foreign policy-making that had prevailed until that point.

The Cold War

Historians disagree about the origins of the Cold War, that permanent state of crisis and tension between, principally, the United States and the Soviet Union, which lasted from the late 1940s to the late 1980s. The liberal school of western scholars blame the aggressive, expansionist actions and rhetoric of the Soviets, particularly in eastern Europe, for provoking the conflict, for between 1945 and 1948 the Soviet Union gradually installed puppet regimes in East Germany, Poland, Hungary, Czechoslovakia and Bulgaria. Moreover, with the spread of communism to other countries, including Romania, Yugoslavia and, in 1949, China, many in the West perceived a Moscow-directed plan to conquer the world for communism.

Revisionist historians, however, point to American political and economic aggression, backed by the threat of military force. Certainly, the United States was determined to create a post-war economic order that would serve its own interests. In 1944, the United States called an international meeting at Bretton Woods, New Hampshire. The outcome of that meeting was that while the United States would promote economic growth through the loan and investment of billions of American dollars, the world, including the British empire, would have to open itself to US trade.

The Bretton Woods agreement created two new powerful instruments for American economic domination: the International Bank for Reconstruction and Development – or the World Bank, as it is often called – and the International Monetary Fund (IMF). Primed with American finance and dominated by American administrators, these two institutions would help to ensure that the world would provide the United States with necessary export markets and outlets for capital investment.

Although many countries stood to gain from increased American investment, they were aware that the price to be paid was economic subordination to the United States. Thus, the British prime minister, Winston Churchill, resisted American terms at Bretton Woods: 'US officials, however, simply steamrolled over London's objections' (LaFeber, 1989, p. 411).

If a close ally such as Great Britain was fearful of the consequences of the new American economic domination, it is not surprising that the Soviet Union was deeply suspicious. Although the Soviet Union and United States had been allies during the Second World War, this had been a marriage of convenience. Even as the United States entered the war, Senator (later, President) Harry Truman said the Soviets were as 'untrustworthy as Hitler and Al Capone' (Hunt, 1987, p. 156). Soviet communism and American capitalism lay at opposite ideological poles and each viewed the progress of the other as a threat to its own existence. Thus, while President Franklin D. Roosevelt had hoped that the wartime collaboration with the Soviet leader, Josef Stalin, might continue after the war, the old mutual suspicions quickly re-emerged.

To the Soviet Union, the United States represented not merely an economic threat but a military danger as well. This danger was most dramatically embodied by America's exclusive possession of the atomic bomb. When the United States had used the bomb to end the war with Japan, it had done so, in part, to save the lives of thousands of American troops who would surely have been killed in the course of a traditional invasion. Yet the atomic devastation of Hiroshima and Nagasaki was also intended 'to make clear to the world that the United States was ruthless enough to drop the bomb on live targets' (McCormick, 1989, p. 45).

Thus, American foreign policy-makers hoped that they could exploit their atomic monopoly and practise 'atomic diplomacy' upon the Soviets. Unfortunately, the Soviets reacted to these pressures in ways that only heightened tensions: 'atomic diplomacy reinforced Russia's security fears, strengthened its disposition to control its Eastern European buffer zone more tightly, undermined soft-liners on German policy, and led Soviet leaders to create a crash atomic bomb project of their own' (McCormick, 1989, p. 45).

Containment

Wherever the responsibility for the Cold War should lie, the fact is that in the years following the Second World War, relations between the United States and the Soviet Union deteriorated rapidly. Rightly or wrongly, from the American viewpoint the Soviet Union was an aggressive, expansionist state, armed with a messianic ideology that saw war with international capitalism as inevitable. This was the prism through which American policy-makers viewed not merely Soviet conquests in eastern Europe, but the activities of all communists throughout the world.

The decisive episode for US foreign policy came in 1947 and arose from the civil war taking place in Greece between local communists and royalists. Up to this point, Britain had been backing the royalists in an attempt to prevent the emergence of the first communist government in western Europe. Britain, however, was bankrupt and informed the United States that it could no longer sustain its effort. It also had to withdraw support from Turkey, which was coming under pressure from its Soviet neighbour.

President Truman and his secretary of state, Dean Acheson, decided that the time had come to confront the Soviet threat. They had been primed

for a new policy by the ideas of George Kennan, an American diplomat in Moscow. Kennan believed that the Soviet Union was inherently aggressive and must 'be contained by the adroit and vigilant application of counterforce at a series of constantly shifting geographical and political points'. Thus, the policy of containment was born. Truman decided in 1947 that Greece and Turkey were the places to begin application of the doctrine.

The Truman administration was ready to transform the United States into the 'world's policeman' but he needed to persuade the American people and a Congress controlled by the opposition Republican party that such a new departure was necessary and in the best interests of the United States. At a meeting with congressional leaders in February 1947, Republican senator Arthur Vandenberg reportedly told Truman that if he wanted to get aid for Greece and Turkey from Congress, he would have to 'scare hell out of the American people'. President Truman duly obliged in his address to Congress on 12 March 1947. In so doing, he gave his name to the Truman Doctrine, that is, a policy of global containment.

There followed some forty years of Cold War and the American application of containment. This involved wars in Korea and Vietnam and a readiness to intervene almost anywhere in the world if a crisis arose. In a real sense, the US outlook was on a permanent footing and this necessitated a revolution in the foreign policy-making process.

The foreign policy-making process

The transformation in US foreign policy wrought by the onset of the Cold War called into being the modern foreign policy-making process. The Constitution of 1787 had indicated the broad powers of the president and Congress in this field. It was, however, only when foreign policy assumed the scale and importance that it did in the Cold War, that a massive and elaborate set of arrangements was needed to serve the nation's new global crusade.

The separation of powers in foreign policy

Constitutional powers of the president	Constitutional powers of the Congress
■ Commander-in-chief of the armed forces	■ To declare war
■ To make treaties	■ To ratify or reject treaties
■ To nominate ambassadors and top foreign policy-makers, e.g. the secretary of state	■ To confirm or reject ambassadorial and government nominees
■ To 'receive' representatives of foreign governments	■ To 'raise and support' armies

The constitutional framework

In keeping with its overall strategy, the Constitution of 1787 divided the power to make foreign policy between the president and the Congress. Thus, while the president was made responsible for the negotiation of treaties with foreign nations, they must be approved by a two-thirds majority of the Senate (Article II, Section 2(ii)). And while the president is commander-in-chief of the armed forces, only Congress has the power to declare war (Article II, Section 2(i) and Article I, Section 8(i), respectively). Thus the great constitutional scholar Edward Corwin described this sharing of power as 'an invitation to struggle for the privilege of directing American foreign policy' (1957, p. 171).

Growth of presidential power in foreign policy

It is clear beyond doubt that, today, the president has predominant power in the foreign policy-making process. This does not mean that the president's power is absolute. Nevertheless, the presidency has distinct advantages over other policy-makers, especially Congress, and some of these are traceable to the original constitutional design. For example, the president (and vice-president), as the only office-holder chosen by a national electorate, can lay claim to be the main political embodiment of the nation. The president was also clearly intended to perform the role that we now call head of state, by virtue of his power to appoint and receive ambassadors.

Moreover, foreign policy decisions often require a measure of secrecy, specialised knowledge, cohesion and the ability to act decisively. All these characteristics play to the strengths of the executive branch rather than a Congress composed of 535 autonomous and often parochial individuals, whose deliberations are conducted largely in public. If, as is often asserted, foreign policy-making is inherently authoritarian, then the presidency is the American governmental institution that comes closest to fitting the bill.

However, it was the expansion of American defence commitments, as much as constitutional logic, that made the presidency so dominant. The Cold War called into existence a permanent standing army of unprecedented proportions, peaking in 1968 at the height of the Vietnam War. This enhanced the constitutional powers of the president by bringing to the fore his responsibilities as commander-in-chief and head of the foreign policy-making bureaucracy.

The Cold War as crisis

The Cold War was a permanent crisis in American foreign policy because it constituted a continuing

Table 10.1 US armed forces, selected years, 1950–2003

Year	Thousand personnel				
	Army	**Navy**	**Marines**	**Air Force**	**Total**
1950	593	381	74	411	1,459
1955	1,109	661	205	960	2,935
1960	873	617	171	815	2,475
1968	1,570	764	307	905	3,546
1975	784	535	196	613	2,128
1980	777	527	188	558	2,051
1985	781	571	198	602	2,151
1990	732	579	197	535	2,044
1993	572	510	178	444	1,705
2003	499	382	178	375	1,434

Source: *Statistical Abstract of the United States*, 2004–5

threat to national security. It was, moreover, a crisis that could lead to nuclear war at any given moment. In such a climate of fear and danger, American foreign policy underwent a *qualitative*, as well as quantitative, change. Now it became unwise, perhaps even foolhardy and unpatriotic, to challenge presidential predominance in foreign policy. This did not mean that presidential conduct of foreign policy was beyond criticism, but at no point until the failure in Vietnam in the early 1970s did Congress attempt to wrest a significant measure of foreign policy-making power from the president.

This was true even when explicit powers of Congress were involved. For example, although Congress alone possesses the power to declare war, it was content to allow the president to initiate wars, as well as less significant military actions, without its approval. Thus, neither President Truman (Korea) nor President Johnson (Vietnam) sought or obtained a declaration of war from Congress.

By the early 1970s, some believed that such developments in foreign policy-making powers had helped to create an 'imperial presidency' (Schlesinger, 1973). According to this view, presidential power was now more akin to that wielded by an emperor than an elected chief executive in a democracy. If so, however, it must be said that Congress had willingly acceded to the surrender of

much of the substance of its constitutional powers. The Vietnam War did mark something of a turning point in presidential–congressional relations in foreign policy-making. Nevertheless, it remains the case today that there is simply no alternative to presidential leadership in conducting foreign affairs, especially when a crisis is involved. To a considerable extent, this is due to the fact that the president sits at the apex of a vast network of foreign policy-making bureaucracies.

The foreign policy-making establishment

Until the Cold War, the US government had made do with relatively few foreign policy-making institutions and personnel. The State Department, whose main responsibility is diplomacy, was created in 1789, as was the Department of War. In 1798, a Department of the Navy was added, but there was no further growth in specifically foreign policy-making institutions until the Cold War.

In 1947, Congress passed the National Security Act. This created a Department of Defense, combining the previous War and Navy departments and adding a new military service, the Air Force. The Act also created the National Security Council and the Central Intelligence Agency (CIA). Together with the State Department and the president himself, these three institutional products of the Cold War have dominated American foreign policy-making ever since.

Let us look briefly at each of these five main players.

The president

The character and interests of the individual president can go a long way in explaining the substance and management of American foreign policy in any given period. Some presidents are far more interested in foreign policy than domestic policy. In recent times, Presidents Richard Nixon and George H. Bush stand out as 'foreign policy presidents', whereas Presidents Lyndon Johnson and Bill Clinton at least attempted to devote their main energies to domestic rather than foreign policy.

On the other hand, events often compel a president to devote his energies to foreign affairs. President Johnson intended to focus on domestic policy, but Vietnam blew his presidency off course. Likewise, President George W. Bush had few international aspirations until the events of 9/11.

However, in an increasingly interdependent world, the dividing line between domestic and foreign policy has become blurred. For example, when President Carter imposed a ban on grain sales to the Soviet Union, as punishment for the latter's 1979 invasion of Afghanistan, he did not foresee the impact this would have on America's grain farmers. So badly hit were they by the loss of income from these sales that they prevailed upon the arch anti-communist Ronald Reagan to drop the ban when he replaced Carter in the White House.

Thus, it has become common today to talk of 'intermestic' issues and policies – issues with significant implications for both international and domestic politics. Since Congress will usually try to assert its influence when domestic – and therefore intermestic – policy is at issue, the president can by no means be guaranteed a free hand in such cases.

The State Department

Of all the agencies and federal bureaucracies engaged in foreign policy-making, the State Department is, in principle at least, the first among equals (Kegley and Wittkopf, 1987, p. 372). It was created in 1789 for the purpose of conducting US foreign relations. It also houses bodies with specialised functions, such as the Agency for International Development (AID), the Arms Control and Disarmament Agency (ACDA) and the United States Information Agency (USIA).

Apart from the relatively small number of top political appointees to the State Department, its thousands of employees are true bureaucrats, that is, career specialists who tend to spend their whole working life in the department. As such, the State Department can reasonably claim to be the most authoritative and wide-ranging source of information and perspective upon the world outside the United States.

For all that, the State Department is not only a much-criticised body, but some presidents have regarded it as untrustworthy and consequently have preferred to rely on others as their principal source of policy advice. There are various reasons for this distrust, although in many ways they all relate to the same point: that the president and his personal advisers believe that State Department personnel are out of tune with domestic political perspectives and demands. In the first administration of President George W. Bush, Secretary of State Colin Powell had less influence than National Security Advisor Condoleeza Rice or Secretary of Defense Donald Rumsfeld. The main reason was that Powell was less in tune with the president's own inclinations and those of the president's electoral supporters. Ultimately, the bureaucrats of Foggy Bottom (the area of Washington where the State Department is located) are too independent in their judgements and too distant from the White House inner circle to dominate, or even lead, foreign policy-making.

The Department of Defense

Often referred to as the Pentagon, because of the shape of the building in which it is housed, the Department of Defense is a powerful player in the foreign policy-making process. It has the vital task of ensuring that the United States is militarily capable of defending the nation and its interests, both at home and abroad. This responsibility immediately confers great power and influence upon the Pentagon, particularly during a prolonged period of international crisis, such as the Cold War.

However, there is more to the power of the Defense Department than its formal role, important though that is. One of the keys to Pentagon power is the enormous American defence budget.

The massive expenditures by the Defense Department attract two major sources of support: arms manufacturers and the Congress. The arms industry is eager to support Pentagon requests for ever larger and more sophisticated military hardware, since it stands to gain massive profits from

Table 10.2 Federal expenditures on national defence, selected years, 1960–2005

Year	Total expenditure ($bn)	Percentage of federal outlays	Percentage of GDP
1960	53.5	52.2	9.5
1965	56.3	42.8	7.5
1970	90.4	41.8	8.3
1975	103.1	26.0	5.7
1980	155.2	22.7	5.1
1985	279.0	26.7	6.4
1990	328.4	23.9	5.5
2000	341.6	16.4	3.0
2005 (est.)	518.1	18.8	3.7

Source: *Statistical Abstract of the United States*, 2005

supplying these weapons. Congress, or more specifically those members of Congress whose districts and states benefit from arms industry employment and the presence of military bases and installations, are also keen on high defence expenditures. In his farewell address of 1961, President Eisenhower felt moved to warn the country about the so-called military–industrial complex that threatened to push defence budgets beyond what was necessary and what the country could afford.

The National Security Council

The National Security Council (NSC) was created by Congress in 1947 to advise the president in ways that would lead to the better coordination of foreign policy among the various key institutions. In line with these objectives, Congress required that the president, vice-president, secretaries of state and defense, the chairman of the joint chiefs of staff and the director of the CIA must all be members of the NSC. It also created a new post of 'special assistant to the president for national security affairs', often referred to more briefly as the national security advisor (NSA). From time to time, different presidents have added others to the membership of the NSC, for example, the Treasury secretary and the attorney-general.

It was not until the Nixon administration (1969–74) that the national security advisor achieved great prominence. This was due mostly to Nixon's determination to reduce the power of the foreign policy-making bureaucracy, particularly the State Department, and to his appointment of Henry Kissinger as NSA.

Kissinger increased the number of professional staff on the NSC to about 150, compared with a dozen or so under Kennedy (Hilsman, 1990, p. 137). This allowed him to produce policy

---

Box 10.3

The military–industrial complex

Extract from President Eisenhower's farewell address, 1961

'This conjunction of an immense Military Establishment and a large arms industry is new in the American experience. The total influence – economic, political, even spiritual – is felt in every city, every statehouse, every office of the Federal Government. We recognize the imperative need for this development. Yet we must not fail to comprehend its grave implications. Our toil, resources, and livelihood are all involved. So is the very structure of our society.

In the councils of government we must guard against the acquisition of unwarranted influence, whether sought or unsought, by the military–industrial complex. The potential for the disastrous rise of misplaced power exists and will persist.

We must never let the weight of this combination endanger our liberties or democratic processes . . .'

recommendations that rivalled those of State and Defense. Combined with the fact that President Nixon simply placed greater trust in Kissinger than in any other adviser, this ensured that the NSC and Kissinger became the principal source of foreign policy advice to the president.

Ultimately, the power of the NSA depends upon how much any president chooses to rely on him or her. Condoleeza Rice was a close and trusted NSA to President George W. Bush and, like the influential Henry Kissinger in the Nixon years, was made Secretary of State in the president's second term.

The Central Intelligence Agency

The mere mention of the CIA brings to mind the issue of covert activities. Yet although the CIA has rightly become synonymous with American espionage and secret operations in foreign countries, it was not created with these in mind. Rather, as its name suggests, it was founded in 1947 to provide better intelligence about the world that the United States was now seeking to lead. Almost immediately after its creation, however, the CIA acquired responsibility for covert operations. This was prompted by the communist coup in Czechoslovakia in 1948, after which President Truman authorised the CIA to undertake sabotage and subversion in such a way that, if these operations were discovered, the US government could plausibly deny responsibility for them (LaFeber, 1989, p. 459).

Since then, the CIA has become the most notorious and controversial institution in American government. It has claimed, or been charged with, responsibility for such acts as interfering in Italian elections since 1948 in order to ensure victory for the Christian Democrats against their communist opponents; installing the Shah on the Iranian throne in 1953; planning and executing the bungled Bay of Pigs invasion of Cuba in 1961; devising Operation Mongoose, a series of assassination attempts on President Fidel Castro of Cuba in the 1960s; helping to organise the murder and overthrow of the elected Marxist president of Chile, Salvador Allende, in 1973; and blowing up oil terminals and other targets in Nicaragua during the Reagan administration.

However, the notoriety of the CIA and the extensiveness of its activities, should not be confused with the question of its power in the foreign policy-making process. True, the CIA has some of the characteristics of a 'state within a state' (Hilsman, 1990, p. 201). Its need for secrecy, both in intelligence-gathering and in covert operations, has meant that it is left largely free of normal outside scrutiny and accountability.

On the other hand, it must be remembered that the CIA is responsible to and under the control of the president. For all the mythology of the CIA as a 'cowboy operation' engaging in reckless and unauthorised secret operations, it is more accurate to see it as a highly professional bureaucratic agency acting at the behest of the president or the NSC. Indeed, this was the conclusion reached by the Pike Committee of the House of Representatives after it had examined CIA covert operations between 1965 and 1975: 'the CIA, far from being out of control, has been utterly responsible to the instructions of the President and the Special Assistant to the President for National Security Affairs' (Dumbrell, 1990, p. 153).

Bureaucratic politics

It can be seen, then, that the president is not short of advice on foreign policy from within his administration. Yet such an array of potential influences can be a problem, as well as a source of strength. Ideally, the American foreign policy-making bureaucracies should produce rational and effective decisions. However, the American foreign policy-making establishment is prey to what is called 'bureaucratic politics'.

Bureaucratic politics sees the president less as someone who commands the agencies created to serve him, and more as someone who struggles to manage and contain their separate wills. Each organisation is parochial in outlook and reluctant to entertain novel or rival ideas; it also seeks to expand its own influence and range of responsibilities. The negative results of these characteristics are several: organisations compete rather than cooperate with each other. This in turn leads to dogmatic and exaggerated viewpoints being expressed in the hope that this will maximise the organisation's power when the inevitable bargaining begins between different agencies. As a result, foreign policy decisions are often incremental and insufficiently responsive to new circumstances, as well as lacking clarity and coherence.

Non-governmental influences

Public opinion

It is generally agreed that public opinion is much less influential in the making of foreign policy than it is in domestic policy. From the perspective of most members of the public, foreign policy is figuratively and literally distant from their everyday lives. Unlike the core domestic issues of employment, the cost of living and education, for example, most foreign policy issues make little impact upon the consciousness of the average American.

This general indifference to foreign policy issues leads to low levels of knowledge about them. This in turn helps to make the foreign policy-making process one that is dominated by elites, thereby reinforcing its intrinsically authoritarian nature. In this respect, foreign affairs provides a major exception to the democratic openness of the general American policy-making process.

This frequently means that the public accepts whatever policy decisions the president makes and supports them enthusiastically. In times of crisis, this is termed the 'rally round the flag' phenomenon. In short, most of the time, presidents lead, rather than follow, public opinion on foreign policy.

However, none of the above should be read as meaning that public opinion is irrelevant to foreign policy. In the first place, presidents do pay considerable attention to public opinion poll data on foreign affairs. Any politically astute president will wish to know 'the outer limits of consent' of the American public, if only in order to gauge the possible repercussions of any decision he takes.

Secondly, under certain circumstances, the public *does* take a strong interest in foreign policy and may have clear policy preferences. This is particularly true where US military action is being contemplated and has become more critical in the wake of the defeat in Vietnam.

Pressure groups

Unlike the general public, certain pressure groups know and care about foreign policy. For example, both business and labour groups take a close interest in trade policy because it directly affects the profits and jobs of their members. Thus, business groups lobbied strongly in favour of President Clinton's decisions in 1994 to lift the trade embargo on Vietnam and to renew China's 'most favoured nation' trading status. In both cases, American business saw great opportunities for investments and profits in these former enemy nations, and hence countered pressures from those who wished to punish China for its human rights abuses and Vietnam for its alleged foot-dragging over the fate of US prisoners of war.

As well as groups motivated primarily by economic interests, there are those which can be termed 'ethnic lobbies' (Dumbrell, 1990, p. 176). The American-Israeli Public Affairs Committee (AIPAC), for example, is often credited with a major role in maintaining strong American commitment to Israel and, indeed, there is some evidence to support that. However, given the strong pro-Israeli stance of the US government for a variety of reasons, it seems likely that AIPAC helps to maintain rather than determine US policy on this issue.

As with public opinion, then, the influence of pressure groups over foreign policy is more limited than in the domestic sphere.

Foreign policy since the end of the Cold War

We have seen that in the era of the Cold War, the United States developed a new international grand strategy – containment – and a new foreign policy establishment – the National Security Council. But what of these two pillars of American foreign policy when the Cold War which engendered them disappeared?

It is difficult to exaggerate the fundamental changes in international politics represented by the end of the Cold War. Gone was the rigid, bipolar confrontation that sucked in virtually every nation

Figure 10.1 President Ronald Reagan and Soviet leader Mikhail Gorbachev were equally pleased to bring the Cold War to an end.
Source: © Miroslav Zajic/Corbis

on earth and threatened them with nuclear annihilation. Gone was the conflict that obliged the United States to maintain a massive standing army and a network of alliances all around the globe. Gone was the need to engage in proxy wars in places like Korea, Vietnam, Afghanistan, the Horn of Africa and Central America. Above all, gone was the great superpower rival, the Soviet Union, with its ideology and economy in ruins. Truly, the end of the Cold War was an occasion for rejoicing in the United States. As the sole remaining superpower, the United States regained the unequalled military status that it enjoyed briefly at the end of the Second World War.

The new world order

However, for a brief period in the early 1990s, it seemed that the United States had found the solution to its foreign policy dilemmas. President Bush, flushed with the success of the American-led multinational force in expelling Iraq from Kuwait in 1991, announced the arrival of a 'new world order'. He set out a vision of a global order in which the United States continued to offer leadership, but other nations assumed a greater responsibility for the human and economic costs of keeping the peace and maintaining stability.

This new world order was founded upon 'universal' values of capitalism, liberal democracy, free trade and the renunciation of aggression as an instrument of foreign policy. Nations which transgressed the new order by using force should expect to be met by the collective force of the international community, especially the United Nations. The United States would offer military leadership to the international community, but would not attempt to turn this into a *Pax Americana*.

The Bush concept of a new world order struck some familiar themes in American foreign policy.

Box 10.4

The new world order

'Twice before in this century after world wars, US presidents have led efforts to create an international mechanism for collective resistance to aggression – first, President Wilson and the League of Nations and then President Roosevelt and the United Nations. Yet, now, with the end of the cold war, in the Persian Gulf for the first time an international body – the UN – has played the role dreamed of by its founders – orchestrating and sanctioning collective resistance to an aggressor. The potential for the UN to continue to play this role, and the new willingness of many nations to contribute money and military units, are the foundation stones of a new era of international security – a new world order characterized by a growing consensus that force cannot be used to settle disputes and that when the consensus is broken, the burdens and responsibilities are shared by many nations.

The new world order is neither a *Pax Americana* nor a euphemism for the US as a world policeman. It is simply an attempt to deter aggression – and to resist if necessary – through the collective and voluntary action of the international community.'

Robert Gates, Deputy National Security Advisor, Address to the American
Newspaper Publishers' Association, Vancouver, 7 May 1991

Thus, American values were, in fact, universal values and the United States a political and social model to which other nations aspire. The idealist tradition in American foreign policy also appears in the advocacy of collective security and the implicit assertion that US policy is geared to the good of the international community as a whole, rather than the entrenchment of American power.

However, 'even the most favourable reading of the diplomacy and rhetoric of the "new world order" project could not fail to ignore its central affirmation of the primacy of American global power' (McGrew, 1994, p. 220). Yet if the new world order suggested an America still hankering to play the role of the world's policeman, US foreign policy under President Clinton had a significantly different emphasis.

The Clinton administration came in for sustained criticism for its alleged failure to define a coherent agenda and strategy for US foreign policy (Haas, 1997; Naim, 1997/98). Yet as Michael Cox has argued, Clinton did have such an agenda, although it was based squarely on economic self-interest:

Clinton (like Ronald Reagan) assumed office with a fairly clear view of the world and the sort of policies he would have to pursue in order to enhance American power. Of course, unlike his neo-conservative predecessor, his main interest was not in the evil empire but in the world economy; and the principal means he hoped to use to mobilize Americans behind his policies was not anti-communism but raw economic self-interest.

Cox, 1995, pp. 22–3

Three basic schools of thought could be discerned in the post-Cold War debate over US foreign policy: American primacy, neo-isolationism and new internationalism (McGrew, 1994, pp. 226–34).

Those who advocated American primacy were motivated by a mixture of realism and idealism. They believed that the United States must maintain and enhance its preponderance of power in the world in order to shape the world in ways that favour American economic interests and political values. Along with these powerful elements of realism goes the belief that it is America's historic mission to universalise its political and economic values.

Neo-isolationists also blend realism with idealism in their desire to return to the foreign policy principles and practices of the early republic. They advocated 'selective engagement' with the outside world, guided in this by economic self-interest. They saw the end of the Cold War as an opportunity to focus attention once again on domestic matters, rebuilding a strong, prosperous and stable society at home.

New internationalism viewed neither neo-isolationism nor primacy as a realistic option. On the one hand, nations are too interdependent to permit successful partial withdrawal from the world, and on the other, power is too fragmented to allow the United States to reassert its primacy for very long. Instead, the United States must pursue multilateralism, offering leadership to, but not attempting to dominate, institutions such as the United Nations. The new internationalism envisioned the United States as one of many nations enjoying peace, security and free trade and offering international leadership based economic strength and moral standing.

As President George W. Bush took office in January 2001, it appeared that his administration would lean towards neo-isolationism. The terrorist attacks of September 11th, 2001, however, put an end to that.

The War on Terror

It is difficult to underestimate the impact of the terrorist attacks on New York and Washington on September 11th, 2001. The United States suffered an unprecedented and spectacular mass murder in its political and economic heartland. The whole world, not simply America, reacted with shock and horror. The response of the US government was bound to be on a scale that reflected the magnitude of the blow inflicted by the 9/11 terrorists. Yet it is important to remember that the crisis did not occur in a political vacuum. How the federal government reacted, both in domestic and foreign policy, was powerfully shaped by existing structures and patterns of thought. While this did not rule out some striking new developments in American

politics and government, it did mean that those developments were constrained by familiar political practice and culture. The political reaction to 9/11 thus provides a revealing case study of the adaptability of the American political system when called upon to react to extraordinary external events.

Institutional developments after September 11th, 2001

The attacks of 9/11 were quickly and correctly perceived in the United States as an act of war against the nation. Within minutes of the attacks on the World Trade Centre in New York and the Pentagon in Washington, President Bush told his vice-president, Dick Cheney: 'We're at war' (Woodward, 2003, p. 17). We have already seen that the onset of crisis, especially war, in the United States triggers increased expectations of and enlarged powers to the American president. As Americans mourned as a nation, they instinctively looked to their president for the appropriate response and action. It did not matter in the slightest that President Bush had been elected by a minority of those who had voted and in the most controversial of circumstances. The people rallied around their president and looked to him for leadership.

During that first day, President Bush employed the institutions of the presidency to discuss policy options: meetings were called of the National Security Council and of an informal 'war cabinet' of leading advisors. It was not until the day after the attacks that the president met with congressional leaders. And while they reminded the president that they should be a full partner in formulating America's response, they also pledged bipartisan support for him. This simply confirmed a familiar pattern: for all the reassertiveness of Congress in recent decades, when a major crisis occurs, the president takes the lead and Congress follows.

President Bush, however, exploited the crisis caused by the terrorist attacks to shroud White House decision-making in unprecedented secrecy. While some greater measure of secrecy may well have been required for security purposes, Congress, the media and the public were often excluded from knowing what information the president was using

Figure 10.2 Chief of staff Andrew Card informs President George W. Bush of the terrorist attacks on New York while the president is visiting an elementary school in Florida.
Source: © Getty

to arrive at policy decisions. As one observer wrote: 'A case in point is the near-total secrecy in which the Department of Homeland Security was hatched. No cabinet secretary was consulted, nor were most senior advisors. The largest government reorganization in half a century, involving huge numbers of civil servants and tricky questions of government relations, was decided upon by a handful of people . . . and without serious consultation with Congress' (*The Economist*, 1 November 2003). Yet, despite being excluded from executive branch deliberations on the creation of the Department of Homeland Security, Congress approved it by overwhelming majorities in both houses.

The Homeland Security Act of 2002 was a radical measure in that it brought together under one roof some 170,000 federal employees then operating in a myriad of agencies, such as the United States Coast Guard, the Immigration and Naturalization Service, the United States Customs Service and the Federal Emergency Management Agency. In the 2004 budget, it received $31 billion, almost double the figure allocated to homeland security activities before September 11th, 2001. In other ways, however, the creation of the department, the fifteenth of the Bush cabinet, was a familiar response to national crisis. Indeed, in his message sending the bill to Congress, President Bush compared his proposal to that of President Truman when responding to the onset of the Cold War crisis. Truman had created both the Department of Defense and the National Security Council in the National Security Act of 1947.

Like the Homeland Security Act, the National Security Act brought together existing agencies and personnel in the quest for better coordination of security intelligence and more effective defence against security threats. While President Bush, as a conservative Republican, often spoke out against big, centralised government, he pushed hard for the creation of this new cabinet department. Many members of Congress had reservations about this development. Democrats were concerned about employees' rights and civil liberties and some Republicans were wary of yet more federal bureaucracy. Despite this, the Act was passed by

Box 10.5

The USA Patriot Act of 2001

The basic thrust of the legislation was to enhance the powers of the Federal Bureau of Investigation (FBI) and the Central Intelligence Agency (CIA) to monitor individuals' private communications. Even before 9/11, the executive branch had been trying to persuade Congress to cut back on the restraints imposed upon intelligence-gathering that had been introduced in the wake of the revelations in the 1970s about illegal wire-taps and other abuses of individual privacy. Previously rejected on civil liberties' grounds, the campaign to strengthen intelligence-gathering capacities became irresistible following the terrorist attacks. Democratic senator Patrick Leahy, who negotiated the bill directly with the White House, acknowledged that he yielded 'much more power [to the executive branch] than he had originally intended. But he was prepared to swallow hard and support it. To do anything else was politically impossible' (*Washington Post*, 27 October 2002, p. W06).

The main provisions of the Act modified the Foreign Intelligence Surveillance Act of 1978 to allow a considerable expansion of secret intelligence-gathering. Such activities now cover all crime, not just terrorism, and extend the access of the intelligence and law enforcement services to more kinds of private information. Furthermore, government agencies are permitted much greater powers to share information and have thus blurred the distinction between foreign and domestic activities. Another important feature is broader powers for the attorney-general to detain indefinitely non-citizens suspected of terrorist activities. Nevertheless, Congress did not give the executive branch carte blanche. Many of the Act's provisions are governed by 'sunset clauses' and hence will cease to apply in 2005 unless renewed by Congress. Moreover, intelligence agencies still need the approval of a special court, albeit at a reduced level of scrutiny, before they can conduct surveillance operations. In this sense, the USA Patriot Act remains within the framework of the Constitution's founding principles of separation of powers and checks and balances.

majorities of 90–9 in the Senate and 299–121 in the House of Representatives. Once again, the Congress felt bound to support a major presidential initiative to deal with a security crisis. The Department of Homeland Security, however, experienced familiar problems of bureaucratic management. Ridge struggled to bring all the different agencies together, and when he resigned at the end of President Bush's first administration, it was felt by many that the new department had not fulfilled its aims as well as it was hoped.

The tradition of increased presidential responsibilities and powers in times of crisis was further exemplified by the passage of the USA Patriot Act in 2001. (Its title reflects a growing tendency in the United States to manufacture symbolic acronyms for legislation: the full name is thus the Uniting and Strengthening America by Providing Appropriate Tools Required to Intercept and Obstruct Terrorism Act). The constitutionally prescribed legislative process was not changed in the wake of 9/11: the president could propose legislation but still only Congress could enact it. What did change dramatically, however, was the political pressure on Congress to rally around the president, as the nation had. When President Bush proposed the measures on 19 September, Attorney-General John Ashcroft asked Congress to pass it within a week and without amendment. He warned that any delay could assist terrorists in launching another attack. Congress responded by dispensing with its normal practice of holding committee hearings, investigating the need for the legislation and producing reports, and the bill was signed into law by

---

Box 10.6

Congressional oversight: the Joint Inquiry into 9/11

As we saw in Chapter 7, one of the most important powers of the Congress is that of oversight. This requires Congress to monitor and evaluate the administration's performance, to criticise where necessary and to propose appropriate reforms. Unsurprisingly, the Senate and House of Representatives launched a Joint Inquiry into the events of September 11th, 2001, and published its findings on 10 December 2002. The report criticised the FBI, CIA and NSA (National Security Agency) for their particular failures but also made clear that there were systemic failures that needed urgently to be addressed:

'In short, for a variety of reasons, the Intelligence Community failed to capitalize on both the individual and collective significance of available information that appears relevant to the events of September 11th. As a result, the Community missed opportunities to disrupt the September 11th plot by denying entry to or detaining would-be hijackers; to at least try to unravel the plot through surveillance and other investigative work within the United States; and, finally, to generate a heightened state of alert and thus harden the homeland against the attack.

No-one will ever know what might have happened had more connections been drawn between these disparate pieces of information. We will never definitely know to what extent the Community would have been able and willing to exploit fully all the opportunities that may have emerged. The important thing is that the Intelligence Community, for a variety of reasons, did not bring together and fully appreciate a range of information that could have greatly enhanced its chances of uncovering and preventing Usama Bin Ladin's plan to attack the United States on September 11th, 2001.

Our review of the events surrounding September 11th has revealed a number of systemic weaknesses that hindered the Intelligence Community's counterterrorism efforts before September 11th. If not addressed, these weaknesses will continue to undercut U.S. counterterrorism efforts.'

President Bush on 26 October 2001. The Act covered over three hundred pages and significantly amended some fifteen existing laws. Yet it was rushed through both houses of Congress in a bipartisan spirit and with little substantive debate. The final vote in the Senate was 98–1 and in the House, 357–66.

The National Intelligence Reform Act 2004

Yet another institutional change to come out of the 9/11 attacks was contained in the National Intelligence Reform Act of 2004. The major innovation was the creation of an intelligence supremo, the National Intelligence Director (NID), to head a new National Intelligence Authority. In the wake of the numerous criticisms of the performance of the various intelligence agencies before and after September 11th, 2001, the Bush administration deemed it necessary to bring all the agencies together under one authority. Again, there are echoes here of the 1947 amalgamation of several branches of the armed forces into a Department of Defense and the creation of the National Security Council to bring together various security-related officials. Now as then, the National Intelligence Reform Act clearly indicates that even in the most critical areas of national security there is a problem in getting different agencies to work together effectively.

The War on Terror and US foreign policy

Along with the early neo-isolationism of the Bush administration came a preference for unilateralism. This was most clearly demonstrated by the repudiation of the Kyoto Protocol on climate change, which had been endorsed by President Clinton. The administration also refused to sign up to the International Criminal Court, a multilateralist attempt to punish war criminals. And it championed a greatly expanded programme of National Missile Defense (NMD), which effectively tore up the Anti-Ballistic Missile Treaty of 1972. On the other hand, President Bush showed relatively little interest in using American power to solve international problems that did not directly threaten US interests, most notably the Israeli–Palestinian conflict.

The Bush administration was fully aware of US primacy in the post-Cold War international system, its position as the world's sole superpower and its unique power to impose its will on others. It intended, however, to exploit that primacy only when a clear US self-interest was at stake. The attacks of September 11th, 2001, intensified some of the existing inclinations of the administration, but also brought forth new policies. Rolled together, they constitute what has become known as the Bush Doctrine.

As John Dumbrell has pointed out, the Bush Doctrine is clearly based on the neo-conservative world view that was developed in the 1990s and is most loudly advocated by the group The Project for the New American Century. But it was 9/11 that turned a neo-conservative agenda into the foreign policy of the United States (Dumbrell, 2003, p. 238).

Speaking in early 2003, in the context of his belligerent policy towards Iraq, President Bush stated: 'After September 11, the doctrine of containment just doesn't hold any water. My vision shifted dramatically after September 11, because I now realise the stakes, I realise the world has changed' (Jervis, 2003, p. 372).

What was it about the attacks that brought George Bush to such a realisation? Most obviously, they emphasised America's vulnerability to terrorist violence. The National Missile Defense programme might one day make America invulnerable to a nuclear attack, but it could not deter or protect against the likes of Al Qaeda. And while domestic measures such as the creation of the Department of Homeland Security were vital, they too were no substitute for a new foreign policy that would take the fight to the terrorists.

As at the height of the Cold War, the United States is now globally engaged and determined to snuff out threats wherever they occur. Again in the manner of the Cold War, all states are called into play and all are presented by the United States with a simple black or white option. On 20 September 2001, addressing Congress, President Bush said: 'Every nation, in every region, now has a decision to make. Either you are with us or you are with the terrorists. From this day forward, any

Box 10.7

The Bush Doctrine

According to Robert Jervis (2003, p. 365), the Bush Doctrine has four key elements, as follows.

Regime change

A conviction that a state's political system is a powerful determinant of its foreign policy. This in turn leads to the belief that the US must promote regime change, if necessary by use of military force, as in Iraq.

Pre-emption

Great threats must be countered by new, vigorous policies, especially preventive war – otherwise referred to as pre-emption. Quite simply, this means that the United States need not wait to take military action until a group or state constitutes a clear and present danger. The mere fact that the president believes that there may be a significant threat at some future date justifies an American attack.

Unilateralism

A willingness to act alone, if necessary. No outside approval, such as a UN Resolution or the consent of allies, is required before America can launch a war. As President Bush was to say in his 2004 State of the Union address: 'America will never seek a permission slip to defend the security of our country.'

US primacy

A conviction that world peace and stability requires the United States to exercise its primacy in the international system. This primacy is based in part on economic and cultural power, but above all it is based on a military might that far outstrips that of even its closest rivals.

---

nation that continues to harbour or support terrorism will be regarded by the United States as a hostile regime.' In January, 2004, he reiterated the long-term and global nature of the War on Terror: 'Twenty-eight months have passed since September 11th, 2001 – over two years without an attack on American soil. And it is tempting to believe that the danger is behind us. That hope is understandable, comforting – and false. The killing has continued in Bali, Jakarta, Casablanca, Riyadh, Mombasa, Jerusalem, Istanbul and Baghdad. The terrorists continue to plot against America and the civilised world.'

Yet another echo of the Cold War was the fact that the new policy was accompanied by a vastly increased defence budget. Just as NSC-68 in 1950 spawned a massive defence build-up, so too did the policy response to 9/11. President Bush asked Congress to approve the largest increase in defence expenditures since the first Reagan administration. Part of the defence build-up was to develop forces and weaponry that the administration believed were more suitable to fight post-Cold War conflicts – smaller, fast-moving troop units and technologically advanced weaponry.

The war against the Taliban

The first deployment of US forces in the War on Terror was the invasion of Afghanistan, with the goal of overthrowing its Taliban government. The Taliban sympathised with Al Qaeda's ideology and sheltered Osama Bin Laden and many of his supporters. In effect, Afghanistan had become the home base of Al Qaeda and it was able to plan attacks and train its combatants under the protection of the Afghani government. When the Taliban refused to hand over Al Qaeda, the United States and its allies went to war in October 2001 to remove it from power.

The decision to go to war in Afghanistan received widespread support, both domestically and internationally. Although some opposed the war and others thought it was fraught with dangers, the fact is that most people and governments deplored the 9/11 attacks and deplored the Taliban for harbouring and supporting those who committed them. The United Nations passed a resolution condemning the attacks and called on all member states to help track down those who had organised them. The North Atlantic Treaty Organisation (NATO) invoked Article 5 of its charter, which treated the attack on the United States as an attack on all NATO members. The United States Congress, in terms strikingly similar to the much-criticised Gulf of Tonkin Resolution of 1964, authorised the president to use 'all necessary and appropriate force' against all organisations or individuals who had planned, executed or in any way aided the attacks.

Despite the breadth of international support for action against the 9/11 terrorists and those who supported them, President Bush chose to fight an essentially American war against the Taliban government of Afghanistan. This decision reflected American military primacy in the international system: only the United States was capable of fighting such a war with confidence and success and the United States did not need military alliances or support to do so. That President Bush accepted the participation of some allied forces reflected political rather than military concerns. American military primacy was also confirmed when the Taliban were ousted from government within two months of the start of the war.

The war against Iraq

If the war against the Taliban embodied certain aspects of the Bush Doctrine, especially regime change, the war against Iraq made clear the implications of other of its aspects, especially unilateralism and pre-emptive war. Much controversy surrounds the 2003 war on Iraq – or Gulf War 2, as it is sometimes called. Unlike the war in Afghanistan, the war in Iraq split the United Nations, NATO allies and, indeed, the American nation.

Iraq's brutal dictator, Saddam Hussein, had been a thorn in the flesh of his neighbours and the United States for many years. However, it is also the case that the United States, the United Kingdom, France and several other western states had sold arms to Saddam and even provided his troops with intelligence when it suited them. This was true, for example, during the long and bloody Iran–Iraq war of the 1980s. Saddam lost all support, however, when Iraq invaded Kuwait in August 1990. In January 1991, a US-led international force expelled Iraqi forces from Kuwait and proceeded to subject Saddam's regime to a number of military controls. Among these were UN weapons inspectors, whose task it was to find and destroy Saddam's programmes for developing weapons of mass destruction (WMDs). Saddam did his best to make life difficult for the inspectors and in 1998 they were withdrawn by the UN because they were finding it impossible to carry out their duties satisfactorily. At that point, it was unclear whether Saddam still possessed any WMDs. That was still broadly the situation when George W. Bush became president in January 2001 and when the 9/11 attacks took place.

Much of the controversy over the war on Iraq concerns the question of whether President Bush went to war in the belief that Saddam, still armed with WMDs, represented a 'clear and present danger' to his neighbours and the world in general, or whether he went to war for other reasons, with the WMD threat being used largely as a pretext. Indeed, it is argued that the Bush administration

Figure 10.3 The US struggles to define its enemy in the wake of 9/11.   Source: © Mark Fiore

exploited the WMD issue and 9/11 itself in order to justify a war that had been the goal of the Bush presidency from the very first day.

These disputes remain to be definitively resolved. It is, however, clear that certain members of the Bush administration were pushing for Saddam's removal from the very start. This was particularly true of Secretary of Defense Donald Rumsfeld and his assistant secretary, Paul Wolfowitz. They believed that it had been a mistake at the end of Gulf War 1 to leave Saddam in power. Such was their fervour for the removal of Saddam that, in the immediate aftermath of 9/11, they sought to persuade the president that Iraq, not Afghanistan, should be the first target in the American war on terror: and this despite the fact that Wolfowitz himself rated the likelihood that Saddam had a role in the attacks as, at most, 50 per cent (Woodward, 2003, p. 83).

It is also clear that one of the consequences of 9/11 was to heighten concern that, if Saddam did still possess WMDs, he might at some point cooperate with the likes of Al Qaeda and aid a devastating terrorist attack. In 2002, President Bush publicly adopted a more aggressive stand towards Iraq. In his January State of the Nation address, the president said that Iraq, along with Iran and North Korea, formed an 'axis of evil' in the world. In April he declared his policy towards Iraq to be 'regime change', and in June he declared he would launch pre-emptive wars against countries that he believed were a threat to the United States (Woodward, 2003, p. 330). Although the Bush administration reluctantly accepted the return of UN inspectors to Iraq as a means of resolving the WMD question, the president continued to threaten war. Thus in October 2002 he urged Congress to give him authority to use force against Iraq. Congress duly obliged, but unlike the Authorization of Force Resolution relating to Afghanistan, the Joint Resolution on Iraq was not near-unanimous. The vote in the Senate was 77–23 and in the House 296–133. Clearly the president was still in a position to command the trust and loyalty of the Congress, but the unity on how best to pursue the War on Terror had cracked.

The United States invaded Iraq in March 2003, and President Bush felt able to declare an end to the war in May of that year. However, in the years since then, it has become clear that the United States may have great difficulty winning the peace in Iraq. If it fails to do so, the much criticised Bush policies of pre-emption and unilateralism may be discarded by future administrations. What will not change in the foreseeable future, however, is the pre-eminence of the United States in the international system and the tendency of the United States to play its leadership role with reference both to its self-interest and to its founding values.

Discussion points

1. What do we understand by the terms *idealism* and *realism* in the context of American foreign policy?

2. What are the major constraints upon presidential power in foreign policy-making?

3. Has the United States been an imperial nation?

4. Has the administration of George W. Bush fundamentally altered American foreign policy?

Further reading

There are many useful introductory texts on the making of American foreign policy, but among the best are C. Kegley, E. Wittkopf and J. Scott, *American Foreign Policy: Pattern and Process* (6th edn, London: Wadsworth, 2002) and B. Jentleson, *American Foreign Policy: The Dynamics of Choice in the 21st Century* (2nd edn, New York: Norton, 2004). A very readable and balanced history of US foreign policy is W. LaFeber, *The American Age: US Foreign Policy at Home and Abroad since 1750* (2nd edn, New York: Norton, 1994). For an assessment of post-Cold War foreign policy, see M. Cox, *US Foreign Policy after the Cold War: Superpower without a Mission?* (London: Pinter, 1995). Bob Woodward has written two readable and well-informed accounts of George W. Bush's foreign policy: *Bush at War* (London: Simon and Schuster, 2003) and *Plan of Attack* (London: Simon and Schuster, 2004). Another excellent work on the impact of 9/11 on US foreign policy is R. Crockatt, *America Embattled: September 11th, Anti-Americanism, and the Global Order* (London: Routledge, 2003). Robert Jervis has written an excellent account of the Bush Doctrine in 'Understanding the Bush Doctrine', *Political Science Quarterly*, vol. 118, no. 3, 2003, pp. 365–88.

References

Commager, H. (1974) 'Myths and realities in American foreign policy', in Commager, H. (ed.) *Defeat of America: Presidential Power and the National Character* (New York: Touchstone).

Corwin, E. (1957) *The President: office and powers* (New York: New York University Press).

Cox, M. (1995) *US Foreign Policy after the Cold War: Superpower without a Mission?* (London: Pinter).

Dumbrell, J. (1990) *The Making of US Foreign Policy* (Manchester: Manchester University Press).

Dumbrell, J. (2003) 'The Bush Doctrine', in Edwards, G. and Davies, P. (eds) *New Challenges for the American Presidency* (New York: Pearson).

Haas, R. (1997) 'Fatal distraction: Bill Clinton's foreign policy', *Foreign Policy*, vol. 108, Fall, pp. 112–23.

Hilsman, R. (1990) *Politics of Policy Making in Defence and Foreign Affairs* (2nd edn, Hemel Hempstead: Prentice Hall International).

Hunt, M. (1987) *Ideology and US Foreign Policy* (New Haven, Conn.: Yale University Press).

Jervis, R. (2003) 'Understanding the Bush Doctrine', *Political Science Quarterly*, vol. 118, no. 3, pp. 365–88.

Kegley, C. (ed.) (1991) *The Long Postwar Peace* (London: HarperCollins).

Kegley, C. and Wittkopf, E. (1987) *American Foreign Policy: Pattern and Process* (5th edn, Basingstoke: Macmillan).

LaFeber, W. (1989) *The American Age: United States Foreign Policy at Home and Abroad since 1750* (London: Norton).

McCormick, T. (1989) *America's Half-century: United States Foreign Policy in the Cold War* (Baltimore: The Johns Hopkins University Press).

McGrew, A. (1994) 'The end of the American century?', in McGrew, A. (ed.) *The United States in the Twentieth Century: Empire* (London: Hodder & Stoughton).

Naim, M. (1997/98) 'Clinton's foreign policy: a victim of globalization?', *Foreign Policy*, vol. 109, Winter, pp. 34–45.

Schlesinger, A. (1973) *The Imperial Presidency* (Boston: Houghton Mifflin).

US Bureau of the Census (2005) *Statistical Abstract of the United States* (Washington, DC).

Wildavsky, A. (1975) 'The two presidencies', in Wildavsky, A. (ed.) *Perspectives on the Presidency* (Boston: Little, Brown).

Woodward, B. (2003) *Bush at War* (London: Simon & Schuster).

Index